A GUID

TEF Study Guides

This SPCK series was originally sponsored and subsidized by the Theological Education Fund of the World Council of Churches in response to requests from many different countries. The books are inter-cultural, ecumenical and contextual in approach. They are prepared by and in consultation with theological tutors from all over the world, but have from the outset been as widely used by students and parish groups in the West as by those for whom English may be a second language. The text and pictures are regularly amended to ensure that both scholarship and relevance to contemporary issues are kept up to date. Fully revised editions are marked (R). Titles at a slightly more advanced level are marked (A).

General Editors: Daphne Terry and Nicholas Beddow

TEF Study Guide 30

A GUIDE TO JEREMIAH

Michael J. Hunter

First published in Great Britain 1993
Society for Promoting Christian Knowledge
Holy Trinity Church
Marylebone Road
London NW1 4DU

Unless otherwise stated the Scripture quotations
in this book are from the Revised Standard Version
of the Bible (Ecumenical Edition), copyrighted
1973 by the Division of Christian Education of the
National Council of the Churches of Christ
in the USA.

The photographs are reproduced by courtesy
of the British Museum (p. 9), the Mansell Collection
(p. 17), Church Missionary Society (pp. 40 and 137),
Church Urban Fund and Stefano Cagnoni (p. 148)
and Camera Press Ltd.

(British Library Cataloguing-in-Publication Data
A catalogue record for this book is available from the
British Library
ISBN 0 281 04627 1
ISBN 0 281 04628 X (special edition for Africa,
Asia, S. Pacific and Caribbean)

Typeset by Latimer Trend & Company Ltd, Plymouth
Printed in Great Britain at the
University Press, Cambridge

Contents

Preface

A book such as this incurs many debts, often unconscious ones. Its first draft was begun and completed in Uganda, and the final version produced with encouragement from the congregation of the Church of St Joseph of Arimathea in Wolverhampton.

My fascination with the Old Testament began as a theological student, and was further stimulated by the opportunity of spending six weeks in Israel. I owe much to those who helped lay some of my 'foundations' at that time. These foundations were developed during nine years in Uganda, where the field of the Old Testament was my primary teaching responsibility. To my staff colleagues and successive generations of students at Bishop Tucker Theological College, Mukono, I owe a deep debt of gratitude for the stimulus and happiness of those years.

I should like to express particular thanks to those who at some stage have read and commented on all or part of the manuscript. These include the Rev. Samuel Tusuubira and the Rev. Dr. Kevin Ward, both fellow-tutors at Bishop Tucker College, the Right Rev. Simon Chiwanga, Anglican Bishop of Mpwapwa in Tanzania and formerly Provincial Secretary, and the Rev. John Hamlin, formerly President of the Thailand Theological Seminary and then at Trinity Theological College, Singapore. To the Church Missionary Society I am grateful for support throughout our time in Uganda and subsequently for additional support in the form of a sabbatical.

The Rev. Nicholas Beddow first encouraged the suggestion that I write this Study Guide and since then he and Daphne Terry have given valuable help and guidance in a whole variety of ways. It goes without saying that the defects of the finished work are my responsibility and not that of others.

My family have been understanding and supportive throughout and my wife Linda has not only been sympathetic when Jeremiah has detained me but has also commented thoroughly on the whole manuscript, checked references and – as if this were not enough – planned and drafted the maps.

Few have known greater heartache than Jeremiah; I dedicate this book to all who know such heartache in their own following of Jeremiah's Lord, and in particular to members of God's Church in Uganda.

MICHAEL J. HUNTER

Using this Guide

The plan of this book follows much the same pattern as other biblical Guides in the series.

In his general *Introduction* the author outlines some of the difficulties faced by readers who are exploring the Book of Jeremiah for the first time, and some of the ways in which recent work by theological scholars has helped to overcome them. He explains the line of approach followed by the Guide as a whole, and points to use of the Special Notes, which deal in detail with the historical and religious background to Jeremiah, the way in which it was edited and put together, and the life and witness of the prophet himself.

Study of the Bible text has been divided into shorter or longer sections according to the continuity or otherwise of subject matter. Some cover relatively short passages where important themes are discussed in detail. Others deal in a more summary way with whole chapters, or groups of chapters, whose content overlaps with that of other sections. The treatment in each section normally consists of:

1. An *Outline* of the passage summarizing its main theme or themes;
2. An *Interpretation* of the message contained in the passage as it applied to the people to whom it was addressed, and as we should understand and apply its teaching in our lives today;
3. *Notes* on particular words and allusions of possible difficulty, especially as relating to the history of the time, and to comparable passages and references in other parts of the Bible.

STUDY SUGGESTIONS AND QUESTIONS

Suggestions for further study and review appear at the end of each section. Besides enabling students working alone to check their own progress, they provide topics for discussion, some of which may involve individual or group research. In most cases they are divided into three main sorts:

1. *Review of Content:* to enable readers to ensure that they have fully grasped the ideas and points of teaching studied;
2. *Bible Study:* to show how the ideas and teaching in each passage relate to those in other parts of the Bible, and how the work and words of the prophet were understood and passed on by writers of the New Testament as well as the Old Testament.
3. *Discussion and Application:* chiefly to help readers clarify their own ideas and beliefs, and relate Jeremiah's message to their own

lives as Christians and to the work of the Church today. The best way to use these Study Suggestions is: first, re-read the Bible passage; second, re-read the appropriate section of the Guide once or twice, carefully following up any cross-references given; and then do the work suggested, either in writing or group discussion, without looking at the Guide again except where instructed to do so.

The *Key to Study Suggestions* (p. 238) will enable students to check their work on questions which can be checked in this way. In most cases the Key does not give the answer to a question: it shows where an answer is to be found.

Please note, however, that all these suggestions are only *suggestions*. Some readers may not wish to use them. Some teachers may wish to select only those which are most relevant to the needs of their particular students, or to substitute questions of their own.

BIBLE VERSION

The English translation of the Bible used in the Guide is the *Revised Standard Version Common Bible (Ecumenical Edition)* (RSV). Reference is also made to the *New English Bible* (NEB), the *Jerusalem Bible* (JB), the *Good News Bible* (GNB) and the *New International Version* (NIV) where these help to show the meaning more clearly.

MAPS AND TIME CHART

The three maps at the end of the book give a general view of ancient South-western Asia, a closer view of the countries of Palestine and the two Israelite kingdoms, and the towns of Judah mentioned in Jeremiah. The time chart on p. 11 sets out in order the events in Judah and in the surrounding nations at the time, as described in Special Note A.

FURTHER READING

The bibliography on p. 237 lists some books which readers may find useful for further study of Jeremiah and his message, and the history of Israel and of prophecy in the Old Testament.

INDEX

The Index includes all the more important names of people and places and the main subjects which appear in Jeremiah or are discussed in the Guide.

Introduction
Approaching the Book of Jeremiah

SOME DIFFICULTIES

The Old Testament Book of Jeremiah is a big book and can appear confusing. If we try to read right through it, we find many things we do not understand. There are several reasons for this:

1. It comes from a *different period of history*. Jeremiah lived over 2,500 years ago, from approximately 645 to 580 BC. Most of us do not know much about the history of that period; this makes it more difficult to understand parts of the book.

2. It comes from a *different culture*. Whatever part of the world we come from, our culture is different from that of Judah in the time of Jeremiah. It can be difficult to understand people from another culture whom we meet face to face; it is much more difficult when we can only meet them in the pages of a book and cannot ask them questions.

3. It comes in a *different form*. Most books we read are arranged and written in a style we find familiar. Each chapter is about a different theme, one chapter leads on to the next, etc. The book of Jeremiah has a very different approach and we do not naturally understand how the material is arranged or see how the book's argument is proceeding. This can discourage us.

4. It comes from the *Old Testament*. Here we read of the history and faith of Israel before the coming of Jesus. For Christians the events and teaching of the New Testament are central, and we may tend to think of the Old Testament as outdated or irrelevant.

For reasons like these we may be tempted to give up reading Jeremiah and concentrate on other books that have a more immediate appeal. This would be a mistake, because the book of Jeremiah has many important insights and its study can be very rewarding. To ignore the Old Testament because we have the New is rather like missing the first half of a play because we are going to watch the second; it makes what we see incomplete.

SOME RECENT APPROACHES

Earlier this century there was quite widespread agreement among scholars who studied Jeremiah. More recently scholars have used a wide variety of approaches to explore the book, and several major new works on Jeremiah have been published. As a result there is now a great range of views about the historical figure of Jeremiah and the development of the book that bears his name.

It has become clear that the book has been produced as the result of a long and complicated editorial process. Some recent scholars have concentrated on trying to trace its historical development from the original activity of Jeremiah to the finished version of the book. Their approach is not unlike that of peeling layers from an onion. They try to identify different contributions made at different stages in the process, and discuss whether or not they can be in harmony with each other. They reach many different conclusions about the historical Jeremiah. Some believe that there is good reason for linking almost all the material in the book with the prophet Jeremiah, while others argue that the historical Jeremiah is so buried by other material which has been added that we can know little about him with certainty.

Other scholars recognize that our understanding of how the book developed historically influences our approach to it. At the same time they are more concerned to discover the message of the finished book as we now have it. So they explore the main themes and the balance and tensions that may exist between them.

THIS GUIDE'S APPROACH

In this Study Guide we try to find one way through the difficulties of exploring Jeremiah. We need to know something of the historical situation lying behind the book, so we shall look at this when we study the opening verses of the book (1.1–3) and in Special Note A (p. 7). The time chart (p. 11) summarizes the events of the period. We shall use our understanding of this history and of the cultures of Jeremiah's day to make clearer the meaning of passages in the book.

The translation of Jeremiah in our Bibles is based on the Hebrew text, which is not always easy to understand. At times we shall refer to the Greek version of Jeremiah to help our understanding. (Some scholars in fact believe it to be older and closer to the 'original' version of Jeremiah than is our Hebrew text.) Special Note C (p. 44) briefly comments on the book's editors, while Special Note F (p. 142) considers the way the whole book developed.

But the chief concern of the book of Jeremiah's editors was to show God's dealings with His people through the prophet Jeremiah. They wrote to communicate their understanding of God and His ways. So we need to look at the book as a whole if we are to discover its intended message. Then we can think how to apply it to our own situations. We know, of course, that the New Testament takes the Old Testament story further, and enriches and develops the Old Testament's understanding of God. However, we need to take the Old Testament itself seriously, so that, once we have grasped its message, we can consider how we should apply it today or, as Christians, modify it in the light of the fuller gospel and our own particular contexts.

Because our chief concern is to explore the main themes of the book, we shall not go into great discussion of whether particular passages can be traced back directly to the prophet Jeremiah. In Special Note D (p. 90) we consider what we can reasonably accept as historically certain about his life. When we talk of 'Jeremiah' we shall not always try to distinguish between the prophet and the book that bears his name. The message of Jeremiah will refer to the content of the finished book rather than necessarily to particular insights of the prophet himself.

We shall find repetition of both language and themes as the editors tried to stress the points they wished to make. By the time that we have looked at the whole book we shall have thought about all the major themes that emerge. Once we have these clear, then we can wrestle to apply them in our own situations. If this Study Guide helps its readers to do this, it will have fulfilled its purpose.

STUDY SUGGESTIONS

1. What are the main reasons why we may find the Book of Jeremiah confusing when we first look at it?
2. What different sorts of approach have scholars made to the Book of Jeremiah?
3. What different attitudes do scholars have towards the historical person, Jeremiah?
4. Which do you think is more important for us to understand:
   (a) How the book of Jeremiah reached its final form?
   (b) The meaning of its final form?
   Give your reasons.
5. What approach to the Book will this Study Guide use?

1.1–3
The Times of Jeremiah

OUTLINE

The opening verses of the book tell us a little about Jeremiah's background and the time when he prophesied.

V.1: The family and home of the prophet.

V.2: The time when Jeremiah was called to begin his work as a prophet.

V.3: The period in which his work as a prophet continued.

INTERPRETATION

HIS FAMILY

1. *A Priestly Family*. Many societies have religious leaders who are believed to stand in a special way between a god or gods and the members of the society. These leaders may be male or female and have titles such as holy man, diviner, guru or priest. In ancient Israel they were known as priests. In the early days of the nation of Israel it was possible for all kinds of people to act as priests in the community. However, as early as the time of the Judges it was thought better, if possible, to have a Levite as priest, though others could also do the work of a priest (see Judges 17. 1–13). Exodus 32. 25–29, Numbers 3.6–13 and Deuteronomy 10.6–9 give three accounts of how God selected the tribe of Levi for priestly work and, as time went by, the right to act as a priest became restricted to those considered to be members of this tribe. By the time of Jeremiah only Levites could act as priests, and so, since Jeremiah's father, Hilkiah, was a priest, Jeremiah and his family must have been Levites.

We have no evidence that Jeremiah ever functioned as a priest, but he would have been brought up familiar with the priestly teaching. This meant that he should have known the law well, for the priests were supposed to be the guardians and teachers of the law in society.

2. *From Anathoth*. Anathoth was a small village about 5 kms north-east of Jerusalem, (see Map 3, p. 236). It was far enough from the capital to be a distinct community, but near enough to be in close touch with what was happening there.

Over 300 years earlier, when Solomon became king, there had been two leading priests in Jerusalem. One of them, Zadok, became

Solomon's chief priest. The other, Abiathar, had supported Solomon's rival, Adonijah, and was banished by Solomon to his home in Anathoth (see 1 Kings 2.26–27). Jeremiah was not necessarily a descendant of Abiathar, because Anathoth was a Levitical city (Josh. 21.18), i.e. one where many Levites could live. But stories about Abiathar must have been preserved in the small community, and they would have influenced all the other Levites in the village.

THE TIMES IN WHICH HE LIVED

An outline of the history of Judah in the time of Jeremiah is to be found in Special Note A, p. 00.

The period that began with the reign of Josiah was one of very great change in Judah's fortunes. For many years Assyria had been the major power in Ancient South-western Asia and, since the time of King Ahaz nearly 100 years before Josiah, Judah had, to a greater or lesser extent, been under Assyrian influence. By 640 BC, when Josiah came to the throne, the power of Assyria had declined and was no longer great enough to enforce Judah's submission. A few years after Josiah's accession, Judah's leaders launched a reform, involving both political and religious changes. The discovery of a scroll described as 'The Book of the Law' gave the reform a distinctive religious emphasis, which included attempts to bring the conduct of worship under stricter control and to centralize it in Jerusalem.

The reform led to great controversy and, although it achieved some success while Josiah was alive, it was repudiated by the majority after his death, only to be reinstated as a test of orthodoxy by the end of the Exile.

After Josiah's death there followed a period of turmoil, with a swift decline in Judah's fortunes matching the rise of the power of Babylon. There were deep divisions both between those advocating different foreign policies and also on religious issues. Before long Judah was reduced to paying tribute to Babylon; successive rebellions led, first, to the deposing of King Jehoiachin and his exile to Babylon together with many leading citizens in 598 BC and, subsequently, to the exile of King Zedekiah and the destruction of Jerusalem and its Temple in 587 BC.

WHEN DID JEREMIAH PROPHESY?

Most of the dated material in the book of Jeremiah is linked with the reigns of Jehoiakim and Zedekiah. Many of the prophecies are not dated. There are no prophecies linked with the short reigns of

Jehoahaz and Jehoiachin: this may be either because their reigns were too short to be mentioned in a brief historical summary, or because the prophet was silent during them.

Because very little material in the book can be linked with any certainty to the reign of Josiah, some scholars have suggested that the reference in v. 2 is to the prophet's birth, and that his active work as a prophet only occurred later. However, there is one prophecy linked with Josiah's reign (3.6–14) and these introductory verses are clearly intended to show Jeremiah as active during Josiah's reign. For this reason, to take v. 2 as referring to the call of Jeremiah to be a prophet seems to pose fewer problems than other suggestions.

On this interpretation, Jeremiah was active as a prophet for about 45 years. At first he worked in an encouraging time of reform. Later he saw the fortunes of Judah decline more and more. With the destruction of the Temple in Jerusalem they reached their lowest point. Many people were bewildered, others felt that their God had betrayed and abandoned them. Among all this rapid change and upheaval Jeremiah was called to live and work as a prophet of God.

NOTES

1.1: The words of Jeremiah: The Hebrew for 'words' includes doings and activities. So the phrase is not restricted to spoken messages, but also includes those of Jeremiah's actions and experiences that are recorded.
Hilkiah: This is a common name in the Old Testament which mentions five others with the same name.
1.2: To whom the word of the LORD came: 'LORD' is the translation most English Bibles use for *Yahweh*, the name by which God revealed Himself to Moses (see Exod.3.13–16); (some languages use *Jehovah* rather than *Yahweh*). The words of Jeremiah are significant only because the word of Yahweh has come to him. This is what gives them weight so that they are remembered and recorded. What is now presented is to be understood as God's word for His people.
1.3: The captivity of Jerusalem: This refers to Jerusalem's capture in 587 BC after the Babylonian siege. Although Jeremiah's activity, as recorded later in the book, extends several years after this date, the fall of Jerusalem marked the fulfilment of a key part of his message, as well as being a major landmark in the history of the people of Israel. It is not too much to say that this destruction of Jerusalem is the climax towards which the whole book moves.

STUDY SUGGESTIONS

REVIEW OF CONTENT

1. What does the opening verse mean by the 'words of Jeremiah'?
2. Which two major powers influenced Judah's history during the period of Jeremiah?
3. What kind of political situations existed in Judah during the period of Jeremiah?
4. What internal divisions were there among the leaders of Judah after the reign of Josiah?
5. Why do you think that the introductory verses 1–3 fail to refer to any prophecies of Jeremiah after the fall of Jerusalem?

BIBLE STUDY

6. Compare this introduction with Hosea 1.1, Amos 1.1 and Zephaniah 1.1. What do all these introductions have in common?

DISCUSSION AND APPLICATION

7. Give some modern examples of national leaders being deposed and replaced because of the intervention of a foreign power. What reasons did the foreign powers concerned give for their actions?
8. Josiah met resistance when he tried to reform worship in Judah: why do you think that religious communities often resist change?
9. What experience do you have of attempts to introduce changes in worship? What responses did they meet with? Why do you think this was so?

Special Note A
Judah's History around the Time of Jeremiah

After the death of Solomon in about 920 BC the united Davidic kingdom collapsed into the separate kingdoms of Israel in the north and Judah in the south (1 Kings 12.1–25). They continued as separate kingdoms for the next two centuries, with the relationship between them often tense; frequently there were border conflicts and strained diplomatic relations.

With the growth of the Assyrian empire under Tiglath-pileser III (745–727 BC) and his successors, Judah and Israel came under increasing threat. Israel was especially vulnerable: it was larger and more prosperous than Judah, its land was more fertile and its territory included part of the main road from Egypt to Assyria. Assyrian pressure eventually led to the siege and fall of Samaria, the capital of Israel, in 722 BC (2 Kings 17.1–6). Israel became an Assyrian province, many of its leaders were deported and others were moved in. The northern kingdom of Israel was never restored.

1. JUDAH UNDER THE ASSYRIANS

While Assyria was at the height of its power, Judah, under its kings Ahaz (c.735–715) and Hezekiah (c.715–697), paid it tribute. At one time during his reign Hezekiah rebelled, but this caused a savage invasion by Assyria in which all but Jerusalem was overrun and Hezekiah was forced into submission (2 Kings 18.13–16). Hezekiah's son Manasseh enjoyed a long and peaceful reign (c.697–642), made possible by his continuing submission to Assyria. Among other things this required him to include the worship of Assyrian gods as part of the worship of Jerusalem.

The reasons for this derived from the fact that in the ancient world, as for instance in many African cultures today, religion belonged to the whole of life. It was not possible to divide life into 'religious' and 'secular' aspects. Hence, when a country was conquered its people were expected to respect the victor's gods as well as their own: after all, the victory proved that the victor's gods were more powerful! So some Assyrian worship was an inevitable part of Judah's allegiance to Assyria.

2. JOSIAH AND REFORM

By the time Manasseh died Assyrian power was weakening, and after Amon's brief reign (c. 642—640) Josiah came to the throne. The period that began with his reign was one of very great change in Judah's fortunes. Assyrian power was now too small to compel allegiance and under the new king (and his advisers, for he was only eight when he became king) an independence movement was launched. Parts of this movement are reported in 2 Kings 22—23 and 2 Chronicles 34—35. The nature of the situation required that political and religious aspects of the reform be combined, and the reform went ahead successfully.

At about the same time an old scroll was discovered during some clearing out in the Temple in Jerusalem. This scroll was found to be a copy of 'The Book of the Law', and was probably an earlier edition of what eventually became our Book of Deuteronomy. This 'Book of the Law' became like a text-book for the next phase of the reform, and gave it a fresh religious emphasis. Josiah tried to

'When a country was conquered its people were expected to respect the victor's gods as more powerful than their own.' Scenes on a monument discovered at Nimrud, in what is now Iraq, show Tiglath-Pileser's soldiers carrying off statutes of the 'defeated' gods after capturing a city.

centralize worship in Jerusalem, to purify it from the worship of foreign gods and lead people back to obedience to the covenant God had made with them.

As with many religious reforms, this reform met with mixed success. Some people welcomed it as leading them back to the old way of worshipping the LORD, others resisted it as a dangerous innovation. By the time Josiah died in 609 BC the reform had not made enough progress to be accepted as the 'right way', and its measures faded into the background. Later, in fact, some people regarded Josiah's reformation as the cause of subsequent troubles for Judah (see Jer. 44.16–19).

3. THE COLLAPSE OF THE MONARCHY

During Josiah's reign the political scene was changing rapidly. As Assyrian influence decreased, the power of Babylon increased. In 609 BC, in an attempt to prevent Babylonian supremacy, the Egyptian army marched to the support of Assyria. Josiah tried to oppose this, and led Judah's army into battle with Egypt at Megiddo (see Map 2, p. 235); there he was killed and his army was defeated.

For a major power to put pressure on a lesser one, to arrange the overthrow of one leader and the installation of a new one, was as common in the ancient world as it is today. After the victory over the army of Judah, Egypt claimed the right to appoint Judah's new king. So, three months after Josiah's death, the Egyptian king Neco exiled to Egypt Jehoahaz (also called Shallum), who had succeeded his father Josiah, and replaced him with Jehoiakim, another of Josiah's sons. Jehoiakim reigned from 609 to 598 BC. He first paid tribute to Egypt and then, after Egypt's defeat by Babylon at the Battle of Carchemish in 605 BC, to Babylon.

About 600 BC Judah joined Egypt in a revolt against Babylon. The Babylonian army, under its king Nebuchadrezzar, advanced to deal with the rebellion. As it neared Jerusalem King Jehoiakim died. His son Jehoiachin (also known as Coniah) succeeded him and quickly surrendered to Babylon. Having reigned for only three months he was deported to Babylon with many of the leaders of the community: this is the Exile recorded in Jer. 52.28. The Babylonians placed Zedekiah, another of Josiah's sons and Jehoiachin's uncle, on the throne.

After a few years, Zedekiah in turn joined a rebellion against Babylon. The Babylonian army besieged Jerusalem for 18 months, finally capturing the city in July 587 BC. Zedekiah tried to escape but was captured, blinded and exiled to Babylon: this is the Exile of Jer. 52.29. The conquerors destroyed both city and Temple.

TIME CHART

BC	Judah	Ancient South Western Asia
— 650		
	— 642 Manasseh dies; Amon becomes king	
— 640	— 640 Amon dies: Josiah becomes king	*Assyrian*
		power
		declining
— 630		
	— 627 Jeremiah's call to prophesy	— 626 Nabopolassar comes to power in Babylon
— 620		*Babylonian*
		power
		increasing
		— 612 Nineveh falls to Babylon
— 610	Josiah dies at Megiddo	— 610 Neco comes to power in Egypt
	— 609 Jehoahaz reigns 3 months	— 609 Battle of Megiddo: Egypt defeats Judah
	Jehoiakim becomes king	
		— 605 Nebuchadrezzar comes to power in Babylon
		Battle of Carchemish: Babylon defeats
— 600	Jehoiakim dies	Egypt
	— 598 Jehoiachin reigns for 3 months then exiled to Babylon	
	Zedekiah becomes king	— 594 Death of Neco
— 590	End of Zedekiah's reign	— 589 Hophra comes to power in Egypt
	— 587 Jerusalem falls	
	Many exiled to Babylon	
	— 582 3rd Exile to Babylon	
— 580		
— 570		
		— 568 Nebuchadrezzar invades Egypt
		— 562 Nebuchadrezzar dies
— 560		

11

4. WITHOUT KING OR TEMPLE

Babylon now appointed a governor, Gedaliah, to run the affairs of the conquered territory. He made his base at Mizpah, a town about 13 kms north of Jerusalem (see Map 3, p. 236). Gedaliah had not been long in office when there was a conspiracy against him by a man called Ishmael. Gedaliah was murdered and the conspirators fled to Egypt, forcing Jeremiah to go with them. It may have been this incident which led to a third Exile to Babylon, reported in Jer. 52.30. For the next 50 years Jerusalem remained in ruins and Judah had no independent political existence.

STUDY SUGGESTIONS

1. Which kings reigned in Jerusalem during Jeremiah's time as a prophet? Give the dates of their reigns.
2. Read 2 Kings 22.1—25.30, and use it to make a chart which outlines the history of Judah and Jerusalem in this period. Compare it with the chart on p. 11 of this book.
3. Why was the northern kingdom of Israel more likely to experience foreign intervention?
4. Why did conquest by another power require acknowledgment of that power's gods?
5. What responses did Josiah's reform meet?
6. During the time of Jeremiah which kings of Judah were deposed by which foreign powers?
7. Which two important battles late in the seventh century BC affected the fortunes of Judah?

1.4–19
The Call of Jeremiah

OUTLINE

The rest of ch. 1 is concerned with Jeremiah's commission as a prophet. There are four separate sections which have now been woven together. As well as talking about the call of Jeremiah, the verses also form an introduction to the whole book. Each important theme that we shall find later in the book has a mention here: each theme here will be taken up and developed in subsequent chapters. Vv. 4–10: A record of God's call of Jeremiah and Jeremiah's reaction.

Vv. 11–12: A vision Jeremiah has about the way God is certain to fulfil His word.

Vv. 13–16: A further vision, about an invasion of Judah from the north.

Vv. 17–19: God challenges Jeremiah about his ministry, warning and encouraging him.

INTERPRETATION

THE CALL OF THE PROPHET (1.4–10)

As we read through the Bible we can note how God calls different people for different tasks. God calls Abraham and Moses, the people of Israel, Samuel and David. Jesus calls twelve disciples. Paul is called on the road to Damascus.

In the Old Testament we find many prophets, men and women who received from God a fresh message which they delivered to the nation or to particular people. Every prophet needed to have a call from God. To be able to describe it lent weight to their claim that they had a special message from God. Unless prophets had a 'call experience' many would doubt what they said. To know they had been called would also encourage them in difficult times when people ignored or rejected what they said.

Because a prophet's call was so important it is not surprising that, in the Old Testament books bearing their names, we find some information about the calls of Amos, Hosea, Isaiah and Ezekiel, as we do here about Jeremiah. If we compare them we find certain things in common. We can also find certain links between the call of Jeremiah and the call of Moses described in Exodus 3.

The prophetic call begins with God. People became aware of God's call in different ways. There are as many different ways in which God calls people as there are people. Moses was keeping sheep, Isaiah was in the Temple, Ezekiel was in exile. But, however the call takes place, it begins with God. He selects and chooses particular people for particular tasks. Here we are told that He selected Jeremiah from the moment of his conception (v. 5), perhaps even earlier. God *knew* Jeremiah and set him apart for a particular job – to be a prophet. (The Hebrew word translated '*knew*' is a word used for the closest possible relationship; it has the idea of something deep and intimate and includes personal commitment.)

When we look at human leaders we can see how easy it is for those elected to leadership to be proud of their position. We might imagine that people who were certain God had chosen them for special work would also become proud. In fact, we find the exact opposite is true. Those called often had a *deep reluctance* to accept the call. Sometimes they shrank from it because they knew they were unworthy. Sometimes they felt that they could not do the work because of their own weakness or inadequacy. So Jeremiah, like Moses and Isaiah before him, tries to tell God why he is not the right person for this work (v. 6).

God's response contains *encouragement* (vv. 7–8). Jeremiah is assured that God will both give him the message and help him to deliver it. The message is the word of the LORD and not just the words of Jeremiah (see note on 1.2). Jeremiah will not need to be an inventor who works out his own message and ideas; he is to be an interpreter, passing on what he receives from God. We shall find occasions later (e.g. in 28.11f; 42.7) when Jeremiah had to wait before God's message was revealed to him: even when a prophet has been genuinely called by God, the divine word has to come to him fresh each time before he can speak with God's authority. The prophet's responsibility is to pass on what he is given. Also, he is not to select his audience, choosing those people he thinks will be attracted by what he says – he is to go to those to whom God sends him. The prophet is not a general planning a campaign, but an ordinary soldier at the disposal of his commanding officer.

But together with the encouragement in vv. 7–8 there also comes a *warning*. Jeremiah is warned that he will not have an easy time, but that he must be faithful and do what God requires of him. When God calls someone to do a particular job, however dangerous that job may seem it is even more dangerous for that person to disobey God. A man had been talking about his experiences in a country where there had been a civil war. After he had finished, someone said that he must have been very brave to have stayed in the country during the fighting. The man's reaction was that since he was sure God wanted him in that country it would have been far more dangerous *not* to have been there.

So God warns Jeremiah that to act as God's messenger will lead him to face great difficulties and opposition (cf. vv. 17–19). This is not to stop him from being a prophet but to prepare him, so that from the very beginning he knows that his life will not be easy. Compare Jesus's words of warning to his followers in Luke 9.23.

Finally, after encouragement and warning, there would come some kind of *commissioning*. This could include an action (as here in v. 9) and a declaration of the role or message of the one commissioned (here in v. 10). Only after this was the call complete.

We cannot be certain how far the account in vv. 4–10 depends on Jeremiah's own report. It would be strange if the prophet had not had some kind of call experience, but the present shape of the narrative has been determined by the editors of the book. Some scholars are content to accept these verses as an account of how Jeremiah became Yahweh's prophet. Others, however, see their chief importance lying in their testimony to the fact that Yahweh's words have come through Jeremiah; it is on this basis that all the subsequent chapters are important, for they are the 'words of Yahweh', (1. 1).

VISIONS OF THE PROPHET

Each prophet was an individual. How they were called, how they received and delivered their messages, varied. Their backgrounds, situations and temperaments influenced the ways they carried out their ministry. Very often we do not know exactly how a prophet received a message from God. Verse 4 tells us that 'the word of the LORD came'; no mechanism is described. The phrase is saying that Jeremiah became sure of what God was telling him. We can compare this with Genesis 12.1, 'the LORD said to Abram', or with a present-day comment about 'the message which the LORD has given our speaker this morning'.

Some prophets had visions. Amos 1.1 and Isa. 1.1 both refer to messages which these prophets 'saw'. Ezekiel also received messages through visions. Verse 9 here seems to refer to some kind of visual experience. Although there are few references later in the book to visions, vv. 11–12 and 13–16 report two occasions when God did speak to Jeremiah by visual means:

1. In both these incidents the prophet finds a message from God by means of a natural object. An ordinary sight contains a supernatural meaning. So the pot boiling over, spilling on its south side, is a picture of the way that judgement will approach Judah from the north (see Amos 7.1–9 for other pictures linked with judgement).

2. In the first vision, when we read the English we cannot understand how Jeremiah gets his message. The key is found in the Hebrew, for the Hebrew words for 'almond' and 'watching' are very similar, *shaqed* and *shoqed*. Jeremiah sees one and the message is about the other. We call this a play on words. Sometimes, as here, the two words may be very similar: there is another example in Amos 8.1–2, where the Hebrew words for 'summer fruit' and 'end' are *qayits* and *qets*. In other passages, as later in this chapter, a particular word may be repeated to make a special emphasis. First, the *evil* (i.e. judgement) that comes from the north, v.14, is brought by God because of the *evil* (RSV 'wickedness', but the Hebrew word is the same) of His people, v. 16. Then v. 17 has, 'Do not be *dismayed* by them, lest I *dismay* you before them'.

THE MESSAGE OF THE PROPHET

We shall explore this as we go further into the book. We can note here that in this chapter we find outlined the major themes that the book will develop. We can summarize them as:

(a) Jeremiah is a prophet to the nations in general and to Judah in particular.

(b) The first emphasis in his message is on judgement. Destruction must come, and only when it has come will rebuilding be possible.

(c) Once destruction has come rebuilding and renewal will certainly follow.

(d) Jeremiah's message will be unpopular and he himself will face opposition. But this must not lead him to abandon his ministry, for God Himself has called him, will strengthen him and requires him to be faithful.

(e) Jeremiah feels great hesitation and uncertainty about his ministry.

(f) Behind both the words of Jeremiah and the political events that unfold in the book lie the purposes of God. He directs all that occurs. Neither the leaders in Jerusalem nor those of the great empires determine the fate of the nation.

NOTES

1.6: Youth: The word gives no clear guide to Jeremiah's age. Elsewhere, it can mean a child just born or someone old enough to marry. Here, whatever his actual age, it is Jeremiah's way of stressing his youthfulness and feeling of inadequacy for this work to which God has called him.

1.9: Touched my mouth: The mouth was especially significant for the prophetic ministry which was, above all else, a ministry of the spoken word; compare Isaiah 6.5–7.

1.10: Pluck up ... break down ... destroy ... overthrow ... build ... plant: The images of these six verbs constantly recur in the chapters that follow. The twin themes of Yahweh's destruction of Jerusalem (considered impossible by its people) and His subsequent restoration of it (considered hopeless once the destruction had occurred) are constant refrains in Jeremiah. Most thought is concentrated on the destruction.

1.12: I am watching over: Whatever human rulers may think or say, it is God who actually determines the course of events. The same word is used at 5.6 of the leopard lurking in wait for its prey, and

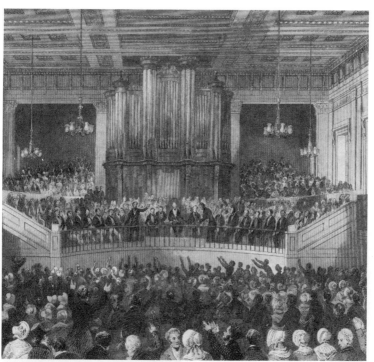

'The prophetic call begins with God.' All through history people have been 'called' by God to speak in His name against the evils of their day. The prophetic words and tireless work of William Wilberforce in the 19th century, supported by anti-slavery societies, led to abolition of the evil practice of slavery in many countries.

such a warning of threatening doom fits well here. But the positive element (**build and plant**, v.10) can also be included, as it is at 31.28.

1.14: Out of the north: To the north lay the main road to Mesopotamia, the direction from which enemies traditionally advanced on Israel and Judah; because of the desert there was no direct route from the east. The north was also often thought of as the home of divine powers hostile to Israel; this too may be in mind here.

1.15: I am calling all ... of the north: In many parts of the Ancient world people believed that different gods were responsible for different countries, and that the fortunes of a country reflected the relative power of competing gods. By contrast, one of the distinct marks of the faith of Israel was the conviction, as here, that their God was the LORD of all history, and that *all* nations came under His authority.

1.16: Their wickedness in forsaking me; they have burned incense to other gods, and worshipped the works of their own hands: The first half of the verse contains the general charge; the people have forsaken God. The second half gives the particular charges; they have offered worship to other gods (breaking the first commandment), and to created objects (breaking the second commandment). Although there were particular sacrifices where incense was burned, here the phrase is probably best understood (as in GNB) to mean sacrifice in general rather than burning incense in particular.

1.17: Gird up your loins: In ancient Israel, as in some countries today, people wore long robes, so before a person ran he would tie up his robe in a belt so that it did not get in his way. This is what Jeremiah was to do: he was to get ready and brace himself for a struggle.

1.18: Iron pillar: At this time iron was the toughest material available. God would make Jeremiah strong enough to be able to resist every threat and attack from his enemies (cf. 1 Cor. 10.13f; 1 John 4.4).

STUDY SUGGESTIONS

REVIEW OF CONTENT

1. What are the typical features in stories about the call of a prophet?
2. What do we mean by a 'play on words'? Why is it sometimes difficult to understand plays on words when the Bible is translated? Give examples of two kinds of plays on words that we find in this section of Jeremiah.

3. Put in your own words six important themes found in this passage which will be developed later in Jeremiah.
4. What do you understand by:
   (a) God 'watching over' His word, v.12?
   (b) The 'kingdoms of the north', v.15?
   (c) 'Gird up your loins', v.17?

BIBLE STUDY

5. Compare the call of Jeremiah with the calls of Moses (Exod. 3.1—4.17), Isaiah (Isa. 6.1–13) and Paul (Acts 9.1–19). Identify the common elements in these stories. What significant differences, if any, are there between them?
6. In John 2.19 Jesus uses imagery similar to that found here in 1.10. What were the different sorts of destruction and new hope that Jeremiah and Jesus were talking of?
7. Compare the emphasis in 1.11f on Yahweh fulfilling His word with Num. 23.19, Isa. 55.10f and Heb. 4.12f. In the New Testament we find that 'the word of God' is used not only of what God has said but also of Jesus; what does this teach us?

DISCUSSION AND APPLICATION

8. In ancient Israel God gave messages to His people through prophets. How do people in your community become aware of God's messages?
9. How would you expect people today to support a claim that they had been called by God?
10. Do you think it natural for people to shrink from taking up positions of Christian leadership? Give reasons for your answer.
11. Like many other Old Testament leaders, Jeremiah faced great opposition. What recent examples can you give of people who were opposed when they spoke out for God? Why were they unpopular? Do you think Christian leaders today should expect to be unpopular?

Special Note B
The Structure of the Book of Jeremiah

When we look at a modern book we expect it to have a clear structure and to develop its themes as it proceeds. Often a quick look at the table of contents or the chapter headings makes the arrangement clear. It may be chronological or thematic, but it will have a definite pattern. Such a pattern is not only a feature of recent books; it is true also of many old books: from within the Bible we could mention the Acts of the Apostles, Paul's letters, Genesis or the books of Samuel and Kings.

In the prophetic books of the Old Testament it is often much more difficult to understand the overall arrangement of the material. We may find close links between two adjacent passages but quite fail to see any connection between them and surrounding material. This is certainly true of the book of Jeremiah: while certain themes are prominent and the overall emphases are plain, the reasons behind the arrangement of some of the material in the book are not at all obvious. While we can identify some natural units, in many places, especially in the first half of the book, we cannot explain the present arrangement of oracles. Probably this does not matter very much, since it is unlikely that a precise arrangement was the chief aim of the editors. So in the remainder of this note we shall identify what appear to be the most obvious units within the book, but will not try to fit everything into a detailed scheme.

1.1–19: Introduction
The opening chapter sets the scene for what will follow. It gives a historical context and mentions most of the major themes to be developed in the book.

2.1—25.38: God's Judgement On His People
The central theme of these chapters is obviously the coming of God's judgement on Judah. The sin of God's people and the nature of God's judgement are explored in various ways in poetic oracles and reports of various incidents. Also included are some poems which are presented as Jeremiah's personal reactions.

While the main theme is clear, we cannot trace a steady development within these chapters. The following substantial sub-units have been proposed:

2.1—6.30: Some have suggested that this collection of short

poems comes from early in Jeremiah's ministry. This is possible but, since most of the material is not dated, we have no way of being sure.

7.1—8.3: A collection of attacks on false worship. (Some scholars have suggested that the whole of 7.1—10.25 belongs under this theme.)

21.1—23.40: Two series of passages concerned with the leaders of Judah. 21.1—23.8 focuses on the kings and 23.9–40 on the prophets.

24.1—25.38: This collection of passages leads from the idea of God's judgement on Judah to that of His judgement on the world. This rounds off the whole section, and prepares us for the later development of the theme of God's judgement on the nations.

26.1—36.32: The Divine Word Comes Offering Hope, But It Is Rejected

Not all scholars agree that these eleven chapters should be grouped together, but the theme suggested is certainly prominent throughout the text. Within these chapters, which are not in chronological order, we can identify the following sub-units:

26.1–24: An account of the responses to Jeremiah's preaching of the 'Temple sermon'. God's invitation to repent is ignored or rejected.

27.1—29.32: Jeremiah proclaims God's word but he is opposed by other prophets who thus reject God's message.

30.1—33.26: These four chapters focus on the theme of restoration and hope, and to some extent mark a break with the overall theme of chs 26—36. However, the hope will only come once the judgement has fallen; so the rejection of God's word is assumed. What is more, in the despair that follows the fall of Jerusalem, any hope seems improbable – thus the natural reaction of the people who earlier rejected God's word of judgement will be to reject this hope also.

34.1—36.32: Jehoiakim formally burns a scroll containing a collection of Jeremiah's messages. This rules out the possibility of further opportunities to respond to God's word. From now on the judgement will be inevitable.

37.1—45.5: The Divine Word of Judgement is Worked Out

Apart from 45.1–5, these chapters are arranged chronologically. They trace the course of events in Zedekiah's reign once the fatal attack by Babylon had begun. Chapter 45 is linked with the same period as ch. 36 and could naturally have followed it. Placed as it now is, it reminds us of ch. 36; the fate that then became inevitable has now been accomplished. Judgement has come, but the promise of chs 30—33 remains valid; Baruch will survive – something new is still possible.

46.1—51.64: God's Message for the Nations

This final major section of the book takes us beyond Israel and Judah to the nations of the world. God's judgement is proclaimed to a range of nations, last of which comes the 'king' of the world, Babylon. With the overthrow of Babylon, the restoration of God's people can begin.

52.1–34: Conclusion

A historical epilogue is used to endorse the accuracy of Jeremiah's message. Since he was right all the time, what he said should be heeded.

The following outline uses the main divisions proposed above to suggest one possible way of viewing the book as a whole. It oversimplifies but tries to suggest how we can see in the material an ongoing development, which may help our understanding.

1.1–19: Introduction.

2.1—25.38: The announcement of the message of God's judgement.

26.1—36.32: The opportunity to repent in response to the message of God's judgement is presented but rejected.

37.1—45.5: God's judgement takes place.

46.1—51.64: Now God judges the judges. Hope for the future can become a reality.

52.1–34: Conclusion.

STUDY SUGGESTIONS

1. Give examples of some biblical books that have a clear structure. Why is it often difficult to understand the arrangement of material in the prophetic books?
2. What are the main divisions of the Book of Jeremiah?
3. The Book of Jeremiah is not arranged in chronological order. Why do you think this is so?
4. What are suggested as major themes of the book?

2.1—3.5
The Sin of God's People

OUTLINE

Chapters 2—6 contain a series of short poems about things that were wrong in Judah and their consequences; 2.1—3.5 is chiefly concerned with how God's people have sinned.

2.1–3: A picture of Israel as she was meant to be – a devoted bride.
2.4–13: Israel's two fundamental evils: turning from God and turning to other gods.
2.14–19: The results of these evils.
2.20–25: Israel has deliberately pursued evil.
2.26–28: Israel's evil will leave the people embarrassed.
2.29–37: Israel's evil means that God's judgement is justified.
3.1–5: A picture of Israel as she is – an unfaithful wife who has become a prostitute.

INTERPRETATION

A GREAT BEGINNING (2.1–3)

In many languages 'once upon a time' is a common way for children's stories to begin. The child's imagination is taken back to a time long before its parents were born, when things were different. This passage does the same. It goes back in history to the time when Israel became a nation, the time of the Exodus from Egypt, the covenant-making and law-giving at Mount Sinai. 'Making a covenant was like getting married', it says; 'God was the bridegroom, the people of Israel the bride'. The Israelites began the journey from Mount Sinai like a bride on her honeymoon, deeply in love with her husband and eager to follow him. Nothing was too much trouble.

Because Israel belonged to God in a special way this was the right way for the people to behave. Like all mankind Israel had been created by God. But, in addition, God had rescued Israel from Egypt and called the people for a special purpose (see Exod. 19.5f). So Israel belonged to God twice over – by creation and by redemption. The people responded with devotion and God gave His special protection and blessing.

If we read only this passage we would think that the wilderness period was a time of perfect peace between God and Israel. We do not have to read far in the book of Exodus to know that this was not the case; there were some big problems, and later some of the prophets pictured the wilderness period as a time of constant rebellion (see Amos 5.25; Hos. 11.1f; Ezek. 20.13–17). Elsewhere in Jeremiah it is clear that there were problems in the wilderness (see 7.21–26, p. 53). The material in 2.1–3 has been selected to make a particular point. When a marriage begins, the relationship is fresh and special: it was like this when Israel became God's covenant people; whatever the failures from the start, there was an excitement and warmth in the relationship with God.

New beginnings are often times of great excitement. We may see it at the birth of a child, or from the dancing in the streets at the overthrow of an unpopular ruler. We find it too in religion. Someone comes to a living Christian faith and their life is marked by a new warmth and enthusiasm. Revelation calls it 'first love' (see Rev. 2.4), and reminds us that we can easily lose it. This is what is in mind here in Jeremiah; despite the failures in the wilderness the faith of the people was real and alive. But now everything has changed.

AN UNHAPPY ENDING (2.4—3.5)

Some writers make their stories end happily, for they think people enjoy that. Jeremiah was concerned to report what he saw. The honeymoon had ended in disaster, the marriage had broken down. This was not God's fault but Israel's; the people had rebelled against God.

1. THE BASIC EVIL – CHANGED MASTERS

In a marriage ceremony bride and groom promise to be faithful to each other. At Mount Sinai Israel had promised to be faithful to God. But the promise had been broken. The verses 2.13 and 17 sum it up: Israel had turned from the true, living God to the Baals, the false, lifeless gods of the Canaanites. Like Hosea before him, Jeremiah uses the strongest language (we might think him much too rude today!); he describes Israel as a prostitute, frantic to embrace as many men as possible.

His chief charge here is that by worshipping the Baals Israel was following a false religion. Many of the Israelite settlers would have seen it very differently. They would certainly have wanted to continue to worship Yahweh, the God who had been with them in the wilderness. But they would also have believed that the productivity of the ground and natural phenomena like wind and rain were caused by the divine powers of the land, the Baals. And so they would have wanted to worship these Baals also.

Such an understanding of how nature operates is still common today in many traditional African and other societies, where the whole of life is seen as religious. Among the Banyarwanda or the Barundi, for instance, the night before seeds are planted the tradition is for husband and wife to engage in ritual sexual intercourse to aid the fertility of the fields. Such practices were far more widespread in Canaanite Baalism, where sacred prostitution was one prominent feature and was no doubt highly attractive. This was no doubt the reason why Jeremiah used such powerful imagery as the prostitute who longs for more men (2.20), and the wild ass on heat (2.24). To most Israelites such practices were not only attractive, they were natural: to Jeremiah they showed that Israel did not really trust Yahweh, for they did not worship Him alone.

Although such problems take different forms today, they remain common, for they arise from confusion between the Christian gospel and culture. The ancient Israelites assumed that their faith in Yahweh should fit with the cultural and religious values of those already in the land. Today, many people in the Western world assume that the values of their society are to be identified with Christian standards. This very easily blinds people to vital aspects of the Christian message.

In other parts of the world there may be tension between Christianity and traditional world views. In very many areas early Christian missionaries often taught or gave the impression that all aspects of traditional culture were evil; in effect the prevailing European world view was sometimes imposed on new converts. In recent years there have been strong reactions against this, and attempts to develop truly indigenous forms of worship and spirituality. This is a slow process, and where the pull of traditional religions remains strong it can be difficult to distinguish between applying genuine Christianity in the appropriate culture (contextualization) and changing Christianity to fit more closely with the local culture's world view (syncretism).

Jeremiah was not only concerned with the religious issue. He also says that the Israelites' politics provided further evidence that the people did not really trust Yahweh. At this time Judah, the only part of the Promised Land still occupied by the children of Israel, was very vulnerable politically, and diplomats were trying to negotiate treaties to ensure its safety. Some of Judah's leaders sought safety in Assyria, others in Egypt. Jeremiah declared that trust in politics had replaced trust in the living God.

Such comments can still be relevant. Political ideologies of different kinds compete, and developing nations are under pressure to take one side or another. The pursuit of improved living standards (so vital in so many parts of the world) or other social goals can take the place of God. Such goals can have real value, but if they totally dominate our world view they have displaced God from His rightful place. For Jeremiah, trust in God must not be hindered by total allegiance to anything else.

2. EVIL COMES IN MANY WAYS

No-one likes to be rebuked. People are often blind to their failings and need to have the wrong spelt out before they are convinced. This passage contains many different word-pictures to bring home to the people their evil. If they do not recognize one kind of evil in themselves, they may notice another.

Their sin reveals itself in a whole variety of evils; things they have done or omitted, and their basic attitudes. They are *forgetful* (2.6–8) of all that God has done for them. They are *rebellious* (2.20, 29f), refusing to take note of the way that God has tried to bring them back to Himself, warning them through the prophets and natural phenomena. Sometimes they *deny* they have sinned (2.23, 35), at others they are *casual* about the seriousness of their sin (2.35; 3.4f). They may plead that they are *helpless* (2.25) because they are not strong enough to resist evil. Their whole behaviour has been *foolish* (2.27f) and leads only to disaster.

Every aspect of their personality is involved. Their *memories* have not treasured what God has done for them or His instructions. They have *never understood* that the choice before them has been between truth and falsehood. Their *wills* have deliberately resisted following what is right. They lack a proper fear of God.

We too easily develop a narrow view of sin. 'I don't get drunk, I have only one wife, I'm not a sinner'; 'I try and help people, that makes me a Christian'; these are common attitudes. Each society has its own versions of such comments. Part of the challenge facing the Christian Church is to show how in one shape or form sin infects every area of society and every kind of person. Jeremiah's attempts to do this did not make him popular, but building and planting could only come when destruction had been effected, 1.10.

3. EVIL BRINGS CONSEQUENCES

Many Old Testament writers had little or no idea about a life after this one. They believed that God's justice must be seen in this world, so they often linked the experience of God's people to their behaviour. The book of Jeremiah does not simply state that people get what they deserve, but it does assert that their evil has brought problems and will bring even bigger ones. It identifies two problems in particular, political and ecological. Political problems will come from powerful enemies, and will lead to a total loss of freedom for

Judah. Ecological problems have already begun: the people's behaviour has led to a change of climate; the rains have failed, poverty and thirst will result.

Christian understanding of the world is influenced by our background and experience and by the New Testament as well as the Old. People who come from the West, where a particular approach to science has led to a division between the 'sacred' and the 'secular', may find it very difficult to see how God can be active in politics or nature. Cultures which see the whole of life as religious avoid this problem, but may still be unable to interpret exactly how God is active in these spheres. But all of us can see only too easily how human evil brings problems – in the political world and in the realm of nature. Exploitation, oppression and greed sow their own seeds of further chaos.

NOTES

2.3: Holy to the LORD: The basic idea of holiness in the Old Testament is of something holy being set apart and dedicated for God. In Israelite understanding the 'first fruits', the first part of the crop, belonged to God and were to be offered to Him in worship. Here the people of Israel are told that they were the first part of Yahweh's harvest of the nations; anyone who interfered with them would face Yahweh's anger.

2.4: Hear the word of the LORD: This is a very common phrase, typical of the way a prophet introduced his message. But this need not mean it was not important. It was an awesome thing for a prophet to declare that his message came from God.

2.5: Went after worthlessness, and became worthless: The Hebrew word translated 'worthless', *hebel*, sounds similar to the word Baal. Jeremiah is implying that Baal is worthless. Brueggemann suggests the translation, 'Pursue a bubble and become a bubble'.

2.7: My land: God gave the land to Israel but it remained His land. The people held it in trust from Him and were not free to do as they pleased with it.

2.8: The priests ... rulers ... prophets: The leaders failed at the very point of their chief responsibility. The priests were required to give God's rulings on issues – but they never consulted Him! The rulers were appointed as God's undershepherds – but they rebelled against Him! The prophets were called to speak in Yahweh's name – but they had turned to Baal!

Those who handle the law: Probably the priests are meant, as at 18.18, though some link the phrase with the 'wise' (meaning the scribes) mentioned at 8.8.

'We can see only too easily how human evil brings problems.' These tombstones show the site of a copper mine in Japan, where many of the workers died because the owners were too greedy for profit to provide protection from the devastating effects of sulphuric acid.

2.10: Cyprus ... Kedar: Cyprus is an island in the Mediterranean, Kedar a name for Arab tribes east of Israel. The idea is 'wherever you go ...'.

2.16: Memphis and Tahpanhes: Two important cities in Egypt (see Map 1, p. 236).

2.18: Egypt ... Assyria: Before Babylon defeated Assyria in 612 BC, Egypt and Assyria were the two major powers in South-western Asia. Probably this verse reflects the existence of two rival groups in Judah, one seeking help from Egypt, the other from Assyria.

2.19: LORD GOD of hosts: In Jeremiah this phrase usually occurs in passages speaking of judgement on God's people and coming disaster. 'Hosts' refers to the heavenly armies/powers of God.

2.20: I will not serve: Judah's assertion of her will recurs as a chorus or motif of her sin (see also 2.25,31; 16.12; 18.12; 22.21; 44.16f).

2.23: The valley: This probably refers to the practices carried out in the valley of the son of Hinnom (see Note on 7.31).

2.27: Who say ... gave me birth: The people are hopelessly confused. In Baalism the 'tree' represented the female goddess, the 'stone' the male god; so even in paganism Judah has things the wrong way round!

2.34: You did not find them breaking in: Judah has killed people without any justification.

2.37: Your hands upon your head: This was a sign of mourning (see 2 Sam. 13.19).

3.1: If a man divorces his wife: The verse appeals to the argument of Deuteronomy 24.1–4, which absolutely forbids the remarriage of a divorced woman to her previous husband if she has since married someone else.

3.2: Bare heights: In Jeremiah this phrase refers to the high places of worship that were found all over the country. Josiah's reform tried to destroy these sanctuaries (see 2 Kings 22—23).

Like an Arab: A desert bandit is meant, one ready to attack and rob travellers.

STUDY SUGGESTIONS

REVIEW OF CONTENT

1. What were the main reasons why Jeremiah attacked the people of Judah?
2. Identify some of the ways in which Judah's sin revealed itself.
3. What links does Jeremiah see between the people's sin and:
   (a) Their politics? (c) The weather?
   (b) Their worship? (d) Their future?

BIBLE STUDY

4. Read Exod. 20.1–17. Which of these ten commandments does the passage we are studying say have been broken?
5. Using a concordance, look up Bible references to 'holy' and 'holiness'. Use these references to build up a picture of what the Bible means by holiness. When you have done this, compare what you have written with what a Bible Dictionary says about holiness.
6. What pictures of sin are given by the following passages?
   (a) 1 Sam. 16.7
   (b) 2 Sam. 11.1–15
   (c) Jer. 17.10
   (d) Luke 10.25–37
   (e) Luke 18.9–14
   (f) Rom. 3.23
   (g) Gal. 5.17–21
   (h) Rev. 3.15–18

DISCUSSION AND APPLICATION

7. What are the common views of sin in your community? How well do they fit with the biblical ideas of holiness you found in Question 5?
8. If you wanted to make points similar to those Jeremiah is making here, what illustrations would you use in your own society?
9. What examples can you give of confusion between the Christian gospel and a particular culture? How far can you see it in Christian mission or missionaries:
   (a) Working in your country?
   (b) Sent from your country?
10. How appropriately do you think that your Church uses the riches of your culture to apply the gospel? In what ways could it do this better?

3.6—4.4
The Call to Repent

OUTLINE

In the previous section we have seen why Judah needed to repent. Now we see what repentance means and what it can offer.

3.6–11: Judah has refused to learn from what happened to Israel.

3.12–18: God pleads with His people to return to Him.

3.19—4.4: A collection of short messages concerned with repentance.

INTERPRETATION

LEARNING FROM HISTORY (3.6–11)

To the north of Judah had been the kingdom of Israel, made up of ten of the tribes of Israel. They had broken away from Judah after the death of King Solomon (1 Kings 12.1–20). Like Judah, they looked back to the Exodus from Egypt as being the time when they became God's special people. But very quickly they had turned away from Yahweh to follow Canaanite gods. Yahweh tried to warn them: He sent prophets; He used natural disasters; but they paid no attention. So finally the Assyrian army came; it conquered the land and forced Exile on many. The nation of Israel was no more.

Judah was Israel's next-door neighbour. The people shared the same faith. They could have learned from what happened to Israel. But they did not. They went on following other gods. They deliberately refused to hear what God had to say to them, and so insulted Him.

History is full of lessons: lessons of success and failure, empires rising and falling, power struggles within governments, oppressors and oppressed, reform and revolution. The writer of Ecclesiastes says that there is 'nothing new under the sun' (Eccles.1.9). He may not be totally right (he never imagined that God would become man!) but there is truth in that statement. History does show a pattern of repetition. This is true of Church history as well as world history. Some of today's heresies are quite similar to those condemned by the Church in earlier centuries. Some issues, such as Church-State relations or contextualization (see p. 25), have recurred again and again in the Church's history. The experience of the Church in earlier years offers many lessons.

Paul says that part of the value of Old Testament history is as a warning, and to teach Christians how they should live (1 Cor. 10.11); the Corinthians would neglect these lessons at their peril. We too are called to learn from the past. If we did, many foolish schemes, many evil and harmful policies would never be put into practice. This would not make the Church perfect, but it would prevent some unnecessary stumbling on the way. Judah was supposed to learn from Israel, the Corinthians from the Old Testament; today's Church in turn is to learn from the whole history of the people of God. Failure to do so has serious consequences.

HOPE IN THE DARKNESS (3.12–18)

Much of the book of Jeremiah makes sad reading. Like Christians in some parts of the world today the prophet is in a tiny minority, and receives some rough treatment. He has an unpleasant message, exposing evil and threatening judgement. He wishes that this were not the case but he lived at a time of darkness, when evil seemed to be triumphing. Nevertheless, from time to time throughout the book, as here in 3.15–18, there are little gleams of light. In chs 30—33 we find a concentrated blaze of light, but even elsewhere there are hints and rumours of it. Why is this?

Some people have suggested that Jeremiah could not make up his mind and kept changing from hope to despair as his feelings changed. Some have thought that he had different messages at different times in his ministry. Others have believed that Jeremiah himself was so pessimistic that he could never have been hopeful, and that the passages about hope must have come from another writer.

There is no doubt that we owe the balance and arrangement of judgement and hope to the editors of the book. They clearly thought that both aspects were important and needed to be presented in tension with one another. If they could do this there seems no compelling reason why Jeremiah himself could not have delivered prophecies of promise as well as doom.

Certainly the finished work shows Jeremiah seeing the sin and evil of the people, their stubbornness and refusal to heed God's message through him. He knew judgement was bound to come and because he cared he felt the hurt deep in his heart. However, although he was often gloomy, we see him not just as a pessimist but as a realist. He not only saw the people's evil and God's threatening judgement. He also saw that even in the darkest situation God remained God. Therefore He could bring hope to a situation that seemed humanly hopeless. Thus Jeremiah could declare that even as he preached judgement, God had a good purpose for the people if they would only repent. Although they had cancer it was still operable, but they must not delay.

The passage also describes this tension from another angle. One of the images already used is that of Judah as the faithless wife (see note on 3.1, p. 29), referring to an Israelite law that such a wife had no right to return to her original husband, and that he was forbidden to take her back if she did return. But now, in this section, we find Judah being urged to repent since, if she does, God may restore her. It is not that God is not offended by her conduct – the offence is deep and bitter to Him. But because His deep affection for her remains, He is prepared to consider even overruling the law (the same kind of tension in God's attitude is shown by Hos. 11.1–9). Legally and morally Judah has no grounds for hope; and yet – with Yahweh – hope remains a possibility.

This is still true. Christian theology affirms that God specializes in bringing triumph out of the wreckage of human disaster. We see the worst that humanity can do in the Cross; out of it God creates the Resurrection. This is His supreme promise that no human situation is beyond His intervention: 'The light shines in the darkness and the darkness has not overcome it' (John 1.5).

This does not mean that evil is to be treated lightly, nor that we should concentrate on the wonders of God's future and ignore the realities of the present. The Church is to be involved responsibly in opposing evil and working for a more just society. But there will still remain much that could lead us to despair, where hope seems absent. In such situations faith is not a despairing optimism but, because God *is* God, a hold on what is truly real. Many years ago Mother Julian of Norwich, a Christian mystic, put it this way: 'All shall be well, and all shall be well, and all manner of things shall be well'.

RETURNING TO GOD (3.12, 14, 22)

A word that Jeremiah uses frequently and in a wide variety of ways is the Hebrew word *shub*, often, as here, translated 'return'. The glimmer of hope in the darkness is for those who return to God in repentance, and only for them. God's people need a real change of heart; they must change the direction of their lives. The people were quite accustomed to this idea since it was a theme in the great Temple services. Sadly, performing the ritual regularly had become just a routine, emptied of real meaning. This was part of Jeremiah's difficulty: he was urging people to repent when they thought that because of the ritual they had already repented and need do nothing further.

Real repentance, declared Jeremiah, was of a quite different kind. People must genuinely return to God. That meant giving up all other religious practices and closely following the law Yahweh had given them. Only then would their lives match their words. This was not something to be undertaken lightly; the consequences should be carefully considered before the step was taken.

One weakness of the Church at times has been a shortage of the kind of commitment that Jeremiah has in mind. A strong desire to see people begin the Christian life has sometimes led the Church to under-emphasize the more demanding aspects of the Christian gospel. When this happens, people can make the mistake of thinking that all that is required on the part of a Christian is baptism or occasional attendance at Church services. Of course the gospel is about the welcome Jesus gives to all who come to Him; but it is also about the challenging demands He makes on those who would follow Him. If the Church is not clear about the whole-hearted commitment of Christians it is bound to be weakened with too many superficial members, committed in theory but not in practice. Jeremiah makes no such mistake. He spells out with great clarity what is needed if the people of Judah are to return to the God they have abandoned. The change must go to the root of their lives.

NOTES

3.8: Sent her away with a decree of divorce: This divorce which the people of Judah had observed was the Exile of the people of the northern kingdom of Israel and the destruction of Samaria, its capital city, by the Assyrians in 722/1 BC. This talk of divorce possibly refers back to 3.1.

3.9: Stone and tree: See note on 2.27.

3.11: Less guilty than false Judah: Judah's people had had the extra opportunity of seeing how God dealt with Israel, so their guilt is the greater.

3.13: Scattered your favours: The picture is again that of the prostitute who distributes favours to attract as many customers as possible.

3.14: I am your master: The Hebrew word for master is *baal*. What Judah offers to the Canaanite baals belongs by right to the true baal, her God.

Zion: 'Zion' is used as a name for Jerusalem. Mount Zion was the hill on which the Temple was built in Jerusalem, just north of the old city of David.

3.15: Shepherds: In the ancient world this was a common title for rulers.

3.16: Ark of the covenant: This was a wooden chest thought of as the throne of the invisible Yahweh. In early days it was taken into battle by Israel's army as a sign of God's presence with them. Later it was placed in the Holy of Holies, the holiest place in the Temple. It contained a copy of the tablets of the Law (the Ten Commandments) and was also supposed to contain Aaron's rod and some manna. There is no mention of it after the fall of Jerusalem and the destruction of the Temple in 587 BC.

3.17: All nations shall gather: When talking of the future, Jeremiah often talks of members of other nations being drawn to Jerusalem. In part they will share in the glory of Israel, but in part they will contribute to it by their service.

3.22b–23: Behold we come to thee ... salvation of Israel: This is a litany of repentance put on the lips of the people by Jeremiah. It illustrates what true repentance means.

4.2: In truth, in justice, and in uprightness: The importance of *justice* (observing what is legally right) and of *uprightness* (being the sort of person who in practice does what is right) is urged by all the prophets. The concern for *truth* is a particular emphasis in Jeremiah, where the falseness of Judah's faith and leaders is often stressed (see note on 7.4).

4.3: Break up your fallow ground: Hosea used this phrase before Jeremiah (Hos. 10.12). It is time for a totally new beginning. The people must start all over again, like farmers breaking completely new ground.

4.4: Circumcise yourselves ... remove the foreskin of your hearts: The people have been deaf and unreceptive to what God has been telling them. They share the physical sign of the covenant, circumcision, but they lack the inward counterpart, openness and responsiveness to God. They must do something about this, for this is what real repentance means.

STUDY SUGGESTIONS

REVIEW OF CONTENT

1. What lessons could Judah have learned from the experience of the northern kingdom of Israel?
2. Suggest reasons why a knowledge of Church history may be useful for Christians today.
3. What is repentance? How large an effect does repentance have on a person's life?
4. Some parts of Jeremiah concentrate on judgement and others speak of hope. What suggestions have been made about how we should understand the relationship between them?

BIBLE STUDY

5. Read the following passages and note the kinds of lessons that are drawn from past experiences of God's people:
   (a) Jer. 26.17–19
   (b) Mark 2.23–28
   (c) 1 Cor. 10.1–11
   (d) Heb. 3.7–19
   (e) Heb. 11.8–19

6. What do the following passages have to teach about repentance?
   (a) Psalm 51
   (b) Joel 2.12–17
   (c) Luke 3.3–14
   (d) Luke 15.11–24
   (e) Rev. 2.1–5; 3.1–3

7. What tensions within God's attitude to His people are suggested by Hosea 11.1–9?

8. The lack of a real commitment is a recurring theme in the prophets: in addition to Jer. 3.6—4.4, read Amos 2.4–12, Hos. 8.1–5, Isa. 1.2–4 and Mic. 3.9–12. Similar attacks on shallow commitment continue in the New Testament: read for example, Matt. 21.28–32, Luke 6.46 and Acts 5.1–11.

9. The way that the material in the prophetic books has been arranged means that often, as here in Jer. 3.6—4.4, we find short messages of hope embedded in larger messages of judgement. Read:
   (a) Isa. 1—5;
   (b) Amos 5.1–27;
   (c) Micah 1—3;
   and then say where a short message, or messages, of hope can be found within each of these passages.

DISCUSSION AND APPLICATION

10. In what ways does your Church try to show both God's hatred of evil and at the same time His longing to welcome the person who repents?

11. What kind of provision do you think should be made for disciplining Church members who fall into sin?

12. How easily do you see stories from the Bible or from Church history as direct lessons for Christians today? Give some examples.

13. In what ways does your Church encourage members to deepen their commitment to God?

14.   At the cross of Jesus
                     Pardon is complete;
                 Love and justice mingle,
                    Truth and mercy meet.

How does an understanding of the Cross begin to help us see how the Old Testament tension between God's love of the sinner and His hatred of sin can be resolved?

4.5—6.30
The Approach of Disaster

OUTLINE

The central theme of this series of short oracles is the approach and certainty of God's judgement. The element of hope appears only at 5.18–19, and is much less noticeable than in the previous section. There is correspondingly less urging of repentance, for the time for repentance is past. Once again the poetry contains a wide variety of vivid images and is full of urgency and passion.

4.5–8: The enemy army is on its way!
4.9–10: Judah's leaders are left speechless.
4.11–18: Judgement is coming like a fierce wind.
4.19–31: The great horror of invasion.
5.1–9: All alike are sinners.
5.10–17: They said God was harmless; now they will see His power.
5.18–19: However, a few may survive.
5.20–29: It is the Creator who is the Judge.
5.30–31: False people love false leaders.
6.1–8: Jerusalem is besieged.
6.9–15: The people have no sense of shame or guilt.
6.16–21: They will not listen to God's warning so they will not be able to hide from Him.
6.22–26: Terror on every side!
6.27–30: The prophet's verdict on the people.

INTERPRETATION

GOD IS NOT POWERLESS

We have seen that the people of Judah were worshipping many gods. They confused Yahweh with the baals, and did not think of Yahweh

37

as having any particularly great power. They paid Him lip service but did not take Him very seriously.

This, says the prophet, is a great mistake, for Yahweh is the controller of creation. The theme of Yahweh as creator occurs often in the Old Testament – in Genesis, in Job and the Psalms as well as in other prophets (see Isa. 40.12–31; Amos 4.13f; 5.8f; 9.5f). Here Jeremiah uses it to declare that because it is the Creator who is the Judge He can harness all the powers of nature to do His will. His judgement is like the blistering east wind, full of sand, that rolls in from the desert (4.11–18). In 4.23–26 the story of creation in Genesis 1 is reversed: mankind and birds are no more, gardens are barren and cities reduced to heaps of rubble, the earth's foundations are removed, the lights are gone and chaos has returned. How foolish to think that Yahweh is of no account – for this is the power He can employ in His Judgement.

But He is not only creator, He is also controller of history. Nations are under His command. Isaiah had described the nation of Assyria as the rod of Yahweh's anger (Isa.10.5). Now Jeremiah sees Yahweh as the one leading the enemy to attack and defeat the people of Judah (5.15–17; 6.1–8). He controls the mightiest army of the ancient world. How foolish to neglect Him; He is well able to punish sin.

Often in the past the Christians' God has been seen by other people as one among a number of divinities, a god whose chief rivals are other gods. Only when people have been convinced that He is the greatest or the only God have they become Christians. Such attitudes remain common for many in Asia, Africa and elsewhere today. In the Western world, however, where people's hopes have centred on progress through science, the advances of materialism or the pursuit of power, His rivals are now more often secular gods than religious ones. Whether we belong to the more technological West or the more religious 'developing' world, if we lose sight of the power of the living God it is natural for us to take Him lightly. To do so, says Jeremiah, will lead us into grave danger.

GOD IS NOT CARELESS

A man once declared, 'God will forgive me, that is his job'. Some people in Judah had a similar idea: 'God will do nothing', they said (5.12). They did not deny His power, but it remained theoretical. He would never use it against them; He was harmless.

Jeremiah totally denied this, declaring that God had strict standards of right and wrong. How people behaved was of great concern to Him. He had done His best to guide and warn them, but the people had taken no notice. Even when their sin was made clear to them they were not the slightest bit ashamed. *They* might not care, but *God* did. They had treated Him lightly; they had played with fire and now they would get burned.

Throughout the world today secular and religious ideologies challenge the Christian view. In many parts of the world standards of right and wrong are changing. Sometimes the idea of God as judge is itself under attack from within Christian circles. 'God is love', we are told, 'He will not hurt anyone'. God *is* full of love, but it is a *holy* love. He is not only grieved by the evil of so many kinds that abounds in the world; He will act once and for all to deal with it. The Cross and the Resurrection are His pledge of that. When His final act comes it will be very hard for those who treat His standards lightly (see 1 Pet. 4.17). Because He cares He will judge.

GOD IS NOT BIASED (6.27–30)

The last passage in this section pictures the prophet as an assayer testing the purity of a metal. He is trying to extract the pure silver from the less valuable matter. But, hard as he tries, he finds no silver at all. He reports His findings to Yahweh: the people are like 'refuse' silver (see note on 6.30); there is no pure metal; all are corrupt, none is without guilt. This is true of leaders and peasants, educated and simple, politicians and priests. All are examined and found wanting. All must face the consequences, for God has no favourites.

Every human society has divisions and favours one section at the expense of another. Class or racial distinctions divide people, so does access to money or to 'contacts'. All too often injustice operates to benefit the more powerful members of society at the expense of the weaker ones. A poor man suffers while a well-paid man who breaks the law has his fine paid by the company. The prophets in Israel spoke against such injustice yet it continued. It still does. But God has no favourites; His judgement will apply to all. None can escape it, none can buy their way out of it, all are liable to it, and the greater a person's opportunities and responsibilities, the more will be required of them. Face up to that, says Jeremiah, for God will judge.

NOTES

4.5: Blow the trumpet: A city watchman blew his trumpet to warn of the enemy's approach. See also 4.19,21; 6.1,7; Hos. 8.1; Joel 2.1; Amos 3.6.

'Too often injustice operates to benefit the more powerful members of society at the expense of the weaker ones.' This happens in many of the world's great cities—as shown here in Calcutta, where shanty homes of the poorest people cluster alongside a towering block of luxury flats being built for the rich.

4.9: Princes: Members of the king's administration, not his personal family. GNB translates well as 'officials'.

4.10: It shall be well with you: This is the false prophets' message which has given people a false sense of security. False prophecy troubled Jeremiah; see 23.9–40 (p. 128) and 28.1–17 (p. 152).

4.15: Dan ... Mount Ephraim: Dan was on the northern border of the old kingdom of Israel; Mount Ephraim was much nearer, just next door to Judah (see Map 2, p. 235).

4.17: She has rebelled against me: The Hebrew stresses the 'me', so we could translate, 'Me it is she has rebelled against'. Similarly in v. 22 we could read, 'Me they do not know'.

4.19: My anguish: This is a good example of the difficulty that recurs throughout Jeremiah, of knowing who is speaking and who is being addressed or spoken about. Most people think the prophet is the speaker here, being personally caught up in the tragedy that is developing. (A few suggest that the words are put on the lips of Jerusalem or Judah, imagining their reaction as judgement overtakes them.)

4.22: They know me not ... how to do good they know not: Only where there is knowledge of Yahweh can there be knowledge of the right way to behave.

4.27: Yet I will not make a full end: If the RSV translation is correct this does not appear to fit well here, and could be a later addition to soften the declaration of judgement. Brueggemann suggests that an alternative way to understand these words is to see them as an expression of reluctance on Yahweh's part because of His deep longing not to destroy His people. As soon as He has pronounced the judgement He recoils from it, as though to say, 'No, I can't do it' (compare Hos. 11.8). We may do better if we understand the Hebrew to mean, 'I will certainly make a full end' (JB); the same applies at 5.10.

4.30: You dress in scarlet ... beautify yourself: A return to the picture of a prostitute. In a last, desperate attempt to find security, Jerusalem tries to make herself attractive to the invader. But it is in vain.

4.31: A woman in travail: The image changes to that of a mother about to deliver her first child. She is helpless and in agony but has no midwife with her, only those who wish her death.

5.10: Make not a full end: See note on 4.27.

5.13: The prophets will become wind ... done to them: In most English versions this verse continues the false prophets' rejection of the message of judgement begun in the previous verse. But it is probably better to see it as a comment on the false prophets; they have rejected the word (of Yahweh) and so they will become wind. See further 23.9–40, p. 128.

5.17: They shall eat up ... with the sword: Brueggemann comments that it is 'not the identity of the army but what it does that is important' and compares the threat here with that posed by the monarchy according to 1 Samuel 8.11–17.

5.18f: But even in those days ... not yours: These verses apparently come from a later time. Some of the people have survived the experience of Exile, and the editor wanted the message to allow for this.

5.21: Senseless people: The people refuse to use the minds God has given them.

5.31: Priests rule at their direction: The Hebrew is literally 'rule at their hands'. Either the priests are under the authority of the prophets or they behave in just the same way.

6.1: Tekoa ... Beth-haccherem: Two towns very near Jerusalem (see Map 3, p. 236): the danger is at the door.

Looms out of the north: See note on 1.14. Evil is hanging over Jerusalem like a sword about to fall on those beneath. Neither here nor elsewhere in these early chapters of the book is the foe from the north identified. This does not matter. For one thing, the lack of identity can make the threat more ominous, since no political or military precautions can be taken. More important, whatever human instrument may be employed acts at Yahweh's direction. He is the controller of all history, and that includes the approaching destruction of Jerusalem.

6.3: Shepherds with their flocks: Invading kings with their armies (see note on 3.15).

6.4f: Prepare war against her ... destroy her palaces: Probably both these verses are supposed to be words spoken by the enemy.

6.9–11: Thus says the LORD of hosts ... very aged: Yahweh speaks in v. 9, Jeremiah replies, and Yahweh speaks again in v. 11b. Jeremiah must make sure that everyone has heard the message. 'Remnant' here is probably those who have not yet heard the message, in which case it is not necessarily those who will survive.

6.14: They have healed the wound ... lightly: The gravity of the situation has not been realized. The NIV reads 'They dress the wound of my people as though it were not serious'; a major injury is treated as though it were a slight scratch.

6.16: Ancient paths: The Law of Moses.

6.17: Watchmen: A familiar term for a prophet (cf. Ezek. 3.17; Hab. 2.1). Note also the link back to 'trumpet' (see note on 4.5).

6.20: Your burnt offerings are not ... pleasing to me: Sacrifice has no value unless it comes from a sincere heart. See 7.21–26, p. 52.

6.25: Terror is on every side: This phrase recurs in the story of Jeremiah's ministry; see 20.3f; 46.5; 49.29. It seems he used it so much that it became a nickname others gave him (20.10).

6.26: Mourning as for an only son: The most bitter sorrow imaginable; there is no-one who can continue the family.

6.30: Refuse silver they are called: To refine silver, lead is first added. When the mixture is melted the impurities are absorbed into the lead and the pure silver is left behind. When Jeremiah does this with the people of Judah he finds there *is* no silver, only the 'refuse': the lead filled with impurities.

STUDY SUGGESTIONS

REVIEW OF CONTENT

1. What aspects of God's power does Jeremiah appeal to in this section? How does he illustrate them?
2. On what basis does Jeremiah here present God as judge?
3. What reasons are given here for God's judgement of Judah?

BIBLE STUDY

4. Compare 4.23–26 with Gen. 1. List the ways in which the Jeremiah passage reverses the account of Genesis.
5. In addition to the passages in Isa. 40 and in Amos given in the text above, read Job 38—39, Ps. 19.1–6 and Ps. 104. What picture of God do these passages present?
6. Christians in Corinth claimed that because they belonged to Christ they were free to do anything. How did Paul treat these claims? See 1 Cor. 6.12–20.
7. We have seen that Judah's loyalties were divided. What loyalties do you think prevented the following from being devoted to God, according to the following passages?
   (a) Samson: Judges 16.
   (b) King Jehoiakim: Jer. 22.13–17.
   (c) The rich young ruler: Mark 10.17–22.
   (d) Ananias and Sapphira: Acts 5.1–11.
   (e) The silversmiths of Ephesus: Acts 19.23–41.
   (f) Felix: Acts 24.1–27.
8. What points about God's control of history are made by:
   (a) Ps. 105?
   (b) Isa. 45.1–6?
   (c) Dan. 2.31–46?

DISCUSSION AND APPLICATION

9. If we believe that God is in charge of history, how does that affect our attitudes towards world events and our prayers for nations and their leaders?
10. What do you see as the chief rivals to God:
    (a) In your society?
    (b) In your Church?
    (c) In your life?
11. Do you think that it is right to maintain the image of God as judge in today's world? Give your reasons.
12. In your country, are there ways in which 'injustice operates to benefit the more powerful members of society at the expense of the weaker ones'? If so, in what ways is the Church active to oppose this?
13. Do you think that there are ways in which your Church favours some people (e.g. on the grounds of race, wealth or sex) at the expense of others? If so, give examples.

Special Note C
The Deuteronomic Editors

2 Kings 22—23 reports a reform carried out by King Josiah. If you read the books of Kings you find that the standard of this reform is the basis by which the kings of Judah and Israel are judged. Most scholars believe that people in favour of these reform measures were responsible for the editorial emphasis in the history of the people of Israel that we find in Joshua, Judges and the Books of Samuel and Kings (often called the Deuteronomic History).

If we compare the outlook of the Book of Deuteronomy with these principles we find that there are many similarities. These occur both in the basic ideals laid down in the reform and also in the style of writing. These basic ideals include the centralization of worship at one sanctuary, the abolition of the worship of various other gods, and the making of the Passover a central pilgrimage festival.

Because of these similarities this theological outlook is often called 'Deuteronomic' or 'Deuteronomistic'. Fuller discussion of this will be found in the Study Guide on Deuteronomy to be published in this series. But we mention it here because there are some similarities between the writing style and theological outlook of parts of Jeremiah and the Deuteronomic History. For this reason, many scholars believe that the editors of our book of Jeremiah combined a loyalty to the teaching and tradition of Jeremiah with a sympathy towards many of the central features of the theology of Josiah's (Deuteronomic) reform. This is why in places in this book we refer to the 'Deuteronomic editors', or to a passage as reflecting a 'Deuteronomic viewpoint'.

STUDY SUGGESTIONS

1. What reasons do scholars have for linking the book of Deuteronomy and the 'Deuteronomic History'?
2. Why are some parts of Jeremiah described as 'Deuteronomic'?
3. What conclusions about the editors of the Book of Jeremiah may be drawn from the style and the ideals of parts of the book?

7.1–15
The Temple Sermon

OUTLINE

Jeremiah 7.1—8.3 accuses Judah of false religious practices. Unlike chapters 2—6, which are poetry, the material is prose and in a style typical of the editors of the book (see Special Note C, p. 44). There are four sections, and the first reports a sermon preached by Jeremiah to people gathered for worship in the Temple. Chapter 26 has a shorter account of the sermon, but then describes how people reacted.

Vv. 1–2: An introduction which gives the setting of the incident.

Vv. 3–4: The 'text' of the sermon.

Vv. 5–7: These verses develop v. 3, giving conditions for God to bless Judah.

Vv. 8–15: These verses develop v. 4, discussing the results of Judah's disobedience.

INTERPRETATION

The sermon is an attack on the faith of the worshippers. There is no doubt that they have a real faith; they are confident that they will remain safe in Jerusalem. Very bluntly Jeremiah declares that their faith is deluded. Because of their behaviour they will soon be driven out of Jerusalem and forced into Exile; at the same time their Temple, in which they trust so much, will become a heap of rubble. What their religious leaders are telling them is in fact a lie, deceiving them totally. Jeremiah declares that for three reasons their faith is false.

1. THEIR FAITH IS SELECTIVE

If citizens of Jerusalem in Jeremiah's day had been asked what lay at the heart of their faith they would most probably have described the covenant with David, and Yahweh's special choice of Jerusalem. In order to understand this we need to outline some earlier history.

King David was one of the great heroes of Israel. Before him there had been a succession of Judges and then King Saul. Saul had only reigned over part of the 'children of Israel' and his reign had ended in defeat. David had changed all that. In his reign the Israelites completed their conquest of the Promised Land. He had led them to victory over their enemies and established Israel as a great power in South-west Asia. Among the changes David made was the establishing of Jerusalem as the nation's capital; it became both a political and a religious centre. After Solomon died and the northern kingdom of Israel broke away Jerusalem remained the capital of the south.

According to 2 Samuel 7 David wished to build a house – a temple – for Yahweh but Yahweh would not permit it. Instead, He promised to establish a house – a line of descendants – for David. Since that time the royal house of David had been firmly established in Judah; there was never any successful challenge to its right to rule in Jerusalem. (The northern kingdom had a very different history, with seven of its nineteen kings being murdered.) Solomon, David's son, built the Temple which was regarded as the special home of Yahweh. It was seen as a sign of His presence with the people, and they thought that this meant that no harm could come to it or to them (see 2 Sam. 7.13, 16). This belief was strengthened further during the reign of Hezekiah (c.715–697 BC), when much of Judah was devastated by the Assyrian army but Jerusalem itself was spared. Although Isaiah said that this sparing of Jerusalem should be seen as a call for repentance, in actual fact many people celebrated it as a great deliverance and a cause for rejoicing (Isa. 22.12f). By Jeremiah's time the dominant feature of the theology taught in Jerusalem was the complete certainty that God would always protect Jerusalem and its citizens.

Jeremiah does not deny the covenant with David, though the book does not say much about it. But it does say that the covenant is by no means the whole of Israel's faith. Other parts of their faith are at least as important. In particular, there is the story of the covenant and Law-giving at Mount Sinai, a story every child in Jerusalem would know. In that covenant the children of Israel promised to do what God commanded them. Now, by concentrating on the Davidic covenant and forgetting everything else, the people had become unbalanced in their faith. Jeremiah agrees that any covenant with God is a great privilege, but insists that the blessings of the Davidic covenant go together with the responsibilities of the Sinai one. Because the people had selected just one part of Israel's belief from the whole, their faith has become distorted.

We too can easily fall into the same trap as Judah, for it is natural to find certain parts of Christian teaching speaking particularly strongly to us. For instance, liberation theologians and others campaigning for social justice make much use of the prophets; civil and religious authorities appeal to the Ten Commandments and Romans 13. Some Christians feel most at home with St Paul, while others find St John an easier companion. Some Christians see the incarnation of Jesus as the centre of faith, others give that place to His crucifixion. Danger comes when we magnify our particular emphasis to the exclusion of other insights, and in effect claim that we have the whole truth. Once this happens it is all too easy to end up with our own version of Christian doctrine shaped to fit our ideas. This can happen when one individual neglects the insights of the local body of Christ, or when a congregation neglects those of the wider body of Christ.

God is too big to fit into any tidy system of ours. One useful thing for any pastor or regular preacher to do is to record the texts chosen and the theme of each sermon; then from time to time to check whether the people are getting a 'balanced diet' of Christian truth or a very narrow selection; whether it is genuine exposition of the texts, or if the same point is being made whatever the text chosen. There is a saying about a nineteenth-century English preacher, 'Ten thousand thousand were his texts, but all his sermons one'!

2. THEIR FAITH IS SUPERFICIAL

To sit an examination is no guarantee that you will pass. What is important is evidence that you have passed; if you rely merely on evidence that you have taken the exam there is no security. The people of Judah were making a mistake as big as this. They thought that because they had the Temple their safety was assured. Their trust lay in a building and its reputation, not in the Lord of the building. The building, which was meant to be a symbol of Yahweh's presence, had become an idol.

The fact that an object is religious does not guarantee that it will not become an idol. Nothing, however precious, can be a substitute for God: if we regard it as such, it becomes an idol. Sometimes even the sincerest and most religious people, without realizing it, substitute an idol for God. Perhaps a particular ceremony or experience is of great importance for a Christian congregation – confirmation, a certain kind of conversion experience, speaking in tongues, etc. These are all examples of ways in which God can bring blessing, but none is like a magic charm, none is an automatic guarantee of God's blessing any more than the Jerusalem Temple was. Any such thing that becomes an end in itself has become an idol.

Jeremiah points out that once there was a temple of Yahweh at Shiloh: if the people visit Shiloh now they will find only a heap of ruins. To the people of Jerusalem the destruction of Shiloh was God's just judgement on the sin of the northerners. They saw themselves in a quite different light, as people to whom, through the Davidic covenant, God had promised His blessing and favour in all circumstances. They believed that God had guaranteed uncon-ditional protection to Jerusalem. Jeremiah's message tries to shatter their self-confidence. It insists that what happened to Shiloh can equally happen to the Jerusalem Temple, for the key to a true faith is not a building but trust in the living God: a trust which is personal and alive now, not just looking back to some past occasion. If someone describes at length how they came to know God ten years ago our response can be, 'Praise God', but also, 'What is happening now?'. No religious building is to be maintained at all costs, for no experience, no ritual, no building – however wonderful – is a substitute for a contemporary faith in the living God.

3. THEIR FAITH IS PARTIAL

This is Jeremiah's third charge against Judah. When the people came in to the Temple for worship they said all the right things, offered all the right sacrifices. But when they went out again, it meant nothing. The beliefs they declared in worship had no effect on the way they lived. On some of the great feast days the Law was read aloud, and the people were reminded of the Ten Commandments that marked the founding of Israel as a nation at Sinai. But the way the people lived totally ignored these commandments. So 7.5f reminds the people of the basic attitudes they were to show, and 7.9 lists some of the commandments. They *said* the right things – but they never *did* them; their faith did not really belong to the whole of their life, only to a religious bit which made no impression on anything else.

One big weakness in some parts of the Christian Church comes when people think that because they have a little religion they do not need any more! When that happens the 'little bit' becomes like an inoculation against an illness – it prevents you from getting the real thing! Christianity becomes something for Sunday; it is not seen as relevant to the business, the schooling, the farming you are involved in. It is something theoretical, not for daily life; you fit it in when you have time.

In reality, the Christian faith calls those who trust God to put the whole of their lives at His disposal. The root meaning of the Hebrew word translated 'worship' in 7.2 is to bow down, to fall at the feet of a master and acknowledge him as master. To call God 'Lord' is to submit to His lordship; no part of life, however special, however small it may seem, must remain outside. It has been said that if we do not call God Lord of all we do not really call Him Lord at all; then we run the risk of His saying, 'Why do you call me, "Lord, Lord", and not do the things that I say?' (Luke 6.46). That was the situation into which the people of Judah had got themselves. We can very easily fall into the same trap.

NOTES

7.2: Gate of the Lord's house: Jer 26.2 says that it was in the 'court of the Lord's house'. We should probably think of Jeremiah standing at the gate separating the inner and outer courts of the Temple. Those coming for worship would have to pass him.

7.3: Lord of hosts, the God of Israel: See note on 2.19 for the first phrase. The second phrase echoes the people's claim that Yahweh is their special God. 'Be warned', says Jeremiah, 'that is a dangerous claim to make'.

7.4: Deceptive words: The Hebrew word *sheqer*, here translated 'deceptive', is often used in Jeremiah: e.g. Judah's repentance is false (3.10); the people swear falsely (5.2); all deal falsely (6.13); the prophets give false messages (29.9).

7.6: The alien, the fatherless or the widow: These groups represent the underprivileged and vulnerable in Judah's society; they should receive special consideration, Exod. 22.21f.

Innocent blood: In 19.4 a similar phrase probably refers to child sacrifice. Here it is more likely to refer to gross injustice, possibly judicial murder like that which Jezebel arranged for Naboth (1 Kings 21); Uriah's murder (Jer 26.23), provides a later example.

7.7: I will let you dwell: Here, as in v.3, some ancient versions, followed by JB, have 'I will stay with you'. The basic meaning is not affected.

7.9: Will you steal ... go after other gods: Six of the ten command-ments of Exodus 20 are mentioned here. As at 1.16, 'burn incense' may be translated 'offer sacrifice'.

That you have not known: Either these gods are recently adopted (i.e. the people have no real experience of them) or (if 'know' has here its deeper meaning: see the comment on 1.5, p. 13) the people have no deep personal relationship with these gods as they have had with Yahweh.

7.10: Stand before me: The phrase is commonly used of a slave or vassal, standing before his master in an attitude of submission.

Called by my name: A common phrase in Deuteronomy and in literature influenced by that book. It includes the idea of Yahweh's claim to authority over that place, and of His presence there in a special way.

We are delivered: Cf. 2.35, 'I have not sinned', for a similar bold but untrue assertion.

7.12: My place ... Shiloh ... at first: Shiloh was the first place in the Promised Land to have a permanent sanctuary. It lay 40 kms north of Jerusalem (Map 2, p. 235) and its sanctuary had once held the ark of the covenant. Later the town and sanctuary had been destroyed: what God did there He can do to Jerusalem also.

7.13: Spoke to you persistently: Literally this is 'rising early and speaking' or 'speaking early and often'. The same phrase occurs at 35.14 and similar phrases are found elsewhere in Jeremiah; literally translated they are: 'rising early and warning' (11.7); 'rising early and teaching' (32.33); 'rising early and sending' (7.25; 25.4; 26.5; 29.19; 44.4). The people who do this persistent speaking are the prophets.

7.14: The house ... the place: God is independent of locality and cult. He remains a totally free agent, not bound by any building or belief of His people.

7.15: Kinsmen ... Ephraim: The northern kingdom of Israel was often known by the name of one of its tribes, that of Ephraim. The Exile that had befallen the northern kingdom could also be the experience of Judah. Judah should not deny that it could happen to her: it could!

STUDY SUGGESTIONS

REVIEW OF CONTENT

1. What was the popular opinion of God's attitude towards Jerusalem, and why did Jeremiah disagree?

2. Put in your own words the meaning of 'worship'. What consequence does this have for our lives?
3. What place did the Law have in the eyes of the people of Jerusalem? What place should it have had?
4. Why did Jeremiah talk about Shiloh to the people of Jerusalem? How did what he said about Shiloh surprise them?

BIBLE STUDY

5. Read 2 Sam.7 and Ps. 89.1–37. From them build up your own picture of the covenant with David. Then read Ps. 89.38–51 to see the reaction when Jerusalem was destroyed. How does this help you to understand the people's reaction when Jeremiah announced the city's destruction?
6. What different kinds of falseness or deception (*sheqer*) do you find in the following references in Jeremiah: 3.10; 3.23; 6.13; 7.9; 8.8; 9.5; 10.14; 17.9; 20.6; 23.25f?
7. In what ways do you think the faith of the following was false or unbalanced and in need of correction?
   (a) The ten spies (other than Joshua and Caleb): Num. 13.1—14.9
   (b) Balaam: Num. 22.1—23.12
   (c) Elijah: 1 Kings 19.1–18
   (d) The Pharisees reported in Matt. 12.9–14
   (e) The Pharisees reported in Luke 11.42
   (f) The Church at Corinth: 1 Cor. 1.10–17

DISCUSSION AND APPLICATION

8. Many of Jeremiah's accusations of falseness were directed against religious leaders. What does that say about the responsibilities of those who preach and teach today?
9. In what ways do you try to get a balanced grasp of Christian truth? If you are a preacher, how do you try to make sure that your preaching is balanced?
10. How should we try to help people who seem to us to be unbalanced in their Christian understanding?
11. Jer. 7.6 refers to the special responsibility of God's people towards the weaker members of society. Who are the weaker members of your society and how is your Church trying to help them? In what ways are you involved?
12. Jer. 7.3 promises physical safety as a consequence of obedience to God. How might we understand this today? What passages could you use to support your understanding?

7.16—8.3
God's Judgement on False Worship

OUTLINE

These passages continue the attack on Judah's worship. Three further problems are exposed.

7.16–20: The people are worshipping a goddess they call the queen of heaven.

7.21–28: Sacrifice and not obedience is central to their worship.

7.29—8.3: On the edge of Jerusalem human sacrifice and astral worship are being practised.

INTERPRETATION

RELIGION IS NOT ENOUGH

As Jeremiah walked around he saw abundant evidence that the people were religious (centuries later Paul would find the same in Athens, Acts 17.16–34). It was not only in the Temple that worship went on. In the streets of Jerusalem and the surrounding towns whole families offered worship to the goddess they called the 'queen of heaven', 7.17f. This refers to Astarte, the Babylonian goddess of fertility; other peoples worshipped her under different names, the Assyrians called her Ishtar. The cakes they made may have been moon-shaped (NEB 'crescent-cakes') or else have had stamped on them an image of Astarte (cf. 44.19).

In the valley of the son of Hinnom just south of the city of Jerusalem was a special place of worship. There, we are told, people used to 'burn their sons and their daughters in the fire' (7.31). This probably refers to human sacrifice to the god Molech (32.34f) which was a feature of some Canaanite worship; we know that it was sometimes practised in Judah (2 Kings 21.6). What, some asked, was more costly than the sacrifice of a member of your own family (cf. Mic. 6.7)? Astral worship, worship of the stars, which was widespread in the ancient world, was also very popular (8.2; 19.13).

No doubt the last phrase of 7.18 exaggerates, and much of this worship was sincere. It may not have been sensible but it was well-meant. And when it came to offering one of your own children as a sacrifice few could have taken that lightly. But to be sincere does not always make you right; it is possible to be sincere and wrong. The passage declares that all these other kinds of worship were totally unacceptable because they were directed not to the true God but to idols, creations of human imagination.

Also, although the people were sincere up to a point, they were wrong because they had forgotten what they should have known very well – how Yahweh had rescued them from Egypt, led them into the Promised Land and stayed with them ever since that time, in spite of their failures. In this history, if they only had eyes to see, was the evidence that required their faithfulness to Yahweh. But they were blind and so their behaviour was irrational.

Such double-thinking in worship remains common today. We see it all over the world in people who call themselves Christians but eagerly search the horoscopes in newspapers. We see it also in many whose belief is a mixture of ideas from Christianity and from elsewhere (perhaps their traditional society, perhaps their industrialized country). It is apparent in pluralistic societies whose members divide their allegiance between two faiths, declaring that all faiths lead to God. We may hear it said, 'You worship God in your way, I'll worship Him in mine'.

Such people may be perfectly sincere; but sincerity does not make their belief true, any more than the sincerity of a Marxist means that there is no God! The basis for any faith needs to be tested to see if it is reasonable. Our minds have been given to us to use, to think sensibly about the faith we profess as well to examine the ground of other faiths. If we take Christianity (or for that matter Islam) seriously, we shall find that its claims are exclusive. To dabble in several different faiths and try to create a mixture from them is shallow thinking; it creates only a nonsense. If we are to take Christianity seriously we must take it on its own terms. Otherwise we shall be like the second-century heretic Marcion, whom the writer Tertullian accused of using a penknife to cut out the bits of Christianity he disliked.

RITUAL IS NOT ENOUGH

We have seen that many sacrifices were offered in the Temple. Now we hear that sacrifice is not the most important thing: nor, although it played a very big part in Israel's faith, was it the oldest part of that faith. When God brought Israel out of Egypt He said nothing about sacrifice. The first priority was the command to *obey* (7.23).

We may understand this in one of two ways: either it concerns the importance of obedience in the time before Israel came to Mount Sinai (Exod. 15.26—19.6); or, more probably, it refers to the fact that the Ten Commandments, the basis of the Law (the Jewish *torah*), contain no command about sacrifice. In either case obedience

Jeremiah saw that much of Judah's worship was 'directed not to the true God but to creatures of human imagination.' We can see such 'double-thinking' in people who call themselves Christians, but eagerly search the horoscopes offered in newspapers or by astrologers like Carroll Righter, who is regularly consulted by Hollywood film stars, and even by political and military leaders.

comes before sacrifice, so that if there is no obedience, sacrifice is unacceptable. This point has been made in 6.19f. On this issue Jeremiah is in close agreement with other prophets who criticize the way sacrifice was practised (see e.g. Isa. 1.10–17; Hos.6.6; Amos 5.21–25; cf. also 1 Sam. 15.22 and Pss 40.6; 69.30f). None of these passages calls for the abolition of sacrifice; they all emphasize that sacrifice is not an end in itself; it is meaningless without obedience. Daily life must be in harmony with what is declared in worship, or the worship becomes an empty shell, an exercise in hypocrisy.

A stress on any kind of ritual to the neglect of Christian belief and behaviour endangers the Church. This can occur not only in Churches which lay great stress on the sacraments, but equally in those which emphasize preaching or fellowship. Worship of any kind can too easily be divorced from the realities of life, whereas what it *should* do is to equip us for these. The nineteenth-century preacher who finished his sermon one Christmas Day by recommending the congregation to study Greek literature is only an extreme example of the way that worship may not be properly related to our situation. Such preaching has become a ritual, empty of real meaning.

Throughout Israel's history God had again and again (7.25; the Hebrew is literally 'rising early and sending' – see note on 7.13) sent prophets to bring His people back to reality, but these were always rejected or ignored, for they made life too uncomfortable. Rather than listening to what the prophets had to say to them, the people concentrated on how they themselves wanted to follow God.

To have our assumptions questioned is always disturbing. Regular worshippers are naturally reluctant to have settled ways and comfortable assurance upset. The Church very easily rejects the voice of criticism, but by doing so may miss the message of God. A congregation may oppose the preacher who does not confirm what they already believe or want to believe; but sometimes worship should upset and not comfort, if that is the word of God for the occasion.

NOTES

7.16: Do not pray: The Hebrew makes it clear that this command was for the present and not permanent. Prayer was a normal part of a prophet's role. (See also 11.14; 14.11f; 15.1; the notes on them, and the discussion on p. 85).

7.19: Is it I ... is it not themselves: The people think they are upsetting God by behaving in this way; in fact they are only bringing problems on themselves.

7.20: It will burn and not be quenched: The people are in control of the sacrifices they offer; they light the fire and later see that it goes out when the sacrifice has been offered, 7.18. But the fire that represents God's anger is quite different – human beings have no control over it.

7.21: Burnt offerings ... sacrifices: A 'burnt offering' was a sacrifice all of which was burnt. 'Sacrifices' translates a general word, here describing communion offerings in which part was burnt and part eaten by worshippers and priests in communion together. The whole verse is ironical: 'Go ahead with your sacrifices, but you might as well eat them yourselves for all the good they will do you!'

7.24: Backward and not forward: In spite of God's instructions to them the people got worse and not better.

7.27: You ... but they: The prophet has the very difficult task of speaking to people knowing that there will be no response.

7.28: Truth has perished: 'Truth' (Hebrew *emunah*) here means faithfulness, trustworthy loyalty to the covenant. This is a mark of God, and His people should reflect His character. Several times Jeremiah mourns the fact that they do not show it; see 5.1,3; 9.3. The right mood is caught by GNB which reads, 'Faithfulness is dead. No longer is it even talked about.'

7.29: Cut off your hair: This was a sign of mourning (see Job 1.20; Mic. 1.16). Possibly it also refers to the long hair which Nazirites (Israelites who had taken special vows, see Num. 6.1–18) grew as a sign of dedication to Yahweh (Judges 13.5): the dedication has gone so the long hair should also go.

Bare heights: See note on 3.2.

7.30: Called by my name: See note on 7.10.

7.31: Topheth: 'Topheth' was an insulting term, combining the consonants of the Hebrew word for 'fireplace' (*tephath*) with the vowels of the word for 'shame' (*bosheth*).

Son of Hinnom: Hinnom is unknown but was probably the father of the original owner of the valley.

7.32: Because there is no room elsewhere: Some translations read, 'until there is no more room', giving a picture of the valley overflowing with corpses.

7.33: The dead bodies ... will be food: There will be no proper burial and, for some, no burial at all. This was one of the greatest disgraces possible in ancient Israel.

7.34: I will make to cease ... the voice of gladness ... of the bride: The note of joy is vital for any living community, however desperate its situation; but now it will disappear. There will be no more weddings for no-one will be left to marry.

8.1–2: The bones ... shall be brought out of their tombs; ... spread before ... : The horror that is to come moves beyond the living to involve even the dead. The ultimate insult was digging up a grave and scattering its contents. Now these contents are to be spread out before the 'gods' they had worshipped.

8.3: Death shall be preferred to life: So desperate is the state of the few survivors that they will wish they had died and not been left alive to mourn the devastation. Only in the most despairing situations in the Old Testament would people wish they were dead (e.g. Jer. 20.14–18; Job 3.3–13, 21f; 7.15f), for most of them had no belief in a hope beyond the grave.

STUDY SUGGESTIONS

REVIEW OF CONTENT

1. What sorts of worship does Jeremiah condemn in this section and for what reasons?
2. What were Jeremiah's objections to the sacrifices offered to Yahweh in the Temple at Jerusalem?
3. How did Topheth get its name?
4. Why is it inconsistent to try and combine total allegiance to the Christian faith with commitment to another religion?

BIBLE STUDY

5. Look up the following references and for each one put in your own words the point you think is being made: 1 Sam. 15.22; Ps. 51.16f; Ezek. 33.25–29; Hos. 8.13; Mic. 6.6–8. How would you relate these ideas to the importance of sacrifice in ancient Israel?
6. Here at 7.20 and elsewhere Jeremiah suggests that the fortunes of the land are linked to human behaviour. What support does Deut. 28.1–24 give to this idea?

DISCUSSION AND APPLICATION

7. Are there any non-Christian forms of worship or religious ideas that appeal to members of your congregation? If so, are they attractive to some because the Church is failing to meet some needs? How does the Church respond to this challenge?
8. Much of the worship of the people of Judah bore no relation to their daily lives. How far can that charge be made of the worship of the congregation to which you belong? In what ways do the worship and the daily life relate? In what ways would you like to strengthen the relationship between worship and daily life?

9. Are there ways in which, in your culture, you could develop ideas about the fortunes of the land and their relation to human behaviour as considered in Question 6?

10. From 7.16–20 we learn that one attraction of the cult of Astarte was that all the family could be involved. Does your Church provide for all the family in a satisfactory way? How do you think it could involve the whole family better?

8.4—9.26
The Horror of Judgement

OUTLINE

This section also contains a number of smaller units. Their recurring theme is the tragedy of the judgement and the horror it brings for all concerned.

8.4–17: This passage explains that because the people have not visited God (in worship) He will visit them (in judgement).

8.18—9.1: A poem expressing the personal reaction of the prophet to the tragedy that is unfolding. His heart aches.

9.2–11: Deceit and falseness is the central idea of several short oracles combined in these verses.

9.12–16: A short prose unit which can be considered as a commentary on Jeremiah's teaching. It links possession of the land with obedience to the Law.

9.17–22: A summons to the people to lament on the magnitude of the disaster. Here it follows as a natural response to the horror described in the previous verses.

9.23–24: These verses, contrasting two very different approaches to life, were originally a wisdom saying about the basis for boasting.

9.25–26: Another isolated oracle which declares that all – inside and outside Israel – will experience judgement.

INTERPRETATION

WORDS – USED AND MISUSED

Much in this section has to do with words. The prophet declares that his message, which comes in words, is from God (8.4). God has given His word (9.13), and the religious leaders claim to have it but they are accused of distorting it (8.8). People were worried about invasion, but these leaders reassured them with words of peace (8.11); however, these reassurances were false words (8.11). Jeremiah is tired of hearing false words (9.2); people deceive their neighbours, for they say nice words but mean evil (9.5, 8). When disaster comes, words and wailing make up the lamentation (9.10, 17–22). And then will follow the awful sound of silence when all the people have gone, birds and beasts are silent and only jackals and vultures will stalk and hover, picking up what scraps they can (9.11).

We cannot imagine life without words: written and read, spoken and heard. They shape the whole of our lives, and are the basic medium of communication. Words are important and have enormous power. Think of the money spent on advertising – manufacturers know the power of words. When there is a coup, one of the new leaders' first objectives is to get control of broadcasting, and then of newspapers. Words influence people: they can speak for truth or against it; they can state something plainly or hint at it; they can be fair or unfair.

The religious leaders of Jeremiah's day claimed that they had and knew and used Yahweh's word; they claimed that their teaching was based on that word. Yet, in fact, what they said and taught was a distortion of the truth. Worse still, many deliberately used words to deceive; they were like the man described in the Psalms whose 'Speech was smoother than butter, yet war was in his heart; his words were softer than oil, yet they were drawn swords' (Ps. 55.21). The letter of James also speaks bluntly about the use of words (see Jas. 1.26; 3.1–12). Like the scribes (Jer. 8.8), Christian teachers today have a special responsibility for the way they use God's words. Christian writers can influence people for or against God; so can preachers. Both must take the greatest care to see that the words they use are appropriate, and do as much justice as possible to the message entrusted to them. Otherwise, they too will make the word of God into a lie. Honest study is the first essential in exploring and explaining God's word: study, because it cannot be understood by a casual glance; honest, because it is dishonest not to convey what one believes.

THE HEARTACHE OF JEREMIAH

We have already seen some of the hard things that Jeremiah had to say to his people; there are more to come. A very large part of his ministry fitted the first part of his commission in 1.10. He was mostly plucking up and breaking down, and it was not for nothing that he gained the nickname, 'Terror on all sides' (20.10). But this does not mean that he delighted in this message of judgement. It is true that in some passages he seems near to despair (as in 9.2 where he can think of nothing better than to get away from the people and their evil), and in others he cries to God to deal with those who oppose him. Nevertheless, he longs for his people to turn back to God: the Hebrew word *shub* (see on 3.6—4.4, p. 33) recurs here several times, five times in 8.4f alone. However, they persist in their own ways, so he is compelled to continue to deliver a harsh message. As he does so his heart is near to breaking, for the people are his people and he feels for them deeply (8.18—9.1). To preach in this way costs him dearly.

There is an important lesson here. Politicians are quick to denounce their rivals, and newspapers are often ready to expose the failures of those in responsibility; they hasten to condemn others. But that is not the way of God. He does not delight in judgement, but is shown as giving His people chance after chance; His nature is merciful, forgiving and patient. Judgement may be inevitable but it always comes with His regret, never His delight. Jeremiah illustrates this well. It hurt him to deliver such scathing judgement; he does not gloat over what the people are going to experience.

Donald Coggan, formerly Archbishop of Canterbury, has said that among the most difficult parts of his ministry were the times when, as a bishop, he had to discipline another Church leader and stop him from working as a priest. It was agonizing, but sometimes it had to be done – and it hurt whoever had to do it. Jeremiah would understand that. He would agree with the person who said that you should only preach about hell if you could do it with tears in your eyes. To deliver any kind of judgement from God is a costly ministry. It cannot be done lightly.

GOD'S VALUES AND HUMAN VALUES (9.23–24)

Jeremiah 9.23f stands quite by itself. Although scholars have suggested various reasons why it is placed at this point, there is no obvious reason that has convinced everyone. But it makes a very important point – God's values are often very different from ours.

Think for a minute about the important people in your country or community. What makes them important or great in the eyes of the world? Possibly they are clever and have several degrees and qualifications. Maybe they are powerful, big men in the government, the army or some other area of public life. Or perhaps they are rich; money talks, it is sometimes said. These verses do not attack such things; there is nothing wrong with degrees, exercising leadership over a nation or having plenty of money. But neither are such things a valid reason for boasting: they are in fact much less important than an awareness of, and a relationship with, the living God. This is what the Bible means by faith.

This is true because God's values are very different from human ones. Indeed, often God turns the world's values upside down. The steadfast love that goes on and on, the justice that does what is right even when it is to one's own disadvantage, these are often unpopular. They are not the way to get on in the world. But they are God's way. The Cross of Christ is the supreme example of how God reverses the world's values: the world judged it a failure – but the world was wrong! In his own day Jeremiah was judged a failure – now we see his true greatness.

We should learn from this. Too easily the Church adopts the world's methods. In a country with many Christians, Church leaders may seek the support of political leaders; the size of the collection is used to judge the effectiveness of the pastor; academic qualifications become the basis of promotion in the Church. When such things happen we are using human means to try and influence the world. We shall fail, for it is not God's way (and in any case the world uses its own methods far more effectively than the Church ever will). Only when the Church is radically different from the world does it really influence the world for God. That is when it shows it has something worthwhile and distinctive to offer. When Paul was weak, then he was strong (2 Cor. 12.10); when the Church renounces the world's weapons, then it can challenge the world!

NOTES

8.7: Even the stork knows . . . time of their coming: All over the world people recognize the changing seasons by the arrival and departure of birds on migration. There is a contrast between the birds who live successfully according to God's natural laws and the people of God who fail to keep the Law that He has given. See Isa. 1.3 for another protest that God's people fail an elementary test.

8.8: The law of the LORD is with us: This obviously refers to some written collection of law but it is uncertain which one; the Book of the Law used in Josiah's reform is one possibility.

The false pen of the scribes has made it into a lie: Either the written law is being distorted by the teaching of the scribes, or Jeremiah is contrasting the written word (interpreted literally?) with the fresh word from God that he is now delivering. In JB the scribes are understood to be the priests, i.e. those who handle the law (2.8; 18.18), but most commentators see a reference to the class of wise men who were responsible for giving advice in Israel (they are also mentioned at 18.18).

8.9: They have rejected: As at 6.19, such rejection includes the idea of despising.

8.10–12: I will give ... shall be overthrown: This repeats the prophecy of destruction in 6.12–15.

8.11: The wound of my people: Not a slight scratch but a fracture, something badly broken.

8.11–12: Peace, peace, when there is no peace ... No, they were not at all ashamed: The indignation is well caught by NEB with, 'All well? Nothing is well ... Ashamed? Not they!'

8.13: When I would gather them ... even the leaves are withered: In most translations this is a further accusation added to those of the previous verses. By contrast, in NIV it is part of God's judgement that comes because of the evils just exposed; barrenness is the consequence of shamelessly forsaking Yahweh.

And what I gave them has passed away from them: The Hebrew is unclear. Different translations offer different suggestions; like the Greek the NEB omits the phrase.

8.16: The snorting of their horses is heard from Dan: Dan was far away on the northern border of the kingdom of Israel. So fierce is the enemy army that even from that distance its approach can be heard. It strikes terror into the heart.

8.17: Adders which cannot be charmed: For the bite of these snakes there is no antidote. Perhaps this is an allusion to the story in Numbers 21, where the effect of the snake bites *could* be taken away.

8.18: Beyond healing: In several versions this phrase (which translates the first word of the Hebrew verse) is understood to refer to the snake bites of v. 17

8.20: The harvest is past, the summer is ended, and we are not saved: Winter approaches and there is no food in reserve; God's intervention has not come.

8.22: Is there no balm in Gilead?: Gilead, to the east of the river Jordan (Map 2, p. 235), was famous for its soothing and healing ointment. The precise substance used has not been identified. 'Of course there is ointment in Gilead', says Jeremiah, 'of course Yahweh is Lord of our people: then why have we not been saved?'

9.2: A wayfarers' lodging place: Any kind of shelter where a traveller might camp for a night. Jeremiah does not want to become a hermit, only to get away from these people; he has had enough of them. (Note how the mood of 9.2–11 is quite different from the concern of the previous verses: we must allow for their coming from different times, but even so the picture of Jeremiah is not always consistent; perhaps this is simply because, being human, he is subject to different moods.)

9.3: They do not know me: Such lack of knowledge was one of Hosea's greatest concerns; see Hos. 4.1. Jeremiah takes after Hosea in this respect.

Says the LORD: JB follows the Greek by omitting this phrase, and so making the verse a continuation of Jeremiah's feelings. In the poetry it is often difficult to tell when the speaker is Yahweh and when it is the poet. Often perhaps their words overlap, with the feelings of the poet expressing also those of Yahweh.

9.4: Every brother is a supplanter: A reference to the story of Jacob and Esau (cf. Gen. 27.36); Gen. 25.26 explains the meaning of Jacob as 'he supplants'. To make the point clear, Bright translates, 'Every brother is as crafty as Jacob'.

9.6: They refuse to know me: Once again we have the assertion that their disobedience is deliberate; see note on 2.20.

9.7: I will refine them: In 6.27–30 Jeremiah was to assay the quality of Judah; now Yahweh will refine them.

9.10: Take up: This translates the Greek; the Hebrew reads, 'I will take up' and is followed by some translations.

9.12–16: Who is the man ... until I have consumed them: This passage is a good example of the outlook of the Deuteronomic editors (see Special Note C, p. 44).

9.15: Wormwood: A plant whose juice had a bitter taste.

9.17–22: Thus says the LORD of hosts ...: This lament is made up of two stanzas, each of three verses; it makes a natural sequel to the devastation described in 9.12–16.

9.17: Mourning women: Professional mourners who earned their living by 'performing' laments for those who had died.

9.21: Death has come up into our windows, it has entered our palaces: This image of disaster uses a picture from Canaanite belief: in one of their traditions the god *Mot* (whose name has links with the Hebrew word for death) enters the palace of the god *Baal* through a window and causes disaster.

9.25–26: Circumcised but yet uncircumcised: The basic idea is that whether or not people are physically circumcised they have remained spiritually uncircumcised (cf. Acts 7.51; Rom. 2.28). Since many of these peoples *did* practise circumcision many English versions emend v. 26.

That cut off the corners of their hair: Either, following GNB, this is linked with some religious practice in honour of their god, or, following NEB and NIV, it should be translated differently as 'all who haunt the fringes of the desert'.

STUDY SUGGESTIONS

REVIEW OF CONTENT

1. What reasons are given in this section to explain why the people were not 'healed' (8.22)?

2. How did Jeremiah feel about having to deliver a message of judgement?
3. In the light of this passage, how would you reply to someone who suggested that human success was a sign of God's being pleased with a person?
4. What kind of words were people likely to hear from the religious leaders in Jerusalem?

BIBLE STUDY

5. Make a list of all the different images that are used in this section to illustrate the evils in Jerusalem.
6. The Hebrew word *hesed*, often, as in 9.24, translated as 'steadfast love', is difficult to translate satisfactorily in English. Read the following verses in which it is found, and then in one sentence summarize what you think it means:
   Gen. 24.12; 39.21; Deut. 5.10; Ruth 2.20 ('kindness'); Pss 44.26; 85.7; 119.64; Hos. 6.6; 12.6 ('love'); Joel 2.13; Mic. 6.8 ('kindness').
7. Compare Jeremiah's heartache here with that of Moses in Exod. 32.11–13, Jesus in Luke 19.41–44, and Paul in Rom. 9.1–3. How important do you think such deep concern is in Christian ministry?
8. Note what Jeremiah has to say here about words, and compare with it:
   Prov. 10.18–21; 12.17–19; 15.23; 18.21.
   Eccles. 5.2,6f; 7.21f; 10.12–14.
   James 1.26; 3.1–12.

DISCUSSION AND APPLICATION

9. When you hear or read things said by the following people, how reliable, in each case, do you expect them to be?
   (a) Politicians
   (b) Journalists
   (c) Advertisers
   (d) Church leaders
   (e) Broadcasters
   (f) Your friends
   What conclusions can you draw from your answers?
10. Why do you think that the Church is often most effective when it is weakest in human terms? Can you give examples of your own Church's effectiveness when it has been humanly weak?
11. By what methods is your Church trying to influence others for Christ? Would you say that these methods fit with the standards of 9.23 or those of 9.24?

12. If you were choosing a new Church leader, in what order would you place these qualities?
    (a) A strong personality
    (b) Effectiveness in fundraising
    (c) A deep concern for people
    (d) On good terms with government leaders
    (e) Prayerfulness
    (f) High moral standards
    (g) Tribe or clan
    (h) Spiritual vision
    What influences your order of preference? What other important qualities, not on this list, would you also wish to include?

10.1–16
Idols and the True God

OUTLINE

This passage compares the worship of those it calls idols with that of Yahweh, the true God. Two themes are combined; (1) the futility of idols and the worship of them, (2) the amazing greatness of the true God. This attack on idolatry is more naturally understood as referring to Babylonian than Canaanite religion. Because of this, and because the ideas in the passage have certain similarities to passages in Isaiah 44 and 46 and Psalms 115 and 135, some scholars may be right in their suggestion that the passage comes from the time of the Exile.

INTERPRETATION

THE FOOLISHNESS OF IDOLATRY

The writer points out that the worship of these other gods is widespread ('the way of the nations', v. 2), and in many cases the traditions of such worship are of great antiquity ('customs', v. 3, refers to something firmly established). But popularity and antiquity are no guide to truth. When we examine such worship in detail we find that people are paying homage to bits of carved wood decorated to look attractive. These statues cannot speak and they cannot move by themselves; there is no life in them (vv. 4,5,14). These beliefs are little more than superstition, based on fears of what people see in the sky (v. 2) They should not convince Israel for a moment, for the people of Israel know the true and living God, the Creator.

Of course, this is not a balanced comparison of two religions. The worshippers being criticized here would doubtless have argued that they were not worshipping the statues; they were just using them as visual aids to help their worship. Many religions today, including branches of the Christian Church, would say the same about statues or pictures they may use. But the writer of this passage is not trying to be objective and neutral, he is urging those who have already discovered Yahweh to continue to follow Him. This other worship had real attractions, and so here the strongest possible language is used to discourage people from being sidetracked. 'You have discovered the truth, so do not let anything else, however impressive it may appear at first, lure you away from Him.'

Because it is not a balanced comparison this passage is not a model for us about how we should discuss with those of other faiths. When we do this we should take these other faiths at their best and not their worst, just as we would wish Christianity to be judged, not on the basis of some of the worst Christian leaders or some of the saddest episodes in the history of the Church, but by the highest Christian standards.

Part of what we can draw from the passage is a reminder of the importance of testing a faith to establish its true value. In terms of widespread popularity and long tradition these other religions had strong support. But when the poet went deeper he found that they were centred around lifeless statues; they did not lead to greater insight into the truth about the living God and greater dependence on Him. This is what must be the fundamental test of all claim to religious truth. Judged by this test these other faiths were total failures, for they were merely man-made. For the people of Judah the test should have been the Torah; for the Christian today it is fundamentally the Bible, with further guidelines coming from doctrinal bases of the various denominations.

Anything that people make must be less than they are themselves. So it cannot possibly give them advice greater than they could work out in other ways. If they worship such a creation their own foolishness condemns them. Today's idols may not be carved statues. For younger people they may be human heroes, pop stars or footballers, or ideals spread by radio and television and newspapers; for the older generation they may be respected traditions. It may be quite easy for us to see the difference between these and the living God, but there may be more subtle idols within the Church. The clothes that are worn or the way the furniture is arranged, certain emphases in theology or the sort of music used in worship may all owe more to human traditions than to Christian truth. If aspects of our faith are merely man-made, and no longer help to point us to the true God, then however widespread they may be, however long they have been followed, they have become idols. In the Christian faith we are not just following the steps of our spiritual ancestors (though we are doing that), we are meeting and serving the true God today.

THE GREATNESS OF GOD

The passage not only illustrates some of the weaknesses of idolatry. By contrast it also points to the sovereignty of God. Yahweh is the God who speaks (v.1). He is alive (v.10), and will be for ever (v.10). He is the creator, (vv.12f), who continues His active control over His creation and has chosen a particular people for His special purpose (v.16).

These are familiar themes. Some of them we regularly affirm in the creeds. We assume their truth in much of our talking about Christianity. But they can very easily become mere words, as meaningless as the idols and empty rituals that the passage condemns. For each of us has our own 'image' of God, an image that is always too small and inadequate. God is greater than we realize, but as soon as we have said that it becomes a phrase without much impact. Our minds must somehow become more open, to let the greatness of God grip us in a new way and remould our thinking, so that we do not limit Him unnecessarily, nor too readily 'invent' Him to match our own pre-conceived ideas.

This is all part of what Paul described as letting our minds be renewed (Rom. 12.2). All around us are human images which dilute our vision of God; we need the concentrated version! One thing that will help us is what the writer is doing here: allowing the facts of God's rule over creation to sink in, letting the mind dwell on them and be shaped by them. To see humanity in perspective in creation is an antidote to false visions of human greatness. When we grasp this, God will grasp us more fully.

The choice in this passage is between submission to the living God, with all the benefits that can bring, and independence from Him, which brings the need to cope entirely from one's own resources. In view of the many passages in Jeremiah where Judah is urged to repent, we might have expected a further appeal here, based on the contrast between Yahweh and idols. But that call is not repeated. Perhaps it is the more powerful because it is unspoken.

NOTES

There are various textual problems with this passage, and the Greek version of the Old Testament omits some verses and rearranges the

'Today's idols may not be carved statues' but they may be equally 'man-made'—for younger people human heroes, pop stars like the Jamaican Bob Marley, or footballers; for the older generation respected traditions about polite behaviour or special sorts of church furniture.

order of others. We shall keep to the order of the RSV, since there is no agreement among scholars about what might have been the original text. Verse 11 is in Aramaic (which became the everyday language in Judah sometime after the Exile) and is a later insertion, probably copied by a scribe. Verses 12–16 reappear at 51.15–19.

10.2: Signs of the heavens: Many people in the ancient world thought that sun, moon and stars were linked with various gods; we noted this when we looked at Jer.7. The 'signs' here may refer to these beliefs in general, or they may concern specific insights such as eclipses or shooting stars.

10.4: Cannot move: According to most translations the nails keep the statue in its place so that it cannot fall over. The NEB reading means that the nails hold the statue itself together so that its pieces 'do not fall apart'.

10.5: Like scarecrows: Literally, this is 'like a post', a piece of wood stuck in a field; it frightens birds away because they think it is a man, but really it is quite powerless, capable of doing neither good nor evil. The idols are similarly powerless; there is no need to fear them any more than to praise them.

10.8: The instruction of idols is but wood: The precise translation of this phrase is difficult but the basic meaning is clear – instruction from idols is as valueless as the idols themselves. The right spirit is conveyed by the NEB, 'Learning their nonsense from a block of wood!'.

10.9: Tarshish ... Uphaz: The location of these places is uncertain. Tarshish may be Tartessus in Spain. Uphaz (which some translate as Ophir) was famous for its gold.

10.11: Thus shall you say ... the heavens: This Aramaic verse was perhaps inserted as a curse on these idols.

10.14: His images are false: See note on 7.4, for the recurrence of 'falseness' as a theme in Jeremiah.

10.15: Delusion: They are a mockery. They claim to have power, to be able to guide and protect the worshipper, but the reality is otherwise.

10.16: Portion of Jacob: This points to the special relationship that existed between Judah (Jacob's descendants) and Yahweh. Taken out of its context (as it often was) it might be misunderstood to mean that God belonged to His people. In fact, of course, it meant the opposite – God's people belonged to Him in a special way, and He had chosen them for a special purpose.

LORD of hosts: See note on 2.19. Here the mood is different; there is no suggestion that God is going to come in judgement on His people; rather, He will protect them. (This is a further reason why some scholars believe that this passage originates in the exilic period.)

STUDY SUGGESTIONS

REVIEW OF CONTENT

1. What should be our attitude if we want to evaluate another religion?
2. What tests can we apply in estimating the worth of another faith?
3. What is one way in which we can increase our awareness of God's greatness?
4. Why do some scholars believe that this passage is likely to come from a time later than that of Jeremiah himself?

BIBLE STUDY

5. Note how the emphasis of the passage is built up by a continual switching of focus between Yahweh and the idols. Make a list of the main points made about the idols, and compare this with a list of the main points made about Yahweh.
6. Study Isaiah 44,46 and Psalms 115 and 135. What understanding of God comes out of these passages?

DISCUSSION AND APPLICATION

7. Do passages like 10.1–16 mean that it is not worth spending time considering any other religion? Give your reasons.
8. Look at the understanding of God that comes out of your answers to questions 5 and 6. Do you think that a visitor would be likely to get such a picture from the worship of your Church? What sort of picture of God do you think a visitor to your Church does get?
9. 'Today's idols may not be carved statues', p. 66. What could be described as popular idols within your country?
10. 'There may be more subtle idols within the Church', p. 66. What things, if any, can you identify which are in danger of being idols within your Church?

10.17—11.17
The Broken Covenant

OUTLINE

The final part of chapter 10 contains several short sayings, basically concerned with God's judgement. Some commentators believe that they naturally follow 9.22. Chapter 11 is quite different. Its first 17 verses are presented as a sermon by Jeremiah on the theme of the covenant that God's people have broken: this is the cause of the coming judgement by God.

10.17–18: The occupants of Jerusalem are warned to prepare to go into Exile.

10.19–21: These verses are a poem put on the lips of Jerusalem, imagining the city's response to the disaster.

10.22: A short saying about the approach of judgement.

10.23–24: Another saying that has links with wisdom: it concerns the sovereignty of God over man.

10.25: A prayer for judgement on the nations that have destroyed Judah.

11.1–17: A sermon proclaiming that Judah has broken the covenant with God and must take the consequences of this.

INTERPRETATION

A SPECIAL RELATIONSHIP

In the ancient world, when two groups or individuals wanted to make a particularly solemn agreement, they made a 'covenant' with each other. As a result of wedding ceremonies husband and wife entered a marriage covenant; nations made treaties (covenants) with one another. The terms of the covenant were drawn up carefully and spelt out clearly so that both parties knew what was expected of them. As long as the two sides kept these conditions they both benefited. It was generally reckoned an advantage for a small power to make a covenant with a greater one: by means of it, in return for allegiance to the greater power, the small power was promised help in case of danger, etc. For the greater power the covenant promised freedom from attacks or rebellion in that area.

Once a covenant had been drawn up it would be officially ratified by a very solemn ceremony. This would include a series of curses called down on any party that should break the covenant. These curses would be in the name(s) of the god(s) of the greater and possibly also the lesser party. Should the covenant be broken the offended party had the right to take up arms against the offender. Similar covenants are known today in some parts of Africa when different clans or tribes make agreements with each other. As in the Old Testament period a solemn ceremony establishes the covenant. For instance, among the Lugbara of north-west Uganda any dispute between clans is discussed by the elders; when agreement is reached it will be sealed by a 'covenant' ceremony which includes the parties concerned drinking from the same calabash as a sign that they are one together. And the 'treaties' made between larger and smaller nations today, for purposes of trade or military protection, are drawn up and solemnly ratified by political leaders in much the same way.

In the Old Testament the relationship between God and His people is often described in terms of a covenant. Genesis 15 and 17 record a covenant between God and Abraham. Then came the covenant made at Mount Sinai (Exod. 19—24). Later there was the covenant God established with David (2 Sam. 7). In each case a very special bond was formed. We have already seen (p. 45) that in the Temple sermon Jeremiah stressed the Sinai covenant which was being neglected in Judah, the covenant to which this passage refers. However, although this covenant was understood to go back to Moses, Jeremiah was not just saying, 'Remember what happened 600 years ago'. The passage refers to the much more recent renewal of the covenant by King Josiah. The covenant is referred to here as though it was written, and probably the 'Book of the Law' (see p. 8) is meant, for this contributed to the development of Josiah's reform (see Special Note A, p. 7).

The mark of this (old) covenant was circumcision, performed at a solemn ceremony. Later (see p. 164) Jeremiah talks of a new covenant which God would establish in the future. The Church sees this as introduced through Christ (cf. Luke 22.20) and baptism as its distinguishing feature. The person baptized is introduced to a very special relationship which is not enjoyed by anyone unbaptized.

AN EXCLUSIVE RELATIONSHIP

In the ancient world such a covenant was binding on both parties. A small power that made a covenant with a larger one was not at the same time free to make another covenant with another large power. In the same way the covenant between Yahweh and Judah required Judah's undivided allegiance to Yahweh. As a result of the covenant the people of Judah could call Yahweh their God; but if they also paid homage to any other god then the whole of their covenant relationship with Yahweh would come crashing down.

In today's world close ties with certain countries or groups rule out equally close ties with others. You cannot be a supporter of capitalism and also a hardline communist; you cannot both support apartheid and be a true member of the African National Congress. The same is true in the sphere of religion. Although certain groups like the Bahai may try to combine elements from various faiths, and although the major religions of the world can learn from one another, you cannot be a committed Sikh and a Hindu, you may not be a Moslem and a Christian. Baptized Christians are of course free to discuss and interact with members of other faiths; we are pledged to support the quest for truth, because God is truth. But the covenant relationship we enter through baptism requires us to be committed before all else to the faith revealed in and through Jesus Christ. Our first loyalty must lie there.

A BROKEN RELATIONSHIP

Judah had not kept the relationship with Yahweh exclusive. Worse still, not only had the people tried to divide their allegiance between Yahweh and other gods, but at times they had left out Yahweh altogether. Because of this, they will experience the consequences of breaking the covenant, for these consequences are part of the covenant terms (cf. Deut. 28). So the Exile in Babylon is presented as the consequence of rebellion against Yahweh.

If there were only the Sinai covenant, that would spell the end of hope for Judah. But overall, the Old Testament (and even Jeremiah itself) points to another hope, one which rests not in human obedience and effort but in God's grace and His willingness to respond in a new way to human sin. The seriousness of that sin is not played down at all, but, despite it, the Old Testament believes that God will offer a new hope. Jeremiah 31 (see p. 164) will refer to a new covenant in which God somehow changes people so that they genuinely desire to do what is right. No longer will their failure to obey the covenant regulations be dominant.

But in Jeremiah's time the outlook was gloomy. After giving a solemn undertaking, Judah had broken the covenant and must take the consequences. At baptism a similarly solemn undertaking is given; it is not to be made lightly. Ecclesiastes 5.5f emphasizes how serious is any dealing with God: 'Better not to promise at all than to make a promise and not keep it. Don't let your own words lead you into sin, so that you have to tell God's priest that you didn't mean it. Why make God angry with you?' (GNB).

NOTES

10.17: Gather up your bundle: The 'bundle' will contain the few possessions the people can carry into exile.

10.19: My wound: As at 8.11, this is something badly broken.

10.20: My tent ... my curtains: As at 4.20 the image is of Jerusalem as a tent whose supporting ropes are broken so that the tent collapses. In Isa. 54.1f also the image of a tent is used, but in quite a different way.

10.21: The shepherds ... do not inquire of the LORD: Here the 'shepherds' are the leaders of Judah. Since 'inquire of the LORD' was a technical term for consulting God, it is possible that the priests are specifically intended; 2.8 adds support to this interpretation.

10.22: Lair of jackals: A wilderness quite deserted.

10.25: Pour out thy wrath ... his habitation: This verse is almost identical with Ps.79.6f, and seems to assume the Exile. For 'Jacob', see note on 10.16. The 'nations' will be considered when we look at chs 46—51 (see p. 205).

11.2: Hear the words: That is, 'Listen to the terms of'.

11.4: The iron furnace: The same description of Egypt is found in Deut. 4.20; 1 Kings 8.51.

11.5: A land flowing with milk and honey: A traditional description of the Promised Land which was often used as a symbol of fertility. Milk and honey are the food of the pastoralist, and describe the land as seen from the desert. 'Rich and fertile', as in GNB, is a good equivalent.

11.6: Proclaim ... in the cities of Judah: This is the only mention of Jeremiah acting as a wandering prophet. It may be an editor's interpretation, especially since it comes in a prose passage; see Special Note F, p. 142.

11.7: Warning them persistently: See note on 7.13.

11.8: Yet they did not obey: Here in vv. 6–8, about earlier Judah, and in vv. 9–13, about the contemporary nation, both the accusation and the punishment that follows the verdict of 'guilty' are described in very general terms. In this way the possibility is left open for the basic charge of covenant breaking to be applied to a whole range of particular situations.

11.9: Revolt: A more accurate word would be 'conspiracy'. Although it is a revolt it is not a public one, for the people still claim to follow Yahweh.

11.10: Their forefathers: This is either a general term for ancestors, or may refer specifically to those who rebelled during the time in the wilderness.

11.13: Your gods have become as many as your cities: The familiar attitude of 'safety in numbers'. Later, in the days of their empire, the Romans believed that their success came because they encouraged the worship of all gods, both their own and those of the peoples they had defeated.

11.14: Do not pray: A further ban on Jeremiah's praying for people. See the discussion on p. 85.

11.15–16: What right has my beloved ... will be consumed: The Hebrew is difficult and various translations have been proposed, but the basic idea is clear. The picture in v.16 is of a tree struck by lightning; it suddenly turns from being luxuriant and fertile to being barren and leafless.

11.17: Has pronounced evil against you, because of the evil: This translation brings out that there is a play on words in the Hebrew, $r\bar{a}'\bar{a}h \ldots r\bar{a}'ath$.

STUDY SUGGESTIONS

REVIEW OF CONTENT

1. What is the purpose of a covenant? In what ways can it be an advantage for nations to make covenants with each other?
2. Explain what we mean when we say that a covenant is 'exclusive.' Why must some covenants be exclusive?
3. Why did the breaking of the Sinai covenant not mean the end of all hope for the people of Judah?

BIBLE STUDY

4. With 11.1–17 compare Gen. 15.1–21; 17.1–21; Exod. 19—24; Deut. 28.1–68.
5. Study 2 Kings 22.1—23.25 and list the main features of Josiah's reform. What similarities do you find with Jer. 11.1–17?

DISCUSSION AND APPLICATION

6. What relationships in your own society are similar to covenant ones? How are they made? What are the consequences of breaking them?
7. In countries where the Christian Church has many members, baptism often becomes just an outward ritual. What can the Church do to try to prevent this?
8. What other faiths do you have contact with? What kind of contacts with people of other faiths do you have? What could you do to develop closer relationships?

9. We have noted that 'the accusation and the punishment ... are in very general terms' (p. 74). Do you think this makes the prophet's words more effective or less effective? Give your reasons.

12.7—13.27
Judah's Sin – Pride and Practice

OUTLINE

At this point we shall postpone consideration of 11.18—12.6 until we look at all the 'Confessions of Jeremiah' together (see Special Note E, p. 107), and go straight to 12.7—13.27, a section which is again focused primarily on the judgement that is coming to God's people. The destruction is tragic but necessary. A short message about the surrounding nations is included. The main story centres round the disintegration of a waistcloth, an act of prophetic symbolism, which also serves as a visual aid to bring Jeremiah's message home.

12.7–13: Yahweh expresses His grief at the tragedy of Judah.

12.14–17: A message for the surrounding nations that have harmed Judah.

13.1–11: The spoiled linen: an acted parable about Judah's pride.

13.12–14: A traditional proverb is stated and applied to the coming judgement.

13.15–17: A short poem about Jeremiah's contrasting emotions in public and private.

13.18–19: How the mighty are fallen! A short oracle about the humbling of Judah's rulers.

13.20–27: A poem declaring that shame is inevitable because the people have gone too far to change.

INTERPRETATION

PROPHETIC SYMBOLISM (13.1–11)

Most of the messages delivered by prophets in the Old Testament were spoken ones. Many of them were quite short, a brief poem finishing with a punch line so that they were easy to remember. To deliver a prophetic message was a very serious act – it was believed that as a prophet delivered a true prophecy God released His power to fulfil the prophecy.

But some messages were not just spoken, they were also acted, or acted and then explained to the people. Such actions were thought to be especially solemn and powerful and are known as *acts of prophetic symbolism*. Many of the great prophets performed such acts. Isaiah gave his sons names with special significance (Isa. 7.3; 8.1–4) and went about naked and barefoot as a sign of coming disaster (Isa. 20.1–4). Ezekiel performed many such actions. Here in ch. 13 we find Jeremiah performing one; we shall meet others later, e.g. with a pottery jar in 19.1–13 and a yoke in chs 27—28.

Such incidents would obviously be particularly memorable (we may ask whether the Church today uses enough visual and dramatic means of communication). But these acts were also believed to be endowed with special power. As the prophet performed the action, the process effecting the message was thought to be set in motion by God. For instance, when Hananiah broke the yoke on Jeremiah's shoulders, as described in ch. 28, the congregation would have burst into applause, because this breaking was thought to make it certain that Exile would end within two years. We should be wrong if we thought that the people believed the prophet had God under control; what they did believe was that when God spoke in this way through a prophet the result predicted was bound to follow.

A PICTURE OF PRIDE (13.1—11)

This particular symbolic action involved Jeremiah's taking a piece of new linen (i.e. good quality) clothing. The precise nature of the clothing is unclear; 'loincloth', 'waistcloth', 'shorts', 'belt', have all been suggested as translations. Jeremiah went and buried it in the ground, left it there, and then later went back and collected it, by which time it was totally ruined. The text says that he did this by the Euphrates. It is very unlikely that the actual river Euphrates is meant, since this would have involved Jeremiah in two journeys, each of 1,100 kms! Either we should imagine Jeremiah acting a parable with the 'Euphrates' marked out on the ground or, since there is no suggestion of this in the text, we should perhaps picture the prophet going to Parah or Perat (the Hebrew for this and for Euphrates is similar), a place 5 kms north-east of Jerusalem.

Various points are made by the story. The linen was meant to cling to a man; now it was spoilt because it had not been used for the right purpose and was good for nothing. The people of Judah were intended to cling to Yahweh but they had not; now they would go to the Euphrates (Babylon) in exile and there they would be spoiled and become useless. The story stresses the pride of Judah. The people felt that they could decide for themselves what gods they should worship and how they should behave (see note on 2.20 for the people's claim that *they* had the right to decide such issues). Now Yahweh declares that they will be punished for this pride: their pride itself will be reduced to ruins by the experience of Exile, and disappear.

The people of Judah do not have a monopoly on pride! We see it in Genesis 3 in the story of Adam and Eve in the garden: their pride, their desire to assert themselves against their creator, is what leads to their expulsion from the garden. Because pride is a sin of attitude, and not always openly visible like murder or theft, it sometimes carries an air of 'respectability'. Yet it claims more victims than many other sins, since it so easily creeps in and can take so many shapes and forms. Not only is there the military pride of the powerful dictator, the scholar's pride in learning, the businessman's pride in profits; there is often religious pride, of which we may be quite unconscious, like that of the Pharisee in Jesus's story recorded in Luke 18.9–14. When pride asserts itself – whether or not we realize it – it prevents us from being shaped to fit our Creator's intended purpose, and so we too are spoiled and useless for God's plan.

GOD'S HEART ACHES TOO (12.7–13)

According to 13.15–17 (and see also 8.18—9.1, p. 59) Jeremiah's heart was aching even as he delivered his message; he was not gloating over the coming disaster. In public he had to keep a firm face, but behind the scenes his tears flowed. But it was not only Jeremiah who was grieved by the situation; God Himself was grieved, and 12.7–13 reads as though it is spoken by Yahweh Himself. There is deep pain in the regret that His own people have turned upon Him in protest and revolt. God Himself intervenes in judgement, but He does not enjoy it. Despite the bitterness apparent in vv. 7–8 there is an undercurrent of internal tension. This tension is captured much more clearly by Hosea, who describes how, when confronted by Israel's sin, God declares, 'My people are bent on turning away from me; so they are appointed to the yoke, and none shall remove it. How can I give you up, O Ephraim ... My heart recoils within me, my compassion grows warm and tender' (Hosea 11.7f).

If God was God, some people might have said, all He had to do was to forgive. But there is a fatal flaw in that argument, for to adopt it means that God will forgive anything and everything. If this

'The people of Judah claimed to decide for themselves what gods they should worship
... Yahweh declared their pride would be reduced to ruins.' At a great Jubilee parade
in Moscow the USSR showed similar pride, in its military might, as units of the armed
services massed before the Defence Minister. In both cases there is a lesson to be
learnt from history!

happens, in effect He renounces His authority over the world. Precisely *because He is God* He will not abandon His hopes for His people (and beyond them for all the world). He continues to set them standards so that His plan for the good of the world may progress. We are back to the understanding of God's love as a holy love (see p. 39). Because it is love – of a kind far beyond our limited human experience – there can be forgiveness; but because it is holy it means that to abandon standards is to submit to evil. Yet even while He administers the punishment, God Himself weeps. One day it will lead to the Incarnation and the Cross, but in Jeremiah's day that was still being prepared.

WE BECOME WHAT WE DO (13.20–27)

We can play with fire, but if we go on doing so we will one day get burned. In the last part of ch. 13 Judah has reached this position; the people have got so used to sinning that they can no longer change their ways. Maybe originally the followers of Yahweh decided to have one, and only one, special service in honour of some other god; Yahweh was very much to the front of their minds at the time. Now He has been relegated to the background, and other gods dominate the people's thinking.

As the Book of Jeremiah makes clear (see discussion of 2.1—3.5, p. 24), the evil of Judah is not a few isolated acts but a deeply rooted attitude that reveals itself in many different ways. But one of the reasons why the evil is so deeply ingrained is that Judah has practised evil so often that it has now become a habit too strong to break. 'I always thought that I was in control and could stop when I wished' could be echoed by thousands of people, whether about gambling, drinking alcohol, lying or any other habit that has got the better of them. Whatever the temptation may be, Jeremiah gives only one recipe for resisting it: 'If you want to avoid that evil becoming a persistent habit, do not start doing it; if you have already started, never do it again'.

No doubt the people could explain why they first sacrificed to Baal: they wanted to understand that faith, they did not want to offend other people, etc. But this is the argument that the end justifies the means; an argument which is fatally weak. However attractive or plausible it may seem, once the decision is taken that an exception can be made 'just this once' or that it can be permitted 'this time only', a foundation has been laid which can lead to endless repetition. In this way the 'means' easily becomes the master (13.21). No-one starts intending to become an alcoholic! 'As now, so later', is a wise saying.

NOTES

12.7: I have ... have ... have: In the NIV these are all future, not past.

12.8: Therefore I hate her: Jeremiah is willing to use forceful language. Yahweh's love has been scorned by Judah and He is not neutral or resigned about it, but bitter.

12.9: Speckled bird of prey: 'Hyena's lair' is the NEB reading, which follows the Greek. In either case the picture is of a creature that feeds on carrion.

12.10: Shepherds have destroyed my vineyard: The vineyard is a common metaphor for God's people (see Ps.80.8–16; Isa.5.1–7). In view of the passage that follows in 12.14–17, the shepherds are probably foreign kings rather than the leaders of Judah.

12.11: No man lays it to heart: Lack of repentance when the evidence of God's displeasure stared the people in the face was a recurring theme in the prophets (see e.g. Isa.22.12–14; 42.25; Amos 4.6–11). The sorrow of God is even more strongly expressed in Lam. 1.12.

12.14–17: Thus says the LORD concerning all my evil neighbours . . .: The theme of these verses will be considered when we look at chs 46—51 (see p. 206). The section is possibly placed here because of the verbal link provided by 'heritage' (vv. 7 and 14).

13.12: Every jar shall be filled with wine: This was probably a well-known proverbial saying; the different English versions translate it slightly differently. 'Jar' was the largest earthenware container used for storing wine.

13.13–14: I will fill with drunkenness . . .: Two different thoughts are mixed in these verses. First, God's judgement will make His people as confused and helpless as those who have drunk too much wine: in the Old Testament, Yahweh's giving drink is a symbol of death, like giving poison (cf. 25.27; Pss 60.3; 75.8; Isa. 51.17). Second, the destruction will be like the shattering of these jars at a drunken party.

13.15: Be not proud: As in 13.1–11, pride is singled out.

13.16: Before he brings darkness ...: The picture is of shepherds guarding their flocks before the dawn, waiting for it to get lighter. In fact, what they think is the twilight before dawn will turn out to be the brightest light left – it is going to get darker, not lighter.

13.17: My eyes will weep ... the LORD's flock has been taken captive: The figure of the LORD as shepherd recurs. In the Greek version it is the whole community that will weep.

13.18: The queen mother: The queen mother was a person of great importance in Judah. If the king is Jehoiachin and the reference to his Exile in 597 BC, the queen mother would be Nehushta (2 Kings 24.8).

13.19: The cities of the Negeb: The Negeb was strictly the arid region lying to the south of Judah; see Map 2, p. 235. Here the term seems to be used more loosely to mean the southern area of Judah.

13.20: From the north: See note on 1.14.

13.21: What will you say ... friends to you: The Hebrew is difficult, and various English translations have been suggested. 'Friends' are probably political allies, as in the NIV.

13.24: Wind from the desert: This is the fierce scorching wind that blows in from the east (the sirocco); Jer. 4.11; 9.16; 18.17; Lev. 26.33 and Ezek. 5.2,12 all contain pictures of Yahweh's scattering of His people as the wind does the chaff.

13.25: This is your lot ...: JB and NEB translate 'portion of the rebel' and 'wage of your apostasy' respectively. They have followed the Greek.

13.27: How long will it be before you are made clean?: Without knowing the tone of voice it is not easy to know what answer is expected. It could be, 'Never', 'After a long, purifying judgement', or, 'Will it ever be?'. See 4.14 for a similar unanswered question.

STUDY SUGGESTIONS

REVIEW OF CONTENT

1. What do you understand by 'prophetic symbolism'? What did the people of Judah believe about it?
2. What message did the incident of the spoiled waistcloth convey?
3. What do we mean when we talk of God's 'heartache'? Why could God not just forgive the people and start again?
4. Why did Jeremiah say that it had become impossible for the people of Judah to change their behaviour?

BIBLE STUDY

5. All the following passages contain examples of prophetic symbolism. For each one identify the nature of the symbolism and the point being made.
   (a) 1 Kings 22.11f
   (b) Isa. 8.1–4
   (c) Jer. 19.1–13
   (d) Jer. 27.1–5; 28.1–16
   (e) Ezek. 5.1–12
   (f) Ezek. 12.1–16
   (g) Hos. 1.2—2.1

6. In what ways do you think that the stories in Mark 4.35–40 and Mark 6.30–44 are like prophetic symbolism, and in what ways they are unlike it?
7. In Jer. 12.7–13 God Himself is pictured as experiencing inner tension. In what ways do the following passages report tensions within God Himself?
   (a) Exod. 32.1–14
   (b) Hos. 11.1–9
8. What other biblical examples can you suggest, of:
   (a) Characters who were dominated by pride?
   (b) Characters who were powerless to resist the evil they had once chosen to follow?

DISCUSSION AND APPLICATION

9. In what ways does your Church use visual means of sharing God's message? Do you think that it uses them enough? For what people do you think that visual methods of communication are especially important?
10. What do you think helps to keep effective Christian leaders from becoming proud?
11. Do you think of God as a figure above the world, controlling everything in it, or as one who is involved in it with a bleeding heart? What effect do you think that these different ideas would have on your life?
12. 'You become what you do' (p. 80). How would you answer someone who said that they had been rebelling against God so much that their life could never be changed?

14.1—15.9
Drought, Defeat and Famine

OUTLINE

The theme of judgement continues through this next section. Central to it are two laments with Yahweh's responses to them.
14.1–9: A lament because of the famine that has overtaken the land.
14.10–12: God replies to the lament by once again telling Jeremiah that there is no point in his praying for the people.
14.13–16: Jeremiah attacks the prophets, accusing them of prophesying falsely.

14.17–22: The lament is renewed: the focus is now military defeat followed by famine.

15.1–4: God's response to the lament again declares His firm resolve that the people must be seriously punished.

15.5–9: A poem asserting that because God is in complete control there is no way that judgement can be avoided. It is described as though it has already taken place.

INTERPRETATION

THE BALANCE BETWEEN NATURE AND MAN

In 3.3 we learnt that the balance of the natural environment was upset because of Judah's sin; now the same theme is taken up more fully. We do not find this theme only in Jeremiah (see e.g. Hos. 4.2f), but in the first part of ch. 14 it is particularly striking. The result of Judah's pride and unfaithfulness is a catastrophic drought. Crops are non-existent, water supplies have dried up, even wild animals that are used to managing on very little water are at the end of their resources. There is irony in this because Baal, whom the people have been worshipping, was regarded as the god of fertility; yet their worshipping of him is what has caused this *lack* of fertility!

Before the Exile there was among the Israelites a deeply held belief that God was not only the creator but that He was also directly in control of the universe and the source and provider for all human needs. And so, if there were problems with crops or rainfall it was seen as a sign of a breakdown in the harmonious relationship between God and His people. The precise manner in which God controlled the environment might not be understood, but poor rains were seen as showing God's displeasure.

We can link this belief with Israel's attempts to understand the relation between sin and suffering. In writings such as Proverbs and Psalm 37 people's sins were thought to be the direct cause of their suffering. Perhaps a bad drought confirmed what Jeremiah already believed about the evil of the people, and was readily understood as God's judgement on their sin.

By contrast, writings like Psalm 73, Job and Ecclesiastes challenge this view, and argue that there is no such simple relationship linking human sin and experience. Nevertheless, although they warn us to beware of versions of Christianity which suggest that there is a way that guarantees human success, they do not deny that human sin has a significant effect on human experience.

In the modern context we can make two points. Firstly, while we do not talk of natural disasters as God's judgement on the sin of those affected, God is regarded as the Lord of nature and so countless prayers are directed to Him concerning adverse weather, harvests, etc. As He is Lord of nature, surely He can bring or prevent rain? (We may note that insurance companies in the Western world describe natural disasters as 'acts of God'!)

Secondly, although we would not regard it as God's direct judgement on men (or at least not express it quite like that) there is ample, and growing, evidence of the serious effect of human greed, carelessness and exploitation on the world's ecology. The alarming rate of deforestation in South America and Africa, the dumping of toxic waste produced by the chemical, mining and nuclear industries, the exploitation of land by those who extract its goodness and then move on rather than trying to replenish what they have taken out; all these produce major problems that affect climate and productivity in a temporary or a permanent manner. We understand nature's balance too little to be able to treat it so carelessly without damage; when human greed controls our behaviour, all too often problems result.

A TIME NOT TO PRAY

In 7.16 and 11.14f we saw God commanding Jeremiah not to pray for the people. Now in 14.10–12 and 15.1 we again hear that prayer is useless and unacceptable. To appreciate the force of this statement we should know that in ancient Israel prayer was an important part of a prophet's task. Prophets not only received and delivered messages from God; they also prayed to God for people (see e.g. 1 Sam. 12.23; 1 Kings 17—18; 2 Kings 19.4). As someone singled out by God for special work and understood to be in a special relationship with God, a prophet's prayer was believed to be particularly effective. It was assumed that prophets would try to use this relationship with God for the good of the people.

So God's forbidding Jeremiah to pray was extremely serious. Jeremiah is called to be a prophet, but he is only to exercise part of the traditional role (at least during certain periods of his ministry). This prohibition goes against all Jeremiah's desires, for he longs that the people should repent and he would dearly love to pour out his heart on their behalf. But he is told that for the time being (the form of the Hebrew means 'do not pray *at the moment*' rather than 'do not pray *ever*') he is not to pray for them. Their sins, and particularly that of worshipping baals rather than Yahweh, mean that such prayers are of no value whatsoever.

Commenting on 13.20–27 (see p. 80) we noted that the people were so deep in their sin that there was no longer any possibility of their returning to Yahweh. This is the context in which Jeremiah was forbidden to pray, for in this situation prayer would no longer have had any meaning. We cannot pray with faith if we know that there is no possibility of the prayer being answered: 1 John 5.16 states that there are problems to which prayer is not the solution.

Despite all the possibilities that the Christian gospel opens up, there can still come times when prayer is not the right option. During the Second World War, Dietrich Bonhoeffer was among those who decided that it was no longer right to pray for Hitler's conversion and wait for God to answer, but that the time had come to try and assassinate Hitler. It was a last resort, an extreme and drastic decision not taken lightly; but those involved felt that the time for prayer had ended. Certainly, in the mercy of God, such situations are rare, but there can be times when it is better not to pray than to utter prayers without faith and with no chance of response.

NOTES

14.2: Her gates: Other English versions read 'cities'; either it refers to the state of Judah's cities in general, or it means that to north and south the land is open and defenceless against any who wish to invade.

14.3: Cover their heads: A sign of mourning.

14.4: The ground which is dismayed: Because of the drought; some scholars understand the ground to be drying up, while others follow the Greek and see a reference to the resulting failure of the crops.

14.6: They pant . . . eyes fail: Even wild animals, used to the struggle for survival, are desperate. Their breath comes in short gasps, their eyes are glazed (probably because they are near death).

14.7–9: Though our iniquities . . . leave us not: As with 13.27 (see p. 82), if we knew the tone of voice in which this was said it would affect our interpretation. Some scholars have suggested that this is a genuine lament or a model of how the people should respond; others see it as a caricature of the artificial way in which the people actually respond.

14.7: For thy name's sake; for our backslidings are many: God's reputation will be judged according to what happens to His people. Many would say that if the people suffered it must be because their God was not powerful enough to protect them. 'Backslidings' includes the Hebrew word *shub* (see discussion of 3.6—4.4, p. 33).

14.8: Thou hope of Israel: The same title for God occurs at 17.13.

14.9: Mighty man who cannot save: A contradiction, for the mighty man was the one who *did* save!

'The result of Judah's pride and unfaithfulness was a catastrophic drought.' And there is plenty of evidence of the serious effect of human greed and carelessness upon the world's ecology, as more and more areas become desert, crops fail, and animals die.

14.10: The LORD does not accept them: Normally in Israel's worship a lament would be followed by an oracle giving assurance; here the precise opposite is found!

14.13–16: The prophets are prophesying lies: See comments on 23.9–40 (p. 128) and 28.1–17 (p. 152).

14.14: Divination: The use by a religious leader of some mechanical means, such as the throwing of dice or bones, to obtain an answer to a question by a worshipper.

14.15: By sword and famine those prophets shall be consumed: Exactly what they say will never happen is what will befall them!

14.18: Prophet and priest ply their trade through the land, and have no knowledge: There are different understandings of this verse. Most English versions have a meaning similar to the RSV, picturing the prophet and priest as travelling round the land, like traders selling their goods, begging for their living but without any real understanding of what was happening. (In JB they give up their call in order to dig, while in NIV they have already gone into Exile.) Lack of knowledge is again singled out; see the note on 9.3.

14.19: We looked for peace, but ... terror: See 8.15.

15.1: Though Moses and Samuel: Moses had persuaded God to change His mind (Exod. 32.11–14; Num. 14.13–20; Ps. 106.23); Samuel was the pioneer prophet and kingmaker (1 Sam. 7.9; 12.23). Who could be more effective in prayer than these men? But now even they would have no influence with God. (It is possible that here and in ch. 1 Jeremiah is deliberately linked with Moses.)

15.4: Manasseh: Manasseh reigned in Judah c.697–642 BC. He negotiated a successful treaty with the Assyrians which ensured political stability and freedom from invasion throughout his long reign. But because of his religious practices the books of Kings refer to him as the worst of all the kings of Judah. His treaty with Assyria meant that he had to include Assyrian worship among his policies. See 2 Kings 21.1–18; 23.26f; 24.3f.

15.7: Winnowed them with a winnowing fork: To winnow is to separate the chaff from the grain by tossing the mixture into the air; the light chaff is blown away. Judah is like chaff, useless, and will be blown away.

15.9: She who bore seven ... her sun went down: Seven is often used in the Bible as a round, full number. The woman had a good number of sons, who were her greatest pride. Now, while in the prime of their manhood and before they could marry, all of them have been killed in battle.

STUDY SUGGESTIONS

REVIEW OF CONTENT

1. Why did the people believe that drought or failures in the harvest occurred?
2. What different views were there in ancient Israel about the relationship between sin and suffering?
3. Why was Jeremiah expected to pray for the people?
4. Why did God forbid Jeremiah to pray for the people?

BIBLE STUDY

5. Compare Deut. 28 and Hag. 1.3–11 with Jer. 14.1–9. What point do they all make?
6. Joel 1 describes the effect of a plague of locusts, and says that this plague is God's judgement on the people. What evidence is there that Joel still hopes that total disaster may be avoided?
7. 'Prophets prayed to God for people', p. 85. Study the following passages and note the importance given to prophets' prayers.
   (a) 1 Sam. 12.19–23
   (b) 1 Kings 13.1–6
   (c) 1 Kings 17.1 & 18.41–46
   (d) 2 Kings 6.11–23
   (e) Isa. 37.1–4

DISCUSSION AND APPLICATION

8. What relevance do you think a passage like 14.1–9 has for:
   (a) A secular scientist who has no belief in God?
   (b) A peasant in a country devastated by a cyclone?
   (c) A shopper in the Western world who buys everything in tins or packets in supermarkets?
9. How do you understand God's control over nature?
10. 'Why should this happen to me?', is a frequent question by people who suffer. What answer, if any, can Christians give?
11. In ancient Israel the prophet was understood to be in some ways standing between man and God. Does the person commissioned to speak for God today have any similar responsibilities to pray? Give your reasons.
12. 'A time not to pray', p. 85. Have there been times when you have painfully decided not to pray for something, even though you longed that it would happen? What kind of things have these been?

Special Note D
Jeremiah The Man

The book of Jeremiah is unique among the prophetic books because of the amount of information it presents about the prophet whose name it bears. Not only are there many stories about incidents involving Jeremiah; passages such as the 'Confessions' (see Special Note E, p. 107) have also been used to shed light on his personal feelings. However, tempting as it can be to try and work out a full biography of Jeremiah, for two reasons this is not possible.

Firstly, and fundamentally, the book of Jeremiah has been put together by editors. Because we are often uncertain of the extent of their editing, we are unable to say how much the material we have reflects Jeremiah exactly, and how much it has been developed. Special Note E, p. 107, explains this point for the 'Confessions'; it applies to other material in the book also. The editors no doubt selected and edited from a much wider range of material. What they included is present because it helped them to make their points more effectively, and not because their chief concern was to give an accurate account of the life of Jeremiah. We should thus be wary of claiming too much detailed knowledge of Jeremiah's life.

Secondly, much of the material in the book is not linked with any particular date: for instance, most of chs 2—25 is undated. Since the material is not arranged chronologically we cannot assign dates to undated material, and so even where we are confident that we have the authentic voice of Jeremiah we cannot trace a detailed progression in the prophet's message or feelings.

This is not to deny that within the book we have faithful records of Jeremiah, and get a good 'feel' of him. But we must beware of trying to compile an outline of Jeremiah's career that goes beyond the evidence available to us. We must remember this as we summarize what we can confidently say about him.

HIS CAREER

Our understanding of Jeremiah 1.2 places Jeremiah's call in 626 BC. As he was still active after the destruction of Jerusalem, his ministry lasted more than forty years. Since the book is silent about any activity during the reigns of Jehoahaz and Jehoiachin, we have four historical periods to consider.

1. JOSIAH

Some scholars have suggested that Jeremiah preached in favour of Josiah's reform, or that he at first supported it but then saw that it did not go to the root of Judah's problems. Such suggestions remain unproven; they usually tell us more about how the scholar concerned views the reform than about Jeremiah's attitude!

Only one passage, 3.6–18, is directly linked to Josiah's reign. The suggestion that much of the material in chapters 2—6 comes from this period is possible but cannot be substantiated. Probably a number of passages in the book do date from this time, but we have no certain way to identify them. Prophecy was quite a common activity and there is no clear evidence that Jeremiah was of particular prominence. He would have been a young man who became established in the course of Josiah's reign. The content of his prophecies presumably anticipated what he would later say in greater detail.

2. JEHOIAKIM

Much of the book's dated material is assigned to this time. Jeremiah was by now a prominent figure who faced widespread hostility and ridicule and was given the nickname 'Terror on every side' because of the nature of his message. He was beaten and put in the stocks (ch. 20), and had to go into hiding (36.19). Though a few people in high places did protect him, he appeared as a voice crying in the wilderness and facing opposition from many quarters, including most of the political establishment. He was charged with heresy on account of his attitude to the Temple (ch. 26), and at one time was banned from the Temple (ch. 36). Although he remained free his safety was uncertain and his life at risk.

3. ZEDEKIAH

By the time of Zedekiah's reign, Jeremiah's unpopularity had grown, and the forces ranged against him were stronger. His political views were now suspect as well as his religious ones. He was considered a traitor for urging surrender to Babylon. For a time he was in solitary confinement; had he not been rescued from that he would certainly have died. Moved from that, he remained in a situation of house arrest or detention until the fall of Jerusalem.

4. THE LAST YEARS

After Jerusalem's fall the Babylonians regarded Jeremiah sympathetically, no doubt because they learned that he had been encouraging

Judah's surrender. They left him free to choose his future, and he decided to remain in the Promised Land. However, with the assassination of Gedaliah, he was compelled to join the subsequent exodus to Egypt. By this time he must have been over 60 years old and he presumably died not long afterwards, no doubt a minority figure to the last.

HIS PERSONALITY

Our chief source for approaching Jeremiah's personality must be the poetic oracles. While they share language, ideas and imagery with those of other prophets, they have (as does every prophetic book) their distinctive flavour, in mood as well as in theology. Their closest relation within the Old Testament is Hosea.

While the oracles use well-known styles, and we have them at the hand of editors, there is no reason to doubt that many of the strong emotions shown go back to Jeremiah himself and that he was intensely involved in his message. Caring about both people and message, it is likely that he would have experienced great internal tensions, for he hated some of the things he was charged to say. When his prophecies seemed unfulfilled he felt betrayed by God; when the people failed to respond he felt bitter and resentful. Constantly in a minority, he became drained emotionally. Given the difficulties of his life, it is not surprising that he sometimes appeared vindictive.

It seems that he faced great pressures for long periods, and that the realities of his experiences as a prophet were very different from his initial expectations. He may not always have been a solitary, protesting figure, and those in high places who helped him may have decreased some of his problems. But he still had to endure great hardship, emotionally and spiritually as well as physically. It is not surprising that his sufferings have sometimes been presented as anticipating the passion of Christ. They were very, very real.

STUDY SUGGESTIONS

1. Why is it not possible to work out a full biography of Jeremiah?
2. What do you think were the chief concerns of the editors of the Book of Jeremiah? What was their reason for using stories about the prophet Jeremiah?
3. In whose reigns was Jeremiah active as a prophet? How long a period did this cover? What was happening in Judah during this time?

4. Which material in the book must be our chief source for insight into Jeremiah's personality? Give your reasons.
5. What kind of pressures did Jeremiah have to face?
6. From your own study of the book, what sort of a person do you think Jeremiah was?
7. In the course of the book as so far studied, what range of attitudes does Jeremiah show:
   (a) towards God?
   (b) towards the people of Judah?

16.1—17.27
The Continuing Tragedy

OUTLINE

Jeremiah 15.10–21 is a further portion of the 'Confessions' of Jeremiah and will be studied with the remainder of that material, see p. 109. The two chapters we now consider contain a mixture of material, often linked by a common word or idea. As a whole the chapters are not particularly coherent, but God's judgement continues to be the central theme.

16.1–13: Jeremiah is commanded to be a solitary figure: for him there will be no marriage, no family, no participation in the community's rites of passage. He is to behave in this way not because these things are bad but as a sign to the people. It is another act of prophetic symbolism.

16.14–15: A declaration that some will return from Exile.

16.16–18: A further short passage concerned with the severity of God's judgement.

16.19–21: Arising from the reference to idols in v. 18 comes a short poem declaring that Yahweh alone is God.

17.1–4: Another short passage which reasserts the deep-rootedness of Judah's sin and the severity of the punishment.

17.5–13: Several short oracles which contrast trust in God with trust in human resources.

17.14–18: A further section of Jeremiah's 'Confessions'; see p. 107.

17.19–27: A passage with instructions about observance of the sabbath.

INTERPRETATION

PREPARED TO BE DIFFERENT

In Jeremiah's society marriage, the raising of a family and participation in the major celebrations of the extended family were seen as essential for all adults. According to 16.1–13 Jeremiah was instructed to abstain from them. Such behaviour would have been quite incomprehensible to his contemporaries, and was doubtless unacceptable to his family and friends. In Special Note D (p. 90), we looked at his personal experience generally; here we consider the fact that he was called to be different.

As a prophet Jeremiah was selected by God for a special role. The commands he received to refrain from marriage and be solitary were linked with the particular message he had to deliver. They were obviously not examples for all to follow! Nevertheless, there is here an important principle, that of readiness to go against the conventions of society, and even the wishes of one's own family, if that should be what God requires.

This is never easy. It is especially difficult in societies where great weight is given to the authority of the elders and to respect for family bonds. In practice most Christians are likely to follow a pattern of life recognizable and for the most part acceptable to the traditional customs of their society (unless these happen to be clearly unChristian). But we must recognize that God may call anyone to be different in a striking way. The sanctity of family life in the Jewish community was (and is) extremely strong. Yet Matthew 19.12 records Jesus as saying that some have made themselves eunuchs for the sake of the Kingdom of Heaven. This should not be understood literally, and refers to people who refrain from marriage on account of particular work for God.

Hard thought is required to see how the Christian faith can best be applied in different cultures. As the example of marriage is raised by the story of Jeremiah we shall consider this a little further. Over the Church's long history a variety of attitudes have developed in its different branches towards the relationship between marriage and ordination. By the eleventh century parish clergy in the Eastern Church were normally married (bishops remaining single), while those in the Western Church were expected to be single. The Western Church's position was made official by the 2nd Lateran Council of 1139. After the Reformation the Roman Catholic Church continued to insist on the celibacy of the clergy, while the Protestant Churches permitted clergy to marry. This remains the basic position today.

The view of the Roman Catholic Church is that a man called to ordination is also called to celibacy. It declares that the calling to the priesthood overrides the 'normal' calling to marriage. Such a ruling can lead to tensions in, for instance, some parts of rural Africa, where men who remain unmarried are only considered as boys. Nor is this only an issue in the Roman Catholic Church. While accepting that most pastors will be married, a Protestant Church may sometimes decide, either because of the particular gifts of an unmarried individual or because of the demands of a certain ministry, that someone who is unmarried should work as a pastor. In such situations the Churches are bearing witness that no culture has the last word on what is right; every culture is at times challenged by the gospel.

Christians will normally accept things in their culture that the gospel regards as neutral. However, there may come occasions when, for some deeper purpose, they are called to go against what their culture regards as not only normal but essential. In Jeremiah there is no denial that marriage is good and is the normal pattern, but the vocation to remain single is perfectly valid. A single person is no less a person, an unmarried Christian is no less a Christian. Similarly, the failure of a married couple to have children does not make their marriage invalid. If human customs clash with the will of God, Christians are called, difficult as it may be, to follow God (cf. Acts 4.19).

A FOUNDATION OF TRUST IN GOD (17.5–8)

Trust lies at the heart of human life. We trust in the chair we sit on; we trust that our employers will pay us our wage; we trust our friends to help us when we have problems. At a deeper level, we rely on the cycle of nature; so we plant and hope for the rains to come and the crops to grow. There may be good years and bad years, but the basic pattern is there. Trust is linked with experience: a young child cries when visiting the doctor because it has not yet learnt to trust that the treatment is for its own good.

Everyone, consciously or not, has a philosophy of life. It may be socialistic or individualistic. It may be religious or not; if it is religious, it may or may not be Christian. Jeremiah contrasts the two basic kinds of philosophy as trust in God (meaning the God of Israel) and trust in human nature. In 17.5–8 this contrast is summarized; the only sensible thing to do is to trust in God, for trust in human nature is doomed to disappointment. When there is such a faith in God it can endure through temporal difficulties and permit individuals to triumph over adversity, with faith strengthened and enriched, rather than weakened, by the difficulties.

This is a common experience where Christians have been persecuted for their faith. Repeatedly, in different parts of the world, there have been attempts to extinguish the Christian Church. All they have succeeded in doing is strengthening the faith and witness of those at the heart of the Church; numbers may have been driven away but the Church itself has become stronger. The writer Tertullian, at a time when Roman emperors were persecuting the early Christians, described how persecution often helps the Church to grow in this way; 'The blood of the Christians is seed'. Even the fiercest opposition will not destroy a true faith.

REMEMBER THE SABBATH (17.19–27)

Within the book of Jeremiah 17.19–27 stands on its own, and in tension with other passages such as the condemnation in ch. 7 of the way various rituals were carried out (see p. 53). In the note on p. 98 we suggest that it probably comes from the post-exilic period. In order to understand these verses in their present context within the Book of Jeremiah we need to see them against the wider Old Testament background.

Genesis makes clear that work was seen as part of God's good purpose for humanity, but it was not to be the sole or the dominant focus of life. So we find the provision of the Sabbath in the Ten Commandments (Exod. 20.8–11) and, in various Old Testament passages, instructions about the way in which it should be observed. There is a balance between, on the one hand, a casual attitude which treats the Sabbath like any other day and, on the other hand, an undue legalism which makes its observance a matter of human regulations.

Within Jeremiah the basic charge against Judah has been that the people have not taken God seriously. In the present passage the observation of the Sabbath is presented as a way in which they can show that they *do* take God seriously.

An important part of the Christian Church's understanding of Sunday has developed from the Jewish understanding of the Sabbath. While legalism can be a threat, because of human nature there is always a danger that greed will triumph over obedience to God and so over our need for worship and rest. In such a situation this charge to observe the Sabbath is an important reminder.

Part of our obedience to God is shown by our giving special place to worship and abstaining from our regular employment. (We need to remember, of course, that in many societies today the provision of basic services and the efficiency of large factories mean that some people have to work on Sundays and rest on other days.) In deciding how we should keep Sunday as a 'holy day' of rest and relaxation we may need to beware of legalism: what is refreshment for us (e.g. digging in the garden or mending a car) may be the work for which someone else is employed throughout the week; what is right in an emergency is different from what is appropriate at other times.

Different people will vary in their approaches. As in worship, there needs to be room for variety of expression and respect of differences in non-essentials. If we reach a position where we think that ours is the *only* way to remember Sunday we have moved away from the spirit of obedience to God into the letter of legalism. If this happens, our dependence on God is being replaced by trust in our own fulfilment of certain regulations.

NOTES

16.2: You shall not: We saw in 14.11f (p. 85) that Jeremiah was forbidden from praying 'at the moment'. The Hebrew here makes it equally clear that Jeremiah is 'never' to marry; it is a permanent prohibition.

16.6: Cut himself or make himself bald: Two kinds of mourning rituals; see note on 7.29 and also 41.5; 47.5; Deut. 14.1; Isa. 22.12.

16.7: Break bread for the mourner ... cup of consolation: This refers to the provision of food, either during the rituals or at the completion of a fast by the mourner(s). In later Judaism the '*consoling cup*' was a special cup of wine drunk by the chief mourner. In many cultures the custom after a burial is to provide refreshment for those present. In certain parts of England the custom is to invite those present at a funeral service back for a funeral tea; if the family can afford it a particular kind of smoked meat is served, giving rise to the expression 'buried with ham'.

16.9: I will make to cease: The same verse is found at 7.34; 25.10 is similar.

16.12: His stubborn evil will: See note on 2.20 (p. 29) for Jeremiah's emphasis on the will.

16.13: There you shall serve other gods: The people of Judah have chosen to worship other gods where Yahweh should have been worshipped. Now they will find themselves in a place where they are expected to worship other gods! (In 24.4–7 the Exile will be seen in a totally different way; it becomes the basis of a new hope and it is those in exile, rather than those left in Judah, through whom this hope will be realized.)

16.14–15: The days are coming ... I will bring them back to their own land: See note on 23.7f which is nearly identical. Placed here, these verses moderate the severity of v. 13, and are likely to be a later addition, perhaps reflecting the hope of a return to Judah by some of the exiles.

16.18: I will doubly recompense: Although most English versions translate to give a similar meaning, we probably do best to follow the NEB, and understand it as an equivalent judgement, 'in full', proportional to the sin rather than double what it deserves.

17.1–4: The sin of Judah ... burn for ever: These verses are not found in the Greek.

17.1: Pen of iron; with a point of diamond: An iron stylus with a diamond (or possibly flint or adamant) point can mark anything. The sin is marked inwardly on their hearts (compare how the new covenant is written on the heart in 31.31–34) and outwardly on their altars.

17.2: Their Asherim: Only here are the Asherim mentioned by name in Jeremiah. They were trees or wooden structures ('sacred poles', JB, NEB) dedicated to the goddess Asherah.

17.6: Shrub in the desert: Whatever the species, it obviously had a stark and naked appearance, reflecting its struggle for life. For the thought in vv. 5–8 compare Psalm 1.

17.9–10: Who can understand it?: These verses possibly originate in Israelite wisdom. In Hebrew 'understand' has the same root as 'know'; here it describes a real grasp of how the heart works.

17.11: The partridge that gathers a brood which she did not hatch: The whole verse is a proverb to the effect that in the long run evil does not pay. The person who has got rich illegally and the partridge both lose what they have. Probably the thought is that of the vulnerability of the partridge's eggs which lie on the ground. Alternatively, it may refer to a belief that the partridge was thought to hatch the eggs of other birds, which then fly off and leave it: ('Kindness killed the partridge' is a Chichewa proverb from Eastern Zambia and Malawi, referring to a story of a partridge which rescued a snake from a fire and then got bitten by the snake.)

17.12: A glorious throne: A reference to Jerusalem, in particular to the Temple within it which was God's throne. To address the throne was to address God Himself.

17.13: Written in the earth: This may mean 'humbled' (NEB) or 'uprooted' (JB). Alternatively, 'earth' may refer to the underworld – i.e. they will die.

17.19–27: Go and stand ... not be quenched: Although the command to keep the Sabbath was a very old tradition in Israel, this is the only passage in Jeremiah about observing it. Since such observance became of very great significance after the exile there is good reason to think that this passage comes from the post-exilic period; compare Nehemiah 13.15–22 for a similar concern.

17.19: The Benjamin Gate: RSV and NEB both emend the Hebrew. If they are right, it probably refers to a gate in the north wall of the city, leading out to the territory of Benjamin: 37.13 and 38.7 refer to the Benjamin Gate. However, there is no manuscript support for this change, and other English versions leave the Hebrew unchanged and translate as 'Gate of the People'; such a gate is not mentioned elsewhere.

17.26: From the land of Benjamin, from the Shephelah, from the hill country, and from the Negeb: From north, west, east and south.

17.27: A fire ... not be quenched: See also 7.20 and compare with Amos 1.4, 7, 10, 12, 14; 2.2, 5.

STUDY SUGGESTIONS

REVIEW OF CONTENT

1. Why was Jeremiah not to marry or attend family celebrations?
2. What difficulties may arise:
    (a) If the Christian faith disagrees with some aspects of our culture?
    (b) If God leads a Christian to behave in a way unacceptable in our culture?
3. Jeremiah sees all philosophies of life as belonging to one of two basic groups: using your own words, summarize these two types of belief.
4. Why do most scholars believe that 17.19–27 comes from a time later than most of Jeremiah?
5. When Christians consider the use of Sundays:
    (a) What extremes should they avoid?
    (b) What other factors should they bear in mind?

BIBLE STUDY

6. How did the following Bible characters go against their culture because of what they believed God required of them?
    (a) Ruth: Ruth 1.1–18
    (b) Joseph: Matt. 1.18–25
    (c) The good Samaritan: Luke 10.29–37
    (d) Peter: Acts 10
7. How many ways can you think of in which Jesus broke the conventions of his day? Give references.
8. Compare 17.5–8 with Psalm 1. What similarities and what differences do you find?
9. Use a concordance to find as many references as possible to the Sabbath. From these references work out what you believe

should be the basic principles that govern the Christian's observance of it.

DISCUSSION AND APPLICATION

10. What examples can you give of any normal patterns of behaviour in your culture which the Church breaks because it sees them as unChristian? Do you think there are other patterns of behaviour it ought to challenge?
11. Do you think that there is a place today for people to make protests as Jeremiah did, by remaining unmarried and not attending parties, etc? Are such people bound to be misunderstood? Give any examples from your own experience?
12. If your culture regards those not married as incomplete or immature, how does it react to Christian leaders who are single?
13. Do most people in your society believe that a life not based on trust in God leads to disaster? What effect, if any, does this have on the Church's approach?
14. What are the common philosophies of life in your society? How close are they to the Christian faith, and how does the Church respond to them?
15. Does your Church require or expect certain behaviour on Sunday? If so:
    (a) Is it applied strictly, or is there room for individuals to apply it according to their own situations?
    (b) Do other people think it is negative and legalistic? If they do, what do you say to them?

18.1–17; 19.1—20.6
Pictures from the Potter

OUTLINE

The material in this section centres around two stories connected with pottery. The first reports a scene in a potter's workshop where, as in 1.11f, through something Jeremiah sees he receives a message from God. The second describes a symbolic action that the prophet performs with a pottery flask. Both stories declare God's sovereignty in punishing Judah for the people's sin.

18.1–12: Jeremiah visits a potter's workshop and is taught by God that the people are like clay in God's hands: when they are spoiled (by sin) He can do what He likes with them.

18.13–17: A poem which argues that Judah is behaving like an idiot. Nature follows a regular pattern and is dependable, but Judah does not.

18.18–23: Another of Jeremiah's 'confessions'; see p. 115.

19.1–13: A story centred around an incident in which Jeremiah breaks a pottery flask as a symbol of coming judgement.

19.14—20.6: The message of the symbolic action is now proclaimed to a wider public. As a result Jeremiah is arrested, beaten and locked up overnight. When he is released he pronounces a message of judgement against the official responsible.

INTERPRETATION

GOD THE POTTER (18.1–12)

If you have ever seen a potter at work on a wheel you know that skill is required. The consistency of the clay must be just right and the potter needs very careful control. Every potter finds that from time to time the clay goes out of shape or collapses and must be completely reworked. This is what Jeremiah saw in the workshop. As he did so he saw also that God is like a potter working with people. He is in complete control and can shape them as He wishes.

The basic reference in this passage seems to be to the children of Israel. If we read vv. 5–6 and then v. 11 we find a straight declaration of God's judgement on Judah. Just as a potter squashes the clay because it is not making the pot wanted, so God will crush Judah because of the people's failure to follow Him. Obviously there is potentially the idea that God may start again and reshape the material for another purpose, but that is not stated here. What is stressed is God's mastery over the clay (the people); they are in no position to resist Him.

A further idea is found in vv. 7–10, where the illustration is applied more widely, not just to Judah but to any nation. God is sovereign over all nations and able to do with each as He wishes. What He will do is related to the behaviour of the nation in question; for instance, if the clay seems to be useless but then starts to be workable it will not be squashed.

The story of God's creation of man in Genesis 2 uses the image of God as a potter shaping man out of the dust (i.e. clay) of the ground. The picture of God as potter is also found elsewhere in the Bible; (e.g. Isa. 29.16; 45.9; 64.8; Rom. 9.19–21). When an illustration is used there is always a particular purpose in view. In applying the illustration we must be careful not to ask of the passage questions with which it is not concerned. The passage under consideration is intended to illuminate God's sovereignty; it is not concerned with human responsibility. (In Romans 9 St Paul does take up the issue of human responsibility in connection with the picture of God as a potter, but that does not concern us here.) Here the concern is only with God's ability to do as He wishes with people according to their behaviour. God is creator, we are creatures: therefore we exist to serve the creator.

The teaching of God's sovereignty is challenged in many ways today. Some people look at developments in technology and scientific understanding and declare that a belief in God is no longer needed or relevant. Others see the scale of disasters and evil present in the world and wonder how there can be a God. 'If God is really in control', they ask, 'Why does He let things be as they are?'

There is no simple answer. Any serious attempt at an answer needs a much wider biblical and theological perspective than is appropriate in this study. But Jeremiah would surely have recognized the problem. For, although in his day scientific understanding was totally different, and people were perhaps more inclined to be religious, then as now God's sovereignty was challenged. In the light of the book of Jeremiah as a whole, the prophet's response to such challenges would doubtless have been an appeal to the importance of faith. Such faith was not a vague hope, a feeling that 'it would be nice if'; it was a strong conviction. For Jeremiah this conviction did not rest on feelings or wishes but on the solid basis of his own personal experience, and also the experience of Israel down the centuries; when tempted to doubt he could fall back on that. For Christians today, not only is there the experience of personal encounter with God, there is also that of the Church down the ages. Behind both are the events of the life, death and resurrection of Jesus Christ, recorded for us in the Bible. At the level of personal relationships we might compare this faith with trust in a friend who has proved reliable and trustworthy in the past. Faith it is, but a faith for which there are good reasons.

THE PROPHET UNDER ATTACK (19.1—20.6)

The incident of Jeremiah's breaking the flask is a further act of prophetic symbolism. Because the performing of the action was believed to set in motion the events it represented, the deed would be taken extremely seriously. This helps us to understand the fury of Pashhur when the act was reported to him, and when Jeremiah proclaimed its significance in public (only a small group witnessed the original act). So Jeremiah was arrested, beaten and chained up (or possibly shut in prison) overnight. No doubt Pashhur saw

Jeremiah saw that God is like a potter, working with people instead of clay. He is in complete control, using immense care to shape them according to His plan. But He may crush them as He crushed Judah if they refuse to obey Him.

himself as doing his job of keeping Temple worship orderly: Church authorities today are unlikely to welcome those who fiercely attack the Church from the cathedral steps! When released the following day, Jeremiah might have been tempted to keep quiet to avoid further trouble. Instead, he charged his accuser with rebellion against God, asserting that Pashhur's behaviour (i.e. his treatment of God's prophet) showed that he was a false prophet himself.

We notice here that God's messenger may suffer opposition (mental or physical) for delivering God's message. Human fear of this possibility must not allow the message to be silenced. To begin the Christian life includes the taking up of a cross, and should not be done lightly. Christian leadership may require public words or actions which are unpopular. This is a risk that any Christian leader must be prepared to face, for Christian leadership introduces us not to a quiet life but to an uphill struggle against the different challenges that our societies pose. We may sympathize with Christian leaders who avoid these, for few of us enjoy being targets of controversy and conflict; but faithfulness to our calling means facing up to the issues.

We also notice the danger that those in positions of leadership within the Church may become blind to the correction of God. Every religious group develops its own hierarchy and particular interests. That is part of human nature. One of the biggest challenges facing any Church is that it be open to the fresh wind of God in renewal, to the exposure and correction of abuses that have crept in. The Church that loses its prophetic voice is a Church that loses touch with the power of God. For instance, we cannot expect a Church that tolerates immorality in its leaders to reflect God to the world. Pashhur's reaction was very understandable, but he was in reality trying to silence the voice of God. Because of that, Jeremiah proclaimed God's judgement. Every time we try to maintain the tradition for the sake of it, or hoping for a quiet life, we risk being deaf to the voice of God. Then we too will come under judgement. Pashhur is a warning to us.

NOTES

18.3: Working at his wheel: The potter's wheel was made up of two stones like mill stones, connected to each other by a vertical axis. The larger wheel was turned by the potter's foot; as the wheel rotated, the potter's hands shaped the clay which lay on the smaller wheel.

18.11: Return: See the discussion on p. 33.

18.12: That is in vain: The situation is desperate. There is no point and no hope any more. The same Hebrew phrase is translated, 'It is hopeless' at 2.25 and Isa. 57.10.

18.14: Does the snow ... cold flowing streams: Although the variations between English translations of this verse show that the detailed meaning is unclear, the basic meaning is straightforward: while nature behaves in an orderly manner and is dependable, Israel does not and is not.

18.15: To false gods: A literal translation would be, 'To emptiness'; JB comes close to this with, 'To a Nothing'.

18.16: To be hissed at: A sign of the terror and horror of the devastation.

18.17: East wind: See also 4.11f; 13.24.

Show them my back, not my face: The people had turned their backs on God (see 2.27; 32.33); now He will do the same to them.

19.1: Flask: The Hebrew word for the flask, *baqbuq*, comes from the gurgling sound made when the liquid was poured out of it.

19.2: Valley of the son of Hinnom at the entry of the Potsherd Gate: For the first phrase see note on 7.31. The Potsherd Gate was presumably a gate into Jerusalem, outside which broken pottery was dumped.

19.3: Kings ... inhabitants: According to 19.1 Jeremiah went with 'elders' and 'priests'. The emphasis in vv. 3–9 is also different from that of vv. 1–2. Many scholars believe that the original incident with the flask is reported in vv. 1–2, 10–11a and that vv. 3–9, 11b–13 represent an expansion of the original story, focusing on Topheth rather than on the flask.

19.4: Profaned: A literal translation would be, 'treated as foreign'.

19.5–6: High places of Baal ... Topheth: See note on 7.31.

19.7: I will make void: In Hebrew this word has the same root as that for 'flask' so the two words are linked by sound.

19.8: To be hissed at: See note on 18.6.

19.9: Siege ... distress: The two Hebrew words sound similar.

19.11: Men shall bury ... no place else to bury: See note on 7.32.

19.13: Houses upon whose roofs: Houses in Israel had flat roofs. For astral worship it was obviously important to be able to see the sun, moon and stars. Each family could have its own worship on its roof.

19.15: Its towns: In NEB a different translation is suggested, 'Blood-spattered altars'; but RSV makes good sense.

20.1: Pashhur ... chief officer in the house of the LORD: This Pashhur is probably the father of Gedaliah mentioned in 38.1. 'Chief officer' is literally 'prince overseer'; he was responsible for order in the Temple and may have been second in authority under the chief priest

(29.26). Since Jeremiah was appointed as 'God's overseer' (see 1.10), there may be deliberate irony in using this title of Pashhur.

20.2: Upper Benjamin Gate: This gate presumably led out of the north side of the Temple area; its location is not known. As it was a Temple gate it should not be confused with the city gate mentioned at 37.13; 38.7.

Jeremiah the prophet: The inclusion of 'prophet' stresses the role of the person thus treated, and so the seriousness of Pashhur's action.

20.3: Terror on every side: See note on 6.25. There may be a connection between Jeremiah's applying this title to Pashhur and the root meaning of the name Pashhur, which has a connection with the Hebrew word for violence. It was a very terrible curse put on the priest.

20.4: Captive to Babylon: This is the first time in the book that Babylon is mentioned by name as the agent of God's judgement on Jerusalem.

20.6: You have prophesied falsely: The description of Pashhur as a prophet may be used loosely and generally rather than being technically accurate.

STUDY SUGGESTIONS

REVIEW OF CONTENT

1. What lesson did Jeremiah draw out from his experience in the potter's workshop?
2. What do you think was the basis of Jeremiah's own faith?
3. Why was Jeremiah unpopular with the authorities?
4. What difficulties is a Christian leader likely to face?

BIBLE STUDY

5. Look up the following passages which refer to God as potter: Gen.2; Isa.29.16; 45.9; 64.8; Rom.9.19–21. What different points is each concerned to make?
6. What different aspects of God's sovereignty do you find in the following passages?
   (a) Gen.1.1–31
   (b) Ps.93
   (c) Isa.40.12–31
   (d) Isa.45.1–7
   (e) Rom.14.9
   (f) Rev.1.9–18
7. What do the following passages tell us about the reasons people had for their faith?

(a) Jacob: Gen.28.10–22
(b) Rahab: Josh.2.1–14
(c) The widow: 1 Kings 17.8–24
(d) Peter: Luke 5.1–11
(e) The Ethiopian: Acts 8.26–40
(f) Paul: Acts 9.1–20

DISCUSSION AND APPLICATION

8. In your experience what are the objections to Christian faith that people raise most often?
9. How would you reply to those who doubt God's control over the world?
10. How would you reassure people that the Christian faith has a solid basis?
11. What reasons can members of your Church give for their faith? What are your own reasons?
12. What helps Church leaders to be open to criticism and correction?
13. How easy is it for your Christian leaders to speak out on public issues? Describe any occasions where this has led them into difficulty.

Special Note E
The Confessions of Jeremiah

In the next two sections of this book we look at a number of passages that are often known as the 'Confessions' of Jeremiah. Although they appear at different places within the book of Jeremiah (11.18 – 12.6; 15.10–21; 17.14–18; 18.18–23; 20.7–18) we shall find it helpful to group them together in this study because they share a common mood and themes. Since we have recognized that it is difficult to find an obvious structure in the arrangement of much of the material in Jeremiah, to extract these passages and consider them together does not greatly affect our understanding of them. It does simplify our looking at their message.

Because of the way that the book of Jeremiah has been compiled we cannot be definite about the origin of these poems. They follow the traditional pattern of the laments used in Israelite worship, so their pattern was no doubt borrowed from the worship of the Temple. Because of this some scholars suggest that these poems may come from the community, or a group within the community speaking as a person, rather than from Jeremiah himself.

Certainly, although the poems are presented as coming from Jeremiah, we cannot use them to discover exact information about the prophet and his feelings. We cannot be sure how far Jeremiah's personal prayers lie behind these poems. However, since the liturgical forms of worship developed to express the feelings of the worshippers, it is quite possible that behind these poems *does* lie either Jeremiah's own anguish or that of an individual or group representative of him.

Whatever their authorship, we can be sure that the poems were not included because the editors wished to shed light on the person of the prophet. The laments' *content* will have determined their inclusion. Just as some Psalms may first have been composed out of individual experience, and then been used in public worship because they expressed a mood felt by many, so the editors of Jeremiah found the 'Confessions' expressing something that they wanted to say.

Perhaps, as some have suggested, the poems' mood of despair and frustration was found to match perfectly the experience of those whose land had been overrun and devastated during the period of the Exile. (A similar attitude is found in the Book of Lamentations, which comes from Jerusalem shortly after the city was destroyed by Babylon in 587 BC; see Special Note I, p. 232.) Either from exiles in Babylon or from those struggling in Judah a similar cry went up to God. The earlier complaints took on fresh life.

Although we cannot be certain of the original context of these poems, there may be some significance in the way that they are now ordered. From the poet's point of view the most despairing comes last. If we look at God's reactions we find that the first confession is followed by a response that is encouraging and reassuring (11.21–23); the opponents in Anathoth will get what they deserve. Omitting the response to Judah, which is indirectly encouraging to Jeremiah (15.13f), the next responses (12.5f; 15.19–21) are stern: 'Jeremiah, stop complaining and get on with your job. I did not call you so that you could shout at Me. Repent of your stubborn attitude, turn back and then, if you are faithful, I will use you in My service.' Finally, the remaining protests meet with no response at all, only silence.

STUDY SUGGESTIONS

1. What do we mean by the Confessions of Jeremiah? What is the value of studying them all together?

2. What suggestions have been made about the origin of these poems? Why can we not be certain whether the poems come from Jeremiah himself or not?
3. Why do *you* think these poems were included in the Book of Jeremiah?
4. Read 11.18—12.6; 15.10–21; 17.14–18; 18.18–23; 20.7–18. Do you think there is any significance in the order in which we now find these poems?

11.18—12.6; 15.10–21
The Confessions of Jeremiah (1)

OUTLINE

See Special Note E (p. 107) for an introduction to the 'Confessions'.
11.18–23: The prophet discovers that his opponents are plotting against him and cries out in protest. He asks God to vindicate him and is reassured that these opponents from his home village will be dealt with.
12.1–6: Jeremiah asks why it is that the opponents of God seem to succeed. In reply, God tells him that his difficulties have hardly begun: the day will come when he looks back on his present troubles as trivial in comparison with his later experiences.
15.10–21: A protest by Jeremiah is followed by an answer from Yahweh (vv. 13f) which is apparently addressed to Judah rather than to the prophet. Then comes a further protest by Jeremiah (vv. 15–18) accusing Yahweh of deception. Finally, Yahweh sternly tells Jeremiah to stop complaining and to get on with the work he has been given (vv. 19–21).

INTERPRETATION

NO SUBSTITUTE FOR EXPERIENCE

Jeremiah's experience as a prophet was not what he had expected, nor what he wanted. We saw earlier (p. 14) that from the beginning Jeremiah was warned that he would face an uphill task. Nevertheless, when the time came, he was not ready for the greatness of the difficulties. Special Note D (p. 90) illustrates some of the opposition he faced; he was in conflict with religious and political leaders, established prophets, ordinary citizens, the people of Anathoth and his own family. The main response to his preaching was ridicule and hostility. He was unsuccessful, unpopular and, worst of all, he felt that his messages, which he was sure came from God, were not fulfilled; so it seemed that even God had let him down.

In spite of the warnings at the start of his ministry he must have set out on his task with high hopes. Prophecy was held in high honour in the land. Micah was a respected name from the past (Jer. 26.18), even if part of his message was ignored! Promises about the protection of Jerusalem were linked with the name of Isaiah (e.g. Isa. 2.2–4; 28.16f). Although Jeremiah was having to destroy and break down, he looked forward to the time when he would build and plant (1.10). But he failed to anticipate the extent of the opposition and the personal attacks on himself.

Many people have such experiences: the missionaries, for instance, who move to a new culture 'for Christ'. Their hopes and expectations are high, but disillusionment may set in. For the practical adjustments needed to live in a strange environment can never be fully foreseen. Romantic ideas about the 'wonder of serving the Lord' seem far distant when the children are fretful, the family is sick, and both food and surroundings are unfamiliar. You can make some intellectual preparations for such difficulties; but you can only begin to come to terms with them practically and emotionally once the experience begins. At the College where I used to teach, students often complain how busy their lives are (probably this is true of most theological colleges); and the staff often tell the students that they will be *much busier* once they start work as pastors in a parish or a secondary school. They find this hard to accept. But after they graduate and come back to visit the College they confess that the staff were right – the demands of being a pastor in a parish *are* far greater than those made of them as students! But it is only the experience itself that convinces.

And these are merely practical problems; very many others may arise – a lack of response to our ministry, hostility or personal differences, apparent failure over many years of steady work. Yet, at the same time, there may be a deep conviction of God's call. God *did* prepare Jeremiah, but only when the difficulties came could Jeremiah grasp what they would be like.

When we reflect, we realize that it is fortunate that we cannot experience the future in advance. If we knew gloomy or depressing facts about the future, we would brood on them. If we had knowledge of exciting events lying ahead, we would lose the surprise and joy of discovery. We can never know just what will be our experience: we are called to live in the present, one day at a time; each day to trust afresh the God who made us and has His plan for us. That is easy to say or write; it is much more difficult to hold onto when the going gets hard – as Jeremiah found out.

TELLING GOD WHAT YOU THINK

Many cultures have traditions in which respect for seniors means that younger people do not criticize them or disagree with them to their face, but accept their decisions without complaint. If that is true about our relationships with our human elders, we might think, how much more true it must be of our relationship with God. In both cases Jeremiah believed that honesty was vital. We have found him in many places (e.g. 6.13; 8.8f) criticizing the leaders of Judah for their mistakes. Now he complains that God has let him down by not fully warning him of the difficulties, by giving him messages to deliver that had not proved true. He felt that God was a deceiver (15.18; 20.7) who made promises but did not keep them. And he told God what he thought. How do we react to this? Was Jeremiah right to feel let down? And was he right to protest to God or should he have kept quiet?

We have just seen that there is no substitute for experience; beforehand, God could only prepare Jeremiah to a certain extent. No doubt God could have told Jeremiah more than He actually did, had He wished, but He did not. We should not think of this as deceit, but rather that God knew there was a limit to the knowledge Jeremiah could cope with at that time (we could compare this with Jesus's remark in John 16.12). A doctor who realizes that a patient has a fatal illness may not reveal it at once, but gradually prepares the patient to receive that information. When God calls a person to faith He knows what lies ahead but it may not be appropriate for the person to know. For one thing, it would detract from the life of faith. For another, the person concerned might turn down the call because it seemed too hard. So in one sense Jeremiah was perhaps right: God could have told him more but He chose not to.

But even if this is true, who was Jeremiah to argue with his creator? To apply the image of the potter differently, as Paul does later in Romans 9.19–21, what say does the clay have in the use the potter makes of it? So was the prophet wrong? Would he have done better to grit his teeth and get on with being faithful? We might appear to find support for this position from God's response to Jeremiah's cries; rebuke or just silence. The protests and anguish of Jeremiah are secondary to his chief task – the delivering of God's message. He is not to wallow in self-pity.

And yet God accepts and uses Jeremiah as he is. The outpourings of an anguished heart are part of Jeremiah. It is partly because of them that God could use Jeremiah, for Jeremiah *did* care! And the

Bible is clear that God is not interested in unthinking followers. He calls His creatures to reflect and respond. Job the questioner is the one who is praised by God, not the friends who just quote the official party line. There is good reason for the book of Ecclesiastes appearing in the Old Testament. God respects honest thought and enquiry.

Because this is so, we can be sure that God appreciates the feelings and ideas that will not be silenced by being told, 'Accept what the Church says', or, 'Just follow the tradition of the elders'. The questionings of Jeremiah have been preserved as part of what is important in his message and experience. Like Ecclesiastes, they may seem particularly relevant to the uncertainties and queries of the present day. We must, of course, keep things in proportion; there is no merit in questioning for the sake of it. The believer's job is not to hurl challenges at God! But when such problems arise we should not pretend that they do not exist; they are not only part of Jeremiah's experience, they are also part of the experience of many men and women wrestling with faith. Because of this, through these passages, as through other parts of the book, Jeremiah still speaks. The honest questioner asks, not in order to doubt, but from a desire to believe. Jeremiah longed to believe and was struggling to do so. (Jeremiah must have been feeling, as we sometimes do, like the father of the boy whom Jesus cured of an 'unclean spirit'; see Mark 9.24.) God respects such struggles.

NOTES

11.19: A gentle lamb led to the slaughter: Compare Isaiah 53.7, but the point made is different. In Isaiah it is the lamb's meekness, here its unsuspecting nature.

11.20: O LORD of hosts ... my cause: This verse is repeated at 20.12.

11.21: Concerning the men of Anathoth: Many reasons could be suggested for the men of Anathoth's dislike of Jeremiah's prophesying. Perhaps it made them uncomfortable, or they thought it was heresy; or they may have been embarrassed by one of their number being such a controversial and unpopular figure.

12.1: Why does ... why do ... thrive?: Psalm 73 shows similar questioning, but develops it in a different way.

12.4: How long ... wither?: A further picture of the land's fortunes being linked to the people's righteousness. See the discussion of 14.1–9, p. 84.

He will not see our latter end: Those English versions which follow the Greek and translate 'behaviour' instead of 'latter end' are probably right.

12.5: Jungle of the Jordan: The area adjacent to the river Jordan would flood in the rainy season and, as a result, be covered with thick, luxuriant vegetation. It would be extremely difficult to move through it. In comparison with the difficulties that lie ahead of him, Jeremiah has so far had a very easy time.

15.10: Not lent, nor ... borrowed: Relationships where money transactions are involved are traditionally among the most difficult. Here there may be implied, 'Lent (and charged interest) ... borrowed (but failed to repay)'.

15.11: If I have not entreated ... pleaded: This verse shows that Jeremiah has acted as an intercessor; cf. also 21.2; 37.3; 42.2. This translation follows the Greek; NEB and NIV follow the Hebrew and have the verse spoken by Yahweh, which reads rather strangely.

15.12: Can one break iron ... bronze?: The point of this verse is unclear. Possibly it means that Yahweh's judgement is unchangeable: if this is the correct interpretation, 'iron from the north' probably refers to Babylon (the foe from the north). An alternative suggestion is that no opposition will be able to overthrow Yahweh's prophet; in this case, 'iron from the north' may just refer to the fact that the best iron came from far to the north of Judah in the Black Sea area.

15.13–14: Your wealth ... burn for ever: These verses are almost identical to 17.3f where they seem to be more appropriate to the context.

15.15: For thy sake: Compare Ps. 69.7 for another example of suffering for the sake of Yahweh.

15.16: Delight of my heart: Once convinced that he was called to be Yahweh's spokesman, Jeremiah was excited and delighted.

15.17: I sat alone: See the discussion of 16.5,8 (p. 94).

15.18: My pain: The word used refers to mental pain.

Waters that fail: If this *does* happen then God is not the fountain of living waters described in 2.13.

15.19: If you return ... not turn to them: Now the command to return (*shub*, see discussion on p. 33) is applied to Jeremiah; it occurs four times in this verse.

15.20: A fortified wall of bronze: This verse uses the same picture and language as 1.18. We can think of it as God renewing His commission of Jeremiah and His warning, as part of that commission, that his life as a prophet will be tough.

15.21: Redeem you: God is also described as redeemer at 31.11; 50.34. This is a central theme in Isa. 40—55; e.g. 41.14; 43.1; 47.4.

STUDY SUGGESTIONS

REVIEW OF CONTENT

1. Why did Jeremiah's experience make him depressed?
2. Why do you think that Jeremiah was surprised by what happened to him?
3. What is meant by the phrase the 'jungle of the Jordan', 12.5?
4. Why do we tend to think that it is wrong to question God? What reasons are there for thinking that it can sometimes be right to question God?
5. Why do you think that God was prepared to let Jeremiah accuse Him?

BIBLE STUDY

6. Compare these protests in Jeremiah with Job 3; Pss 22 and 73; 2 Cor. 12.7–10. What are the different protests about? How much do the speakers care?
7. Read the story of the 'rich young ruler' in Mark 10.17–31.
   (a) Why do you think that Jesus did not begin with gentle encouragement and then gradually lead the rich man on to deep commitment?
   (b) 'We have left everything and followed you.' How do you think that Peter would have looked back on this statement later in his life?

DISCUSSION AND APPLICATION

8. How would you try to prepare someone going to a new area or culture because of their faith?
9. Imagine that friends of yours are worried because they do not know what the future will bring. How would you try to help them to live one day at a time?
10. Do you have friends who feel that God has deceived them or let them down? How has this affected them?
11. Is there room in your fellowship for people who question God? If not, do you think you may be excluding some folk who are really concerned to know Him?
12. Is there room in your fellowship for those who question the Church leaders? What kind of atmosphere does your Church enjoy?

17.14–18; 18.18–23; 20.7–18
The Confessions of Jeremiah (2)

OUTLINE

See Special Note E, p. 107, for an introduction to the 'Confessions'.
17.14–18: Jeremiah cries out to God to deliver him and to punish his opponents. There is no reply.
18.18–23: A statement of the purposes of Jeremiah's opponents is followed by a fierce denunciation of them, in which the prophet calls on God to be brutal in His destruction of these enemies.
20.7–13: Jeremiah declares that God is a deceiver, and yet he finds that he has to go on proclaiming the message he is given. The second half of the section contains assurance that God will not ultimately let Jeremiah down, and finishes with a call to praise which may be an addition to the original lament.
20.14–18: The gloom of Jeremiah reaches its lowest point. He would prefer to have been killed at or before birth rather than undergo what he has actually experienced.

INTERPRETATION

WOE TO OPPONENTS?

One recurring theme in these confessions is the cry to God to deal with those who are opposing Jeremiah (and so opposing God). It also occurs elsewhere in the Old Testament, particularly in some of the Psalms of lament. It is a very understandable reaction to opposition, especially when we remember that at that time there was little assurance of a life after death. In Jeremiah's day, most of those with faith believed that God worked out His plan entirely within the boundaries of this life. The clear declaration of life beyond the grave, as an article of faith, belongs to the New Testament. Within the Old Testament, some writers were groping after it and pointing the way that the New Testament would follow, but they remain a small minority, still struggling towards such a view. For the most part the Old Testament writers believe that God's justice has to be seen in this life, and so they urge God to bring it quickly.

These cries express a strong desire for justice. The accusation in 11.18–23, for instance, uses legal language, charging others with injustice: in particular, the men of Anathoth are declared guilty of the serious crime of trying to silence Yahweh's prophet. At their highest they are also cries for God to come to His own defence, not just to the personal aid of the intercessor. Since God's spokesman and God's people are being oppressed, God's own reputation is suffering (throughout the book of Ezekiel there runs the refrain, 'For the sake of my name', as an illustration of this view). In God's eyes evil *is* evil and there *are* such things as 'righteous anger' and 'perfect hatred', even if our human response rarely shows them.

These points may help to explain Jeremiah's attitude. We may remember that he was under great pressure. We can understand his feelings in such a situation, but we should not copy his attitude here. Within the Old Testament itself are the two great commandments (Deut. 6.5; Lev. 19.18), and, taken as a whole, the Old Testament writers knew that revenge on opponents is not the highest way. They knew that the way of love is greater and higher, even if we do not see what it really means until we come to Jesus. Once we are in the New Testament we are confronted with the 'Father, forgive them' of the Cross, which then becomes our model because, 'As the Father has sent me, even so I send you' (John 20.21).

We can sympathize with Jeremiah; we can feel for his outbursts. There are times when we know similar feelings not far from the surface. The cry of the oppressed and exploited is one that we ought to get angry and concerned about. The overthrow of injustice and cruelty are things about which we should feel passion. When, in the Lord's Prayer, we ask 'Your kingdom come', it is in part for these things that we are praying. But the route for us to take is not that of Jeremiah, but that of his promised successor who, 'When he was reviled . . . did not revile in return' (1 Pet. 2.23, cf. Isa. 53.7). This too is far easier to say than to practise, for it requires a rare combination. A passionate concern for the triumph of justice and the overthrow of evil must be mixed with a continuing longing for the liberation of oppressed and oppressor. That is the direction in which we are called. It is an awesome calling.

BLACK DESPAIR

There are few, if any, passages in the Bible more despairing than 20.14–18. It is often linked with Job 3, and a number of commentators think that it may have inspired the passage in Job; certainly there are similarities of thought. Ecclesiastes 4.3 also expresses the belief that not to be born is better than life, but there it comes more as a world-weary comment than with the passion found here in Jeremiah. This passion came from Jeremiah's twin frustrations, a lack of response to his ministry and the feeling that God had abandoned him.

In these 'Confessions' we see Jeremiah's desperate sense of frustration and his feeling that God had abandoned him. But even in despair he remained faithful to his prophetic calling, warning of the 'terror-on-every-side' Judah would experience, as people in war-torn countries do today when enemy soldiers appear.

Was Jeremiah right? From his own context it seemed so. All that he had to go on was the word of Yahweh, and that word came to seem like a deceiver, promising but never fulfilled. Again we may sympathize with Jeremiah. From our context we can see that ultimately his ministry was not a failure – but we have the advantage of hindsight. Paul received treatment as bitter as that of Jeremiah, and 1 Corinthians 4.9–13 shows his very different kind of response: but Paul knew also the fuller hope that was introduced through Christ and, along with all the hardships, had the joy of seeing Churches that he had planted growing.

Believers are not free from the hazards of human existence, the schemes of human opponents or slander. Nor, this passage warns us, are they guaranteed protection from the experience of despair. It may be humanly rational or totally irrational but it can come to any and does come to some. What has been called the 'dark night of the soul' is a real experience for many of those who have grown closest to their Lord.

Every pastor can testify how the faith of some has been enriched beyond measure by an experience of great distress when God perhaps seemed absent. No secret can ensure that we avoid such an experience; if and when it comes to us we need to be able to face it. When it came to Jeremiah he did not utter smooth words, nor did he try to ignore the difficulties and pretend there was no problem. He faced the problem; he shouted at God about it; but he did not let it stop him from carrying out his commission. He was tempted to do so, but even in despair he remained faithful. His heart was prepared to lead him in opposition to his feelings: that is a measure of his faith.

NOTES

17.15: Where is the word of the LORD? Let it come!: Jeremiah is a figure of fun; the people are mocking the failure of his prophecies to come true.

17.18: Double destruction: As at 16.18 (see note on p. 98) we can think of this as an appropriate destruction; (cf. NEB 'utterly').

18.18: Come, let us make plots against Jeremiah . . .: Put here, this verse can be thought of as a response to Jeremiah's declaration in vv. 13–17; a further plea by Jeremiah comes in vv. 19–23.

Priest . . . wise . . . prophet: The three main groups of religious leaders in Judah. Such official criticism would discredit Jeremiah in the eyes of the people and thus have a severe effect on his ministry.

With the tongue: This could refer to slander, gossip or formal charges. The subsequent verses talk about a plot on his life.

Let us not heed any of his words: JB follows the Greek and has 'let us listen carefully', presumably so that material for charges could be found.

18.19: Give heed ... my plea: The leaders will not respond to Jeremiah (v. 18) so he asks Yahweh for support. 'Plea' in RSV follows the Greek; other English versions follow the Hebrew and have 'adversaries', understanding Jeremiah as asking God to pay attention to what these enemies are saying.

20.8: A reproach and derision: He is unpopular because of the content of his message, and ridiculous because it seems to be unfulfilled.

20.9: In my heart as ... a burning fire: Because he really is God's prophet, there is no way that Jeremiah can resist the urge to prophesy, despite the difficulties that it brings him.

20.10: Terror is on every side: See note on 6.25. Now it becomes a nickname for Jeremiah.

20.12: O LORD of hosts ... my cause: This plea for judgement repeats 11.20.

20.13: Sing to the LORD ... he has delivered ...: The inclusion of this verse is puzzling. Laments do often conclude with praise, either in anticipation of God's help or just as an expression of the praise-worthiness of God despite the situation, and that may be why it is found here. It is addressed to the whole community, not an individual, and this suggests that it has been introduced editorially. **Needy:** The needy person is the one who looks to Yahweh for support, the one with a genuine trust in God.

20.14: Cursed ... not ... blessed: This is emphatic; a deliberate and strong wish.

20.15: A son is born to you: In ancient Israel, as in many cultures today, the birth of a son was the greatest joy imaginable.

20.16: Cities which the LORD overthrew: A reference to Sodom and Gomorrah (Gen. 19.24f) which became proverbial as an example of God's judgement. Similar references are found in Jer. 23.14; 49.18; 50.40; also in Isa. 1.9; Amos 4.11 and Zeph. 2.9.

STUDY SUGGESTIONS

REVIEW OF CONTENT

1. What reasons often lie behind the cursing of opponents in the Old Testament?
2. What shows that the Old Testament writers knew that vindictiveness is not the best way?

3. What should be our attitude when confronted with cruelty and injustice?
4. Why was Jeremiah reduced to total despair?
5. Do situations where God seems absent always lead to depression and despair? Give examples to support your answer.

BIBLE STUDY

6. What relevance might Matthew 5.38f have for us when we are confronted by cruelty and injustice?
7. How do the speakers in Pss. 22 and 73 and 2 Cor. 12.7–10 cope with the apparent absence of God? Compare their reactions with that of Jeremiah.

DISCUSSION AND APPLICATION

8. When we read of brutality against innocent people or the cruelty of one group against another it can make us angry. What should we do with this anger?
9. If we find injustice, should our reaction depend upon whether it is directed against ourselves or against others?
10. The desire for vengeance is deeply rooted in our societies. Are there ways in which the Churches can help to prevent people from being dominated by such a desire?
11. 'A passionate concern for the triumph of justice and the overthrow of evil must be mixed with a continuing longing for the liberation of oppressed and oppressor', p. 116. What can we do to help encourage such an attitude?
12. What would you try to say to someone who felt totally abandoned by God?
13. A common reaction to someone suffering from depression is 'stop being stupid'; would this have been of any value to Jeremiah? Does it have anything to say to our attitude to those suffering from depression?

21.1—23.8
The Royal House of Judah

OUTLINE

In these verses we find oracles concerning various kings of Judah. Their main emphasis is the failure of particular kings, and together they attack and condemn the Davidic house. However, the collection is concluded by three short passages which offer hope for the line of David. Much of the material probably owes its present form to the Deuteronomic editors (see Special Note C, p. 44).

21.1–10: King Zedekiah is told that there is no hope for Jerusalem; only those who surrender to Babylon will have any future hope at all.

21.11–12: This very short passage summarizes the remainder of this section. It stresses that kings are responsible for justice.

21.13–14: The image of fire links this oracle with the previous one; it declares the destruction of Jerusalem, city of the kings.

22.1–9: These verses develop the thought of the previous two oracles – the kings' responsibilities for justice and the approaching doom of Jerusalem.

22.10–12: A short piece lamenting the exile of Jehoahaz.

22.13–19: A direct attack on Jehoiakim, asserting that his reign is immoral and that his end will be shameful.

22.20–23: A further lament for the ruin of Jerusalem.

22.24–30: The exile of Jehoiachin and the end of his royal line are absolutely certain.

23.1–4: God promises that beyond the ashes of destruction He will create a future for His people.

23.5–6: God will raise up for His people a true successor of David.

23.7–8: In the future the centre of Israel's faith will be found in a rescue even more wonderful than the Exodus from Egypt.

INTERPRETATION

RESPONSIBILITIES OF A LEADER

Leadership brings influence which can be used rightly or abused. You can work for the good of those under your authority or exploit them. When new political parties take office they often claim that their predecessors misused their influence. When Idi Amin overthrew Milton Obote in Uganda in 1971 he argued that Obote had been favouring members of his own Langi tribe; Emperor Bokasa of the Central African Republic was accused of having moved large quantities of public funds into his private foreign bank accounts; after President Marcos of the Philippines had fallen from power, reporters were shown the enormous collection of his wife's clothes and shoes: 'Here', they were told, 'is evidence of corruption'.

This is no new problem. Judah's kings were well aware of their duty to uphold justice. Their failure to do so is the chief theme of these chapters. It recurs five times (21.12; 22.2f,13–17; 23.2,5) and only in 22.8f is there any mention of the false worship that is so fiercely denounced elsewhere in the book. This attack on injustice follows in the footsteps of the great eighth century prophets; they too had charged the leaders with injustice. Jeremiah takes up this theme and makes it clear that the privileges of leadership cannot be divorced from the responsibilities. When a king stops behaving like a king, he no longer deserves to be treated as one. The attack on Jehoiakim is particularly fierce.

In ancient Israel people believed that the nation's fate was bound up with the character of the king. A good king would bring blessing to the people but a bad one would bring many problems: see e.g. Ps. 72; 1 Kings 9.3–9. A king's responsibilities included the showing of particular concern to the underprivileged in his country – the alien, the fatherless and the widow – people who had no-one to protect them (see note on 7.6, p. 49). The kings' failures in these areas led to their condemnation.

Every leader faces pressures: pressures from associates, from those who have given support in war or political campaigns, from those in positions of influence, from family or tribe. It can be easy to give in to these pressures, but the leader of a country has a responsibility to the country as a whole. Leaders' priorities and concerns need to be clear enough so that they do not succumb to the pressures and favour some of the people at the expense of those with a less powerful voice. A ruler's true success cannot be judged outwardly by the number of new cars or the splendour of lifestyle. A surer test is whether the rich-poor gap is narrowing or increasing, whether the numbers of the underprivileged are growing or decreasing, whether all have access to proper health care and adequate educational opportunities. Such things make a truer test of leadership. If there is no improvement in these areas then there is a shortage of true knowledge of God. For God has a special concern for the underprivileged (22.16).

For a leader to answer criticism of this kind by a shrug of the shoulders and a comment like, 'I did not know' or, 'I could do nothing' is unacceptable. These are responsibilities of leadership. Failure to know or to act is not a valid excuse.

RESPONSIBILITIES OF GOD

God also has responsibilities. He is the one who has established David's family on the throne of Jerusalem. He has warned them of the consequences of disobedience, yet the disobedience has continued. Now what will He do? If He ignores their failure He is morally inconsistent; if He utterly destroys kings and people, all He has done will seem to no purpose.

Chapters 21—22 imply that the judgement will be total; the line of David is to come to an end (note especially 22.28–30). The kings are bitterly reprimanded for their failures, the whole people will suffer on account of their leaders; (elsewhere the people as a whole are declared guilty; Jeremiah recognizes that not all the blame can be put on the leaders). The certainty of God's judgement is not in doubt. The line of David is ended (22.30).

But the last three oracles portray a very different kind of future, one in which God will raise up a new leader, a successor to David (23.5). So the line of David still has a future. Some scholars have argued that these oracles and the earlier ones are incompatible (but see discussion of 3.15–18, p. 32). Whatever the origins of these two sets of oracles, and whether or not they *both* originate with Jeremiah, the editors of the book must have thought that each had an important contribution to make to a balanced perspective on the monarchy.

By comparison with Isaiah, whose vision of the future centres round Jerusalem and the line of David, Jeremiah says little about the future of the house of David. But his book does contain a few positive references, and these must not be disregarded. Their emphasis is on what *God* will do. Although the line of David ends with Jehoiachin (and after the Exile the monarchy is not restored) God will intervene to see that there is, after all, a true successor to David. This shepherd will rule as kings were meant to, with real justice. As a result the people will enjoy genuine peace and stability. Chapters 30—33 present more ideas for the future (see the discussion on p. 169). For now, we may note that they are presented in very general terms, not in detail; there is no full programme described.

NOTES

21.1: Pashhur ... Zephaniah: This Pashhur is different from the priest with the same name mentioned in 20.1; both men are referred to in 38.1. Zephaniah also appears at 29.25, 29; 37.3; 52.24.

21.2: Inquire of the LORD: This was a technical term for consulting God by means of a religious official.

Nebuchadrezzar: The most successful Babylonian emperor, reigning from 605–562 BC. This is the most accurate rendering of the name though in chs 27—29 and elsewhere in the Bible the spelling Nebuchadnezzar is used; this may reflect an Aramaic version.

Perhaps the LORD: Presumably the incident occurred during Nebuchadrezzar's siege of Jerusalem (588–587 BC); 37.3–10 reports another incident from this time. Whether or not Zedekiah's request was genuine, in view of the might of the Babylonians it would need one of the LORD's **wonderful deeds** if Judah was to survive.

21.4: God of Israel: Much of the imagery in vv. 1–7 uses ideas from Israel's understanding of holy war as found particularly in Deuteronomy (e.g. Deut. 20.10–18). But there is irony, for here Israel's God is fighting *against* His own people.

21.7: Pestilence, sword, and famine: These three are often linked in Jeremiah as accompaniments of enemy invasion.

21.8–9: To this people ... I set before you: 21.7 offers the king and his close associates no hope, but, surprisingly, the people are to be given a choice. However, it turns out to be between two unattractive alternatives: stay in the city and die or desert to the enemy and survive. Deserters run great risks and are always unpopular. The idea of choice is a further link with Deuteronomy (see e.g. Deut. 30.15–20).

21.11: And to the ...: This verse and the next make a heading for the remainder of the material to 23.8. It could be translated, 'Concerning the ...' just as 23.9–40 begins, 'Concerning the prophets'.

21.12: House of David: This is only the second reference in the book to David; the first was at 13.13.

21.13: Inhabitant of the valley ... rock of the plain: Both phrases obviously refer to Jerusalem and its inhabitants, but the exact translation and significance of the first phrase is not clear. It may originally have been a curse on another city which, like a proverb, had become well-known in Judah, and is now unexpectedly applied to Jerusalem.

21.14: Fire in her forest: The forest probably refers to the great hall in the king's palace which used many cedar columns and beams; it was called the House of the Forest of Lebanon (1 Kings 7.1–5).

22.3: Shed innocent blood: Here, as at 22.17, we should think of judicial murder, either literally (cf. Naboth's vineyard, 1 Kings 21) or, more generally, of the perversion of justice which leads the innocent to suffer.

22.4: If you will indeed: This verse reflects the idea common in many parts of the Old Testament, that behaviour determines experience: a good man will have a successful life, an evil one will face problems. Proverbs and Deuteronomy illustrate different aspects of this approach. Jeremiah's experiences would hardly lead him to support such theology as the whole truth, so this verse may well be an editorial addition.

22.5: I swear by myself: For God to swear by Himself was especially solemn; such a picture is only found in a few places (as well as 44.26; 49.13; 51.14, see also Gen. 22.16; Isa. 45.23; Amos 6.8 and Heb. 6.13).

House: There is a double meaning here, with a reference both to the building, as in v.1, and also to the line of Davidic kings (so the NEB translates as 'dynasty').

22.6: Gilead ... Lebanon: The region of Gilead was favoured for its good pastureland, while Lebanon was famous for its great cedars and snowcapped Mount Hermon towering over them.

22.8–9: Worshipped other gods: This is the only reference to false worship in these oracles about the kings, and probably reflects the editors' views (cf. 16.10–13; Deut. 29.22–28; 1 Kings 9.6–9).

22.10: Him who is dead ... him who goes away: Josiah is dead and buried, and no more time should be spent grieving over him. The one who should be mourned is Shallum (Jehoahaz) who has gone into Exile and will never see his homeland again. Note the strength of the link between land and people, a link often now weaker in the Western world but still extremely strong in many other countries.

22.14: Cedar ... vermilion: Cedar was the finest timber for building; vermilion was a very bright red colour, chosen to draw attention to the magnificence of the building.

22.15: You ... your father: The father is Josiah, the son Jehoiakim. One suggested translation of the first part of the verse is, 'Are you playing at being a king by ...?' Jehoiakim was concerned with outward show rather than a king's real responsibilities.

22.16: He judged the cause of the poor and needy: Compare Micah 6.6–8. As at 4.22 there is a link between knowing Yahweh and proper behaviour.

22.17: Innocent blood: See note on 22.3.

22.18: Lord ... majesty: These may represent royal titles by which the king was known. Slight alteration of the Hebrew could lead to 'Father, mother', following from 'brother, sister' earlier in the verse.

22.19: Burial of an ass: An ass was unclean in Israel (Deut. 14.3–8; Lev. 11.1–8), since it neither parted the hoof nor chewed the cud). The main point is how inglorious Jehoiakim's end will be, a stark contrast to his building projects. The books of Kings and Chronicles make no reference to anything special about his burial.

22.20: Lebanon ... Bashan ... Abarim: All three were mountainous areas, and ideal sites from which to spread the message far and wide.
Your lovers are destroyed: Some English versions understand the 'lovers' to be the rulers, while others think they are Judah's allies.
22.21: I will not listen: Once again the will is stubborn; see note on 2.20.
22.22: The wind shall shepherd all your shepherds: The 'shepherds' here are again rulers (see note on 3.15). All English versions manage to capture the play on words in the Hebrew, using 'shepherd' in two different senses.
22.23: Lebanon: Now Lebanon is used as a term for Jerusalem.
22.24: Signet ring: The signet ring bore witness to genuineness and personal authority. To prevent forgery, the owner would hang it on a cord around the neck.
22.28: Despised ... cares for: Psalm 31.12, Jeremiah 19 and 48.38 also use the image of broken pottery. Possibly Hosea 8.8 was in the author's mind.
22.29: Land, land, land: A threefold repetition was especially solemn; here it emphasizes the sadness of the fate.
22.30: Not succeed ... succeed: Another example of one word being used with two different meanings. The achievements of the House of David will be worthless because the line will die out in captivity and the succession will fail. A further wordplay occurs at 23.2 ('attend').
23.3: Out of all the countries ... I will bring them back: Since count*ries* are mentioned, this may refer to those exiled at other times and to places other than Babylon. Elsewhere in Jeremiah the return of exiles from the northern kingdom is certainly intended. 'Bring back' uses the Hebrew word *shub* again (see p. 33).
23.4: Neither shall any be missing: Some modern versions translate rather differently as, 'There will be no more punishment'.
23.5–6: Behold ... our righteousness: These verses occur almost unchanged at 33.15f. Here they provide an explanation of the identity of the shepherds promised in the previous verses.
Days are coming: The phrase occurs 16 times in Jeremiah; many scholars regard it as a common late expression. In the present context the passage asserts that in spite of 22.30 the covenant with David will not fail.
Righteous Branch: The Hebrew word here translated as 'Branch', (elsewhere it is sometimes translated as 'horn'), is found in a number of significant passages in the Old Testament. The earliest is probably Psalm 132.17, and the idea is developed in Isaiah 4.2; 11.1–5 and the present passage. In Isaiah 53.2 it is applied in a different way, and in Zechariah 3.8 and 6.12 it has become a title which was later understood to refer to the Messiah. Here, the end of v.6 is almost

certainly an allusion to the fact that the name Zedekiah means 'the LORD is my righteousness'; most probably it is a comparison between Zedekiah and the truly righteous leader that Yahweh will send; for this reason some prefer to translate as 'legitimate branch'. GNB obscures the link with Zedekiah by translating as 'the LORD is my salvation'. It has been suggested that originally the passage was applied to Zedekiah in opposition to those who regarded the exiled Jehoiachin as the rightful king; this seems less likely.

23.7–8: Behold ... in their own land: These verses also occur at 16.14f, where they fit less well. For the Israelite there was no greater evidence of God's power than the events of the Exodus, now they will be dwarfed by a new deliverance.

North country: See note on 1.14. The main road by which the enemy had come would also be the one by which the exiles would return to their homeland.

STUDY SUGGESTIONS

REVIEW OF CONTENT

1. In these chapters, what is the chief reason given for the condemnation of the kings of Judah?
2. In what ways were the leaders expected to show justice?
3. What do these verses suggest are God's responsibilities?
4. Explain the significance of the term 'Righteous Branch' in 23.5f.
5. What message does the tearing off of a signet ring (22.24) convey.

BIBLE STUDY

6. What understanding of justice and righteousness do you get from the following passages: Deut. 16.18–20; 32.4; Isa. 45.8; Ezek. 18.9; Amos 5.10–24; Mic. 6.6–8; Hab. 2.4?
7. In each of the following passages one or more people is condemned. What different reasons are given for their condemnations?
   (a) Cain: Gen. 4. 1–16
   (b) Solomon: 1 Kings 11.1–13
   (c) The man of God: 1 Kings 13.7–22
   (d) Ahab and Jezebel: 1 Kings 21.1–19
   (e) Nebuchadrezzar: Dan. 4.1–33
   Compare these reasons with the reasons given in Jer. 21.1—23.8 for the condemnation of the kings of Judah.

8. Read the following passages: Ps. 132.17; Isa. 4.2; 11.1–5; Jer. 23.5f; Zech. 3.8; 6.12. What ideas do they suggest about how the 'branch' might be understood?

DISCUSSION AND APPLICATION

9. How do the leaders of your country like to be assessed? In what kinds of ways are they assessed by:
   (a) Other political leaders?
   (b) Newspapers, radio and television?
   (c) Your friends?
10. In what ways is your local Church active on behalf of under-privileged people? What others are there, on whose behalf you think the Church should be active?
11. Do you think that the Church should only be concerned for Christians in need, or that its concern should include needy members of other faiths or none? Give your reasons for your answer.
12. Do members of your society think of God as having serious responsibilities? If they do, what kind of responsibilities do they have in mind? Do you think these are God's main responsibilities? If not, what others would you suggest?

23.9–40
An Attack on False Prophecy

OUTLINE

The remainder of ch. 23 brings together four oracles about prophecy. It particularly concerns the prophets with whom Jeremiah found himself in conflict and whom he regarded as false. The source and nature of their messages are discussed together with the quality of their lives and what will finally happen to them.

23.9–15: These prophets are evil and they will suffer evil.

23.16–22: Because these prophets are self-appointed their message is worthless.

23.23–32: This oracle contrasts the powerlessness of false prophecy with the power of God's message when delivered by His messenger.

23.33–40: A discussion of the role of false prophets which is centred round different uses of the word 'burden'.

INTERPRETATION

LIVES PROCLAIM A MESSAGE

People usually have a family likeness. They may be very like their immediate family, their parents, brothers and sisters. They will also share likenesses with clan and tribal members. These are not restricted to physical appearance; cultural behaviour, mannerisms and speech can all reflect one's background – Simon Peter was identified by his Galilean accent (Mark 14.70).

We are also influenced by people we spend time with. Someone moves to a different area of the country and starts to speak with the local accent. Someone admires a teacher or preacher and tries to do things in the same way. This kind of influence can be deliberate or unintentional.

Jeremiah reckoned that the life of anyone claiming to be a prophet of Yahweh ought to reflect something of Yahweh's character. But he claimed that when he looked at his prophetic rivals they did not. Not only did they fail to rebuke the evils of society but they were actively involved in them (v.14, adultery and lies). The prophets of Israel had been bad enough, for they had led the people in the ways of Baal, v.13. But the prophets of Jerusalem had now gone so far as to encourage the abandoning of morality and the spread of evil in the land, vv.14f. If righteousness was to be found anywhere it should be among the religious leaders; that it could not be found among them showed how bad the situation had become.

Today most of us assume that religious leaders (of whatever religion) should be upholders of the highest standards. If they are found guilty of crime or immorality there is likely to be a lot of damaging publicity, and the reputation of that religion suffers. For the special opportunities that accompany such leadership also involve special responsibilities. It is not enough merely to have behaved properly, leaders must do all they can so that it is clear that they *have* behaved properly. If their ministry is to be credible they must be free from all hint of financial dishonesty or sexual laxity. Disclosures about such misbehaviour by some American TV evangelists in recent years have led some people to question whether any such evangelists are genuine.

Jeremiah was making this charge as part of a heated attack on these prophets, and obviously we are not to think that every false prophet was necessarily immoral. The report in ch. 28 about the conflict between Jeremiah and Hananiah has no suggestion that Hananiah was immoral. But personal morality is very important. The authorities who select religious leaders must take it seriously, and also discipline properly any leaders who lapse in such matters.

Otherwise the faith itself is called into question. No matter how able Christian leaders may be, however brilliant in public speaking or gifted in administration, failure in the moral sphere will bring only harm to their ministry.

HAS GOD CALLED YOU TO DELIVER THIS MESSAGE?

In the picture we receive of Jeremiah his sense of call was fundamental to his life as a prophet. Chapter 1 records his certainty that he had been called; his confessions declare that it was only this sense of call which enabled him to continue as a prophet. He felt that other prophets took such a call far too lightly. When a national football team is to be chosen there are many who hope that they may play; but only those picked by the selectors need turn up for the match, the players do not select themselves. But these prophets had selected themselves to prophesy for God; the idea came from their own minds and not from God. They had run to prophesy when God said nothing about it (v.21).

Just as they had not waited for the call of God, so they did not wait for His message. There is little wonder, therefore, that their messages were also their own inventions. They were quick to announce, 'This is what God says', but they had never consulted Him! A newly appointed ambassador has no authority without the official documents presented to the host country. These prophets were like self-appointed ambassadors without authority or knowledge of their own country's intentions. Because they had not been called by God, their message bore no relation to the mind and will of God for His people. So they declared that Yahweh was 'near', tied and permanently committed to Jerusalem. In fact, Jeremiah proclaimed, Yahweh was 'far off', free and sovereign over the whole earth.

'We are looking forward to hearing the message that God has given our visitor.' A visiting preacher will often be introduced in some such way. But has that message actually come from God? Sometimes it obviously has, but at others we may well wonder if it is not just a human creation. Has the preacher really been in the presence of God? If the answer is 'Yes', the words will carry with them a sense of authority.

There is a solemn warning here for those of us who preach. We learn, once we are used to preaching, that we can stand up and speak. Once we learn this, our sense of dependence on God can decrease. Particularly when we are under pressure we can cut down on time for sermon preparation and on the time spent with God in prayer. We know that we can 'get by'. But preaching is not 'getting by', it is declaring and applying an appropriate part of God's message for that congregation on that occasion. A Member of Parliament informs constituents of what the government is doing. We preach in God's name and not our own: only if we have spent time with God in thought and prayer do we have a right to preach in His name.

THE PROPHETS' EFFECT AND FATE

One word can describe the effect when God speaks – Power! For the impact of God's word is like the impact of a great hammer crushing rock, v.29. It will strengthen the hearers like the finest wheat, v.28. By contrast, the self-appointed prophet achieves no lasting effect. There may be excitement, but it is shallow and short-lived; there may be enthusiasm, but it will change no-one. Even the message lacks originality (just as it lacks authority): it is based on other people's words and illustrations; secondhand, it carries no conviction.

Of course we learn from others. What we have read, illustrations that have struck us, can become part of our thinking and so of our preaching. But that is quite different from just imitating someone else. For the preacher who wishes to see people built up in their faith there is only one reliable way – to get the message from God and present it appropriately.

The last section of this chapter uses repeatedly the Hebrew word *massa*, which refers to something lifted up or carried, a burden. It appears that these prophets were claiming that the message they had was a 'burden' given them by God. Because this would need special intimacy with God, they claimed special authority for their message. Jeremiah says that this claim is false; they are taking God lightly and must face the consequences of this. Verse 33 contains the core of the passage: following the Greek (as the RSV does) the question asked is, 'What is the burden (i.e. the message or concern) of the LORD?'; the answer is, 'You are the burden (i.e. the problem) of the LORD'.

Here is a further reminder of the care religious leaders should take in claiming special authority for what they may say. In some cultures such leaders are naturally given a position of great respect, and people may give a leader's words more weight than they deserve. Leadership confers responsibility but it does not necessarily give a spiritual insight greater than that of others: the Spirit is given to all Christian believers.

NOTES

23.9: Concerning the prophets: This forms a heading to the whole section. Originally some of this material (e.g. vv.11, 33) was also referred to priests.

Broken: The Hebrew word, which occurs frequently in Jeremiah (e.g. 19.11) means 'shattered'. Jeremiah's emotions (cf. 8.18) include turmoil, despair and agony.

23.10: The land mourns ... dried up: For the effect of sin on the world of nature see the discussion of 14.1–9, p. 84. In the Hebrew 'full', 'curse' and 'mourns' all have similar sounds.

23.14: But in the prophets of Jerusalem: Note the contrast with the previous verse and see also the discussion of 3.6–11, p. 31. The way that the prophets of Jerusalem behave makes the sin of the prophets of Baal seem very mild!

Adultery: The context here requires that the word be taken literally. Elsewhere it is sometimes used as a metaphor for encouraging false worship.

Sodom ... Gomorrah: See note on 20.16.

23.15: Behold, I will ... to drink: In 9.15 the same phrase is applied to the people of Judah in general. Here it is used specifically of prophets.

23.18: The council of the Lord ... hear his word: The close relationship between prophet and God is like that of a government leader with the president or prime minister. 'Hear' includes the idea of response, and would be better translated as 'pay attention to'.

23.20: In the latter days you will understand it clearly: It will only be later that people come to understand how the Lord's anger will be executed. This may be a later addition to the text.

23.22: They would have turned them ... doings: Taken by itself, this verse would imply that true prophecy was always effective, in producing repentance. On this basis Jeremiah would hardly qualify! The most that we can say is that *some* would respond and turn; cf. 35.15.

23.23: Am I a God at hand ... and not a God afar off?: 'Am I a god only near at hand and not far off?' (as in NEB) catches the mood. God is universal and not just local, transcendent and not limited. We could paraphrase as, 'Do you really think that I only notice what goes on in the Temple?'. The Greek omits the question, thus making the different though related point that God is not only transcendent but also near enough to know just what is happening.

23.24: Can a man hide ... do I not fill?: These prophets have no vision of the greatness of God, and so no true fear and respect of Him: cf. 1 Kings 8.27; Ps. 139; Isa. 66.1 for passages emphasizing God's sovereignty.

23.28: Let the prophet who has a dream ... but let him who has my word: Elsewhere in the Old Testament dreams are one recognized means by which God communicates to prophets and others, e.g. Gen. 28.11–17; 1 Kings 3.5–15. Here, dreams are given only secondary value – the dream comes into the prophet's mind, the word comes from God. Perhaps there is also a further contrast between the true divine word and a falsely acquired one, however the latter is acquired. In this case, dreams may be singled out because they were prominent in the claims of these prophets, apparently lending credibility to the speaker (God has spoken to this man in a dream!), or because the Hebrew for dream (*halom*) sounded like the message of these prophets (peace – *shalom*).

23.29: Fire ... a hammer: 5.14 and 20.9 also use images linked with fire. The 'hammer' is the forge hammer used to crush and beat all under it (the rock is granite, the hardest of all rocks) into shape. The word is only found twice elsewhere in the Old Testament: in 50.23, where it is used to picture the power that Babylon once wielded, and in Isa. 41.7, where it describes a metal craftsman making idols. God's word is upsetting (as well as reassuring) and if it never strikes us in this way there is something wrong – with us.

23.33: What is the burden of the LORD?: A suggestion less likely than that given in the Interpretation is that Jeremiah's message was described as a burden because it was so gloomy. In this case, the questioner was mocking Jeremiah.

23.36: The living God, the LORD of hosts, our God: The use of three titles for God emphasizes the seriousness of the perversion.

23.39: Lift you up: The Hebrew (followed by NIV) reads 'forget you', but most English versions accept a slight amendment to the Hebrew which makes a further play on the word *massa*.

23.40: Not be forgotten: The people have been incited to forget Yahweh, v.27. The consequences of this will not be forgotten.

STUDY SUGGESTIONS

REVIEW OF CONTENT

1. Why did Jeremiah believe that the lives of many other prophets showed them to be false prophets?
2. How important did Jeremiah believe it is for a prophet to have a call from God? Why did he believe such a call to be so important?
3. What is the effect of a message from a true prophet?
4. In what ways was the false prophets' understanding of God limited?

BIBLE STUDY

5. How does Psalm 139 understand the greatness of God? In what ways is this different from the understanding of the false prophets suggested by the passage under study?

6. Compare with 23.29 the following passages which refer to the effectiveness of God's word: Gen. 1.3,9,24; Isa. 55.10f; Eph. 6.17b; Heb. 4.12f. Do you think all these passages are making the same point? If not, give your reasons.

7. Study carefully 23.33–40. How many times is the Hebrew word *massa* (see p. 131) used? How many different meanings is it given? Note how in John 4.7–15 'water' is used with more than one meaning. Can you think of other passages where Jesus gives a word a double meaning?

DISCUSSION AND APPLICATION

8. Suppose that your Church is considering appointing a new pastor: how might you test whether a person was genuinely called by God to this work?

9. In what ways, if any, have Church leaders you know failed to live up to God's standards? What effect has this had on the Church to which they belonged? Has it had an effect on the wider Church?

10. Does the fact that a pastor seems to have had little success mean that he is failing to do God's will? Compare your answer with Jeremiah's own experience and what he says about the effectiveness of God's word.

11. How much effect on others do you think that the quality of Christians' lives has? It has been said that a preacher's life is his own best or worst sermon. How far do you think this is true? Can a bad man be a good preacher?

24.1—25.38
Judgement on Judah and the Nations

OUTLINE

Up to this point, except for 12.14–17, the message of judgement has been addressed to the people of Judah. Now the scope widens, and while 24.1—25.14 is directed to Judah, the remainder of ch. 25 concerns the world.

24.1–10: Jeremiah sees a vision with the surprising message that God will work out His plans for the future through those of His people already in Exile in Babylon.

25.1–14: A declaration of God's judgement on Judah because of the people's stubborn refusal to listen to His warnings.

25.15–29: A vision of a cup of wrath that God will give the world to drink.

25.30–38: A series of comments on this vision, centering round the image of a lion causing havoc in a flock. The leaders (shepherds or lords) of the nations are the particular focus of the condemnation.

INTERPRETATION

THE GOD OF THE UNEXPECTED

In 1.11–16 are recorded two visions through which God spoke to Jeremiah. This section reports two further visions. The first involves two baskets of figs; possibly they had been brought by villagers to offer to God in worship at Jerusalem. Deuteronomy 26.1–11 describes a very old harvest ritual, and Jeremiah may have had this ceremony in mind, or may even have been attending it. Since only the best should be offered in sacrifice, Jeremiah would have known that the inedible figs were unacceptable to God. The surprise lay in the message that came through the vision.

Jeremiah had declared that the deportation of King Jehoiachin and his associates to Babylon was God's judgement. The natural reaction of those left behind would have been relief that they had been spared. Since they were still in the Promised Land and the holy city of Jerusalem, they thought that God was more angry with those He had sent into Exile than with them.

But Jeremiah's message now declares that assumption to be quite wrong. The good plans God has for His people's future lie with those who have gone into Exile, *not* with those left behind. This comes as a great shock. While there was fierce debate between the two factions, we cannot simply say that Jeremiah was pro-Babylonian, for elsewhere he is very ready to talk about God's judgement on Babylon. No reason is given for this declaration by God. He just declares that He will treat one group as good figs and the other as bad ones; there is no comment on the qualities of the two groups concerned. (In v. 5, 'regard as good' can equally well be translated as 'regard for good', and the GNB translation of this verse is misleading since it implies that the two groups are treated according to their merits; this is not the case.) This decision by God remains unexplained and runs counter to human expectation. What are we to make of it?

God is a God of surprises. He is creator and we remain creatures. We cannot predict what He will do nor how He will do it; nor do we always understand why He acts as he does. Taken by itself, this could make us cynical. But this unpredictability must be taken together with other aspects of God's character and activity, such as His justice, His concern and loving purpose for His people and for the world He has created. Brueggemann has likened God's choice here to His reckoning of Abraham as righteous in Genesis 15.6; in both cases God has acted out of His own free choice, promising new hope in a situation of despair.

What is clear is that, because God is God, we must never conclude that we understand just what He will do, nor that any situation is beyond His ability to resolve. If we think that we understand the way God works we are putting ourselves on His level. There remains no better illustration of God's ability to surprise than His plan for the world's salvation: to an unknown woman in a small village in a corner of the Roman Empire is born an apparently illegitimate baby. As Brueggemann puts it, 'This God seems to *make* the future with those whom the world judges to be *without* a future'.

Because God remains God, an openness to His surprises remains a vital part of faith. In 1958 a new Pope was elected and took the name of John XXIII. He was already 77 years old when elected, and was expected by most people to be a kind of 'caretaker' pope, not changing very much and keeping things steady until he was succeeded in a few years by a younger man who would be likely to provide more significant leadership. However, Pope John's summoning of the Second Vatican Council has proved to be of immense significance. Certainly the most important development in the Roman Catholic Church this century, it has also had enormous influence on relationships between the Roman Catholic Church and other Christian Churches. God remains a God of surprises.

THE JUDGE OF ALL THE EARTH

Jeremiah 1.10 stated that Jeremiah would be a prophet to the nations, and 12.14–17 also concerned God and the nations. Now in 25.15–38 we have a much longer passage on the same theme. (Later, in chs 46—51, we shall find six chapters containing messages for particular nations.) The key to the present passage is perhaps 25.29; since God judges His chosen people (25.18), He will certainly also judge those others whom He has created and who are thus responsible to Him.

No reasons are given here for God's judgement of the nations, but we find that some of the ideas and imagery are related to those used elsewhere in Jeremiah when talking of the judgement of Judah. This is not surprising. Jeremiah and his editors were heirs to a common pool of language and motifs which could be used in many contexts. The precise shaping and application would vary depending on the audience.

'God is a God of surprises . . . promising new hope in a situation of despair . . . "God seems to make the future with those whom the world would judge to be *without* a future".' We cannot predict what His good plans may be, say, for this orphan child growing up in a girls' hostel in India.

Behind the images chosen here lies the belief that all nations, small and great, are accountable to their Creator, whether or not they are directly aware of Him. When all other nations have been considered, Babylon, the greatest of the superpowers of the day, is addressed. It too is subject to the searching examination of God; it too fails. No nation has the power to avoid the test or the purity to pass it. No empire, however much it may dominate the world, will last for ever. Even the greatest empire is transient and will fade away.

In our experience we may find that hard to believe, but our lives are very short in terms of world history. With other prophets Jeremiah shared a burning awareness that God *is* the Lord of the nations. Such awareness helps to prevent despair in the face of domination by a more powerful nation or at the apparent triumph of a regime which persistently violates human rights. Our thoughts and concerns naturally tend to be dominated by our own local crises, and the business of day-to-day living becomes uppermost in our minds, especially when just to survive or to find school fees or medical treatment is a struggle. If we can remember the sovereignty of God we shall have a broader and truer perspective on life. God is the judge of all the world.

NOTES

24.1: Into exile ... Jeconiah: The Exile took place in 597 BC. Jeconiah is a variant form of Jehoiachin.

Princes ... craftsmen ... smiths: The 'princes' were royal officials, not necessarily of royal blood. 'Smiths' (metalworkers) is an uncertain but probable translation. Deportation of the craftsmen and smiths would both hinder attempts to rebuild Jerusalem, and at the same time make the skills of these workmen available to the people of Babylon.

24.2: First-ripe figs ... very bad figs: The first figs of the new crop were considered the very best. The image of bad figs recurs at 29.17.

24.5: I will regard as good: See the comment above, p. 135.

Chaldeans: Strictly, the Chaldeans were those from a particular part of South Babylonia. However, King Nebuchadrezzar and his father Nabopolassar were native Chaldeans, and in their time the term was often, as here, used to refer to the whole Babylonian empire.

24.6: Bring them back: Here and in the following verse ('return') the Hebrew *shub* recurs. See the discussion on p. 33.

Build them up ... not uproot them: These images first occur at 1.10.

24.7: I will give them a heart: This is perhaps the seed of the idea developed in 31.31–34 as the new covenant.

24.8: The remnant of Jerusalem: Those left in the city; they have no future ahead of them.

Those who dwell in the land of Egypt: Either this refers to those who accompanied Jehoahaz when he was exiled to Egypt or it concerns other unknown exiles with anti-Babylonian views. Since the context places the incident before the final fall of Jerusalem, it will not include those who would flee to Egypt after Gedaliah's murder.

25.1: The fourth year of Jehoiakim: This would be 605–604 BC. Strictly speaking, this was Nebuchadrezzar's accession year, since, in Babylonian reckoning, his first year only began with the new year after his accession.

25.3: Persistently: Here and in the following verse it is literally, 'Rising early and sending' (see note on 7.13).

25.6: Do not go after other gods: Compare Exod. 20.5.

25.7: That you might: This is probably a strong way of making the point, rather than suggesting that the people were deliberately showing Yahweh their apostasy.

25.8: Therefore: The judgement to be announced comes as a direct consequence of deliberate sin.

LORD of hosts: This title is again linked with judgement; see note on 2.19.

25.9: All the tribes of the north: This is a general term for invading enemies; 'tribes' would be better translated as 'peoples'. For 'north', see note on 1.14.

Nebuchadrezzar ... my servant: The same description recurs at 27.6 and 43.10. Isaiah 44.28 and 45.1 picture another foreign king, Cyrus, as an agent of Yahweh.

Everlasting reproach: We should probably understand this to refer to the foreseeable future. In this case it will not, in principle, eliminate any future beyond that.

25.10: Banish from them the voice of mirth ... the light of the lamp: Everyday sights and sounds mean so much; in their place is silence and emptiness. A curse in a treaty of Esarhaddon, a seventh-century BC Assyrian king, includes the clause, 'May the sound of the mill and the oven not be heard in your homes'.

25.11 These nations ... seventy years: Only here does this passage mention that other nations will suffer under Babylon; the Greek applies it to Judah by reading 'they' instead of 'these nations'. Seventy years is a large round number, a very long time; it is also used of the Exile at 29.10; 2 Chron. 36.21; Dan. 9.2; Zech. 7.5.

25.12: I will punish the king of Babylon: This is the closest this passage comes to suggesting a return from Exile.

25.13: This book: Any reconstruction of the book is speculative. It is part of a comment which could refer to any collection of Jeremiah's words known to the editor.

Against all the nations: This takes up an idea found in 1.10, and prepares for the transition in 25.14 from concern with Judah's judgement to that of the world.

25.15: Cup of the wine of wrath: For Yahweh's cup of wrath see the references in the note on 13.13f (see also 51.39,57; Isa. 63.6; Nahum 3.11; Rev. 14.10; 16.19). The image intended is probably the simple one of the nations being made drunk and so becoming helpless.

25.18: As at this day: This assumes that the Exile has begun.

25.20: Foreign folk: That is, foreigners living in Egypt.

Uz ... Philistines: In Job 1.1 Uz is somewhere to the east; its precise location remains unknown. The Philistines, to the south-west of Judah, traditionally had five major towns (Joshua 13.3, and see Map 2, p. 235). Gath is omitted here as it was no longer of significance; even by the mid-eighth century BC it was discounted (Amos 1.6–8); Isaiah 20.1 reports an Assyrian assault on Ashdod and the historian Herodotus also reports a seventh century BC Egyptian attack on it.

25.21–22: Edom, Moab ... Ammon ... Tyre ... Sidon: See Map 1, p. 234.

The coastland across the sea: Probably colonies of Tyre and Sidon are meant, the islands and coasts to which their fleet of ships sailed.

25.23: Dedan, Tema, Buz, and all who cut the corners of their hair: The three places named were apparently in the region of Arabia. For the last phrase, see note on 9.26.

25.25: Zimri: The link with Elam and Media suggests that it was in the Mesopotamian region. Some scholars have suggested that changing it to Zimki made it a code for Elam.

Elam ... Media: See Map 1, p. 234.

25.26: After them ... Babylon: The Hebrew is actually *Sheshak*, as at 51.1,41. This is a code for Babylon, obtained by exchanging the first letter of the Hebrew alphabet for the last one, the second for the last but one, etc. The use of such a code was not necessarily to deceive; it had probably become a nickname.

25.28: You must drink: 'Must' brings out well the emphasis of the Hebrew.

25.30: The LORD will roar ... his voice: Compare Amos 1.2.

Like those who tread grapes: A noisy activity, enjoyed by the treaders because, as they tread, they imagine the wine that they will be able to drink!

25.33: Not lamented ... dung on the surface of the ground: This is the greatest disgrace imaginable (cf. 16.4).

25.34: Shepherds ... roll in ashes ... rams: 'Shepherds' is again a term for rulers. 'Ashes' may possibly be 'dust'; in either case the idea is one of mourning. 'Rams' follows the Greek and is adopted by most English versions; the NIV follows the Hebrew, and refers to shattered pottery, but the context suggests that the Greek is more likely to be original.

25.38: Like a lion he has left his covert: Various English translations have been proposed. The most likely meaning is that Yahweh has abandoned the flock.

STUDY SUGGESTIONS

REVIEW OF CONTENT

1. Why would people in Jerusalem have been surprised that God's plan for the future lay with those who had been exiled to Babylon?
2. What reasons does the passage give for God's planning the future through exiles in Babylon?
3. How extensive does the passage declare God's control over other nations to be? Would the other nations realize this?

BIBLE STUDY

4. What is the surprise in the following passages?
   (a) Gen. 17.15–19
   (b) Deut. 7.6–8
   (c) 1 Sam. 16.1–13
   (d) Matt. 28.1–10
   (e) Luke 18.9–14
   (f) 1 Cor. 1.18–25
   What other Bible passages can you think of, where God acts in a surprising way?
5. According to 25.8f, what is Nebuchadrezzar to do as God's servant and for what reasons? Compare this with Isa. 44.24—45.7: what is Cyrus to do as God's servant and for what reasons?

DISCUSSION AND APPLICATION

6. 'We cannot predict what God will do nor how He will do it; nor do we always understand why He acts as he does' (p. 135). What effect does this have on your faith? Do you find it reassuring or disturbing?
7. Does the fact that we cannot fully understand God mean that there is no point in attempting to develop a theology? Give reasons for your answer.

8. What helps us to be open to new ideas and insights for our faith?
9. 'The belief that all nations, small and great, are accountable to their Creator, whether or not they are directly aware of Him' (p. 138). What responsibilities does such a belief carry? What effect does it have on the life of your Church or on your own faith? How far is it of help when one nation overruns another?

Special Note F
The Making of the Book of Jeremiah

A book written today will tell us the name of the author and the date when the book was published; often it will give us other information too. Books written long ago may not give us such information. In the case of St Paul's letters we have information about the author, but we cannot give certain dates to them all. Many of the Old Testament books give no information at all about the author. The book of Jeremiah tells us neither the identity of the author nor the date of composition.

Several passages in Jeremiah refer to a book or a scroll being produced on the instructions of Jeremiah (or Yahweh); for example 25.13 and 51.60 concern a collection (or two collections) of prophecies against Babylon, and 30.2, 36.32 and 45.1 refer to collections addressed to Judah and Israel. Although we cannot reconstruct these books, it is natural to assume that much of their content is present in our finished book in some shape or form. These earlier collections may well mark a step towards the final product.

TYPES OF MATERIAL

One approach to the book's development considers the three basic types of material it contains: prophetic oracles, stories about Jeremiah and prose sermons. The general distinctions between these types of material is clear, even though a particular passage may be difficult to categorize.

1. PROPHETIC ORACLES

Prophets in ancient Israel seem normally to have delivered their messages as short oracles, often only a verse or two long. Very often no accurate record would be made at the time, but because they were short the point made was easily remembered, and because they were delivered as poems the exact words would often stick in people's minds. If people heard a prophet several times they might well remember several things he said, though not necessarily the occasions on which each was said.

If someone later decided to compile a collection of the prophet's oracles, many different people could be asked and a wide range of material collected. This material would probably be separated from its original context, and frequently be an extract from the total content of the prophet's message on a given occasion. There would no doubt be duplicates and variations of some oracles.

Compilers would, therefore, find themselves with a large amount of unorganized material and would need to select and arrange what they wished to include. Selection and presentation would thus depend on compiler, or editor(s). Some such process of compilation lies behind the presentation of the poetic oracles in our book of Jeremiah.

2. STORIES ABOUT JEREMIAH

The stories in which Jeremiah is a central figure have sometimes been called biographical. Such a term is rather misleading, since the main reason for the inclusion of these narratives is not to give us a biography of Jeremiah, but to use stories about him to reinforce particular points which concerned the editors. There is no internal information about the identity of the author of this material. Its style is similar to that of the prose sermons, suggesting that the finished version of both may have been written by the same person or group.

3. PROSE SERMONS

These passages present messages delivered by Jeremiah not as short poems but as prose narrative, more like the sermons with which we are familiar today, though in a summary form. While genuine ideas of Jeremiah may often lie behind these sermons, it is unlikely that they owe their present form to him, since prophets after him as well as before delivered their messages as poetic oracles. The language and some of the theological ideas of these sermons show close resemblances to those found in the Book of Deuteronomy and the Deuteronomic History (see Special Note C, p. 44).

THE DEVELOPMENT OF THE BOOK

While there is no doubt that the book of Jeremiah was given its basic shape by an editor or editors other than Jeremiah, we do not know their identity. The possibility that Baruch (see p. 202) was involved has attractions, but cannot be proved. What is clear is that those responsible had a strong sympathy with Josiah's reform as well as a loyalty to the teaching and tradition of Jeremiah.

Nothing substantial in the book requires a date after the Exile. Both the basic shape of the material and most of the content can be placed without difficulty during the first part of the Exile. We may suggest that during this period some of those who believed (or who came to believe) that God had been speaking through Jeremiah tried to compile a collection of his messages. Possibly they had earlier collections to build on. Some of the material they retained as poetic oracles; other material – perhaps because it had been re-used as sermons or because it was only partly recorded – they transformed into prose which clothed Jeremiah's message in a different style. Some oracles were used more than once; they may have come to them from more than one source.

In addition to this material which owed its inspiration to Jeremiah they also included some other material, which had not originated with Jeremiah but which they believed important and relevant. With all this they combined a number of stories featuring Jeremiah which they thought would reinforce the overall message they wished to emphasize.

We do not know where the book was produced. The stories about Jeremiah in Egypt require some first-hand information from that community, but this does not mean that the whole work was compiled there. As a whole the work displays a sympathy with some of those exiled to Babylon, and declares that the future hope will emerge from this group. This may suggest that the editors were themselves among these exiles, but this can be no more than a suggestion.

Although we cannot identify the editors or place of composition, we can be confident that all the material was included because of its theological content. Much of the content can be linked directly or indirectly to Jeremiah. Other material was understood by the editors to develop and reinforce the message of Jeremiah. His name and authority was thus given to the whole work, in much the same way as all the Law was linked with the figure of Moses.

OUR VERSION OF THE BOOK

The Old Testament in our English Bibles, and in any other modern language version we may use, is based on a Hebrew version known as the Masoretic text. This is the oldest version of the Hebrew that we possess. We also possess the Greek version used by the first Christians, often called the Septuagint.

If we compare these Greek and Hebrew versions of Jeremiah we find many differences. While some of them are little, such as occur in any translation, others are major. The order of the material in the two versions is different (for instance, in the Greek version, the oracles against the nations come in a different order, and are placed after 25.13a and not at the end of the book), and in a number of places the Greek version is much shorter. Although the original version was in Hebrew, some scholars believe that the Septuagint is closer to the original Hebrew than is the Masoretic text that we now have. For this reason the Greek version can be specially useful in places where the Hebrew is unclear. Also, those who try to trace the earlier layers that lie behind the book we have (see Introduction, p. 2) often base their suggestions on the content and arrangement of the Septuagint version.

Because our Old Testament is based on the Masoretic text we shall keep to the order of that text. In this Study Guide we do not normally discuss ways in which the Greek and Hebrew are different, though we do remark on the absence from the Greek of some lengthy passages. When the Notes do mention the Greek it is usually either because the Greek has a quite different meaning or because it helps us to understand the Hebrew.

STUDY SUGGESTIONS

1. What does the Book of Jeremiah tell us about the identity of its author and the date of its composition?
2. What can we reasonably assume to be the relationship between the finished book of Jeremiah and the different scrolls mentioned in the course of it?
3. How did prophets generally deliver their messages?
4. What basic kinds of material does the book of Jeremiah contain?
5. How do you understand the book of Jeremiah to have developed into its finished form?
6. Why do some scholars believe that the Septuagint version of Jeremiah is closer to the original Hebrew than is the Hebrew text that we now have?
7. In what ways can the Greek text help to increase our understanding of the whole book?
8. Does it matter for our understanding of the Book of Jeremiah as the 'word of God' that there are major differences between the Hebrew and Greek texts? Give reasons for your answer.

26.1–24
Conflict with Authority

OUTLINE

This chapter concerns Jeremiah's Temple sermon, reported earlier in 7.1–15. While the earlier account concentrated on the content of Jeremiah's message, this one focuses on reactions to it. As explained in Special Note B, p. 20, this chapter also marks the start of a new section of the book (chapters 26—36), concerned with the possibility of Judah turning in response to God.

26.1–6: A very brief summary of the occasion and content of the Temple sermon.

26.7–9: A statement of the initial reaction of those who heard Jeremiah.

26.10–19: A report about the hastily convened trial of Jeremiah where his prophecy is compared to that of Micah.

26.20–24: An editorial footnote comparing Jeremiah's experience with that of a contemporary, Uriah, who was put to death.

INTERPRETATION

ACQUITTED BUT NOT ACCEPTED

Jeremiah's sermon aroused great hostility. He was arrested and charged with attacking Yahweh, a crime carrying the death penalty. A trial was hastily convened by leading government officials; Temple representatives presented the case for the prosecution and Jeremiah then spoke in his own defence. He argued that since he had been speaking in the name of Yahweh he should be heeded, and any who silenced him would themselves be attacking Yahweh. He seized the opportunity to press his message home further.

The government officials accepted Jeremiah's defence and decided that he should be acquitted. One of those present talked of Micah's prophecy in the days of King Hezekiah. Micah had sternly attacked the Jerusalem leadership and warned of God's severe judgement. Hezekiah had recognized God's voice speaking through Micah, and turned back to God in repentance. It was agreed that Jeremiah should be respected in the same way.

That not all agreed with the verdict can be seen from the experience of Uriah, a contemporary of Jeremiah. After delivering prophecies similar to those of Jeremiah he fled to Egypt, but was extradited and executed. And although Jeremiah was officially acquitted, the last verse of the chapter, coming as it does after the story of Uriah, implies that without the help of a friend at court Jeremiah would have shared Uriah's fate. As it was he was safe – but was liked by few, suspected by many, and ignored by the majority.

Sometimes it is better to be attacked than ignored; at least we are then being noticed! Jeremiah must have found his subsequent experience very depressing. The court had acknowledged that he might have an important word from God, and yet no significant official took much notice of what he said. It was a testimony that people did not really care, that they did not think it mattered. Jeremiah's heart continued to bleed as his ministry went on, but the people just turned their backs on what he said.

Indifference is a great hurdle for any preacher to overcome. We can debate with the passionate atheist or with the convinced 'all faiths lead to God' supporter; our opponent will at least listen in order to argue. But those who don't care cannot be bothered to argue. There is great discouragement when people pay lip service to the following of God, nod their heads or make murmurs of approval during the sermon, but never let it really affect them. In some countries many of the political leaders proclaim themselves as upholders of Christian standards, while their policies move their country in another direction. With their followers they attend Church services on Sundays, while their political opponents are detained without trial or tortured in high security prisons. They proclaim the virtues of their democracy while encouraging subversive activities in other countries. Often they will not actively oppose the Church, because that would be politically harmful to them; instead, they try to tame it, while refusing to listen to anything important it may say. Such was Jeremiah's experience.

A FAITH PREPARED TO SPEAK OUT

No doubt Judah's leaders, political and religious, would have preferred that Jeremiah had never spoken out. Now that he had been acquitted (even if his words continued to be ignored) they must have hoped that he would keep quiet. But, in spite of the problems it caused him, he continued to speak and would not be silenced.

To speak out against State or Church leadership is rarely easy. Those who protest run risks. For opponents of some regimes imprisonment, torture and death are common experiences. The Church worker who speaks publicly against Church policy may sometimes run the risk of being moved to another post or denied promotion. It can be difficult to oppose the hierarchy.

In some countries political leaders claim to uphold Christian standards, yet say the Church should not interfere in public affairs. But if a government's policy seems evil, Christians are right to speak out, like this local group in Britain protesting against lack of proper housing and services for poorer people in the cities.

Yet sometimes we should speak out. If the government's policy seems evil or immoral, if the leaders of the Church seem to be compromising the faith, opposition is right. As far as possible we should avoid confrontation and denunciation. We must focus on major issues and not minor ones. We must carefully decide on what issues we are right to make a stand. When we do make such a stand we must be prepared for the consequences, and not complain if they are unpleasant for us; though we may sometimes be effective, our voices may more often be ignored or repressed. Even if we appear to be completely ineffective, that does not mean that the protest was wrong.

Some protests take the form of mass movements which may combine people of many outlooks, some religious and others not. Others may find the protester a lone voice, easily crushed or despised. Either way, our chief duty is to speak the truth. The consequences of doing so we leave, as Jeremiah did, with God.

NOTES

26.2: Court of the LORD's house: See note on 7.2.

All the cities: That is, the citizens or representatives coming from these places. We should imagine a major festival or a great occasion connected with the early days of Jehoiakim's reign.

Do not hold back a word: The message is to be delivered undiluted and without moderation, cf. 1.17; v. 8 records that this instruction was followed.

26.6: Shiloh: See note on 7.12.

26.7: The priests and the prophets: A general term for the Temple officials.

26.8–9: Laid hold of him, saying, 'You shall die! Why ... without inhabitant?': Jeremiah was charged with denying the promise God had made to David (see, 'Their Faith is Selective', p. 46). To do this was apostasy, which carried the death penalty; the Hebrew emphasizes this, saying, 'You shall certainly die'.

26.10: Princes of Judah: As elsewhere, this refers to leading government officials. By hastily convening a court they prevented the possibility of the angry mob killing Jeremiah in the Temple; such violence they would have thought appalling.

New Gate of the house of the LORD: This gate was by the entrance to the upper court of the Temple (36.10), though its exact location is unknown. In ancient Israel judgements were customarily carried out by elders seated by a gate of the town (cf. Ruth 4.1–12).

26.15: In truth the LORD sent me: If Jeremiah is really God's prophet, then those who oppose him are the ones attacking Yahweh.

26.17: Elders of the land: Though we cannot identify them, these were obviously people influential enough to command a hearing in the gathering.

26.18: Micah of Moresheth ... Zion shall be ploughed ... a wooded height: Micah had prophesied about a hundred years earlier. His home town, whose full name was Moresheth-Gath, lay in the Shephelah, the foothills to the south-west of Jerusalem (see Map 3, p. 236). The quotation comes from Micah 3.12; in its original context it does not state that the judgement can be avoided by repentance.

26.19: Did he not fear the LORD: This is the only testimony in the Old Testament that Micah's preaching was effective in his own day.

Entreat the favour: This is literally 'soften the face' and originates in an old ritual in which an idol was touched during a cultic ceremony as a sign of pacifying the god.

26.20: Uriah ... Kiriath-jearim: This prophet is mentioned only here; his home town lay about 13 kms to the west of Jerusalem, (Map 3, p. 236). We may note that Micah, Jeremiah and Uriah all came from outside the capital, and attacked the Jerusalem leadership. In a collection of letters dating from around this time (the Lachish *ostraca*) there is mention of a prophet passing on a message and possibly being involved in military matters, but there is no evidence that it refers to either Jeremiah or Uriah.

26.22: Elnathan: The same man appears in 36.12 as a cabinet member and is spoken of favourably at 36.25; and 2 Kings 24.8 records that Jehoiakim's father-in-law bore the same name.

Achbor was quite a common seventh-century name so we cannot assume that 2 Kings 22.12,14 refers to the same man.

26.23: Slew him: The translation in most English versions, 'had him killed' is better. Apart from 2 Chronicles 24.20–22 (where it is not actually stated that Zechariah was a prophet) this is the only Old Testament reference to the killing of a prophet of Yahweh, though the New Testament implies that it was a common occurrence (see e.g. Matt. 23.37; Luke 13.34; Heb. 11.35–37).

26.24: Ahikam: Ahikam may have been influential in Jeremiah's acquittal or in protecting him later (it is not unknown for those acquitted to be subsequently re-arrested or murdered!). He had been influential in Josiah's day, 2 Kings 22.12,14, and was the father of the Gedaliah who became governor after the destruction of Jerusalem (2 Kings 25.22; Jer. 39.14; etc.).

STUDY SUGGESTIONS

REVIEW OF CONTENT

1. Within chapter 26, what suggests that Jeremiah's message was not really accepted?
2. Why is it sometimes better to be opposed than ignored?
3. Why do you think that Jeremiah continued to speak out even though it seemed to have little effect?
4. What lesson from past history was used by some elders of the land in Jeremiah's defence?

BIBLE STUDY

5. Compare the unpopularity of Elijah (1 Kings 18.17 and 19.1–3) and of Amos (Amos 7.10–13) with that of Jeremiah.
6. How many of the experiences reported in Hebrews 11.33–40 can you illustrate from your knowledge of the Old Testament?
7. Compare Jer. 26.1–24 with Jer. 7.1–15. Make a list of the links between the passages.
8. In Jer. 26.18f the speakers use past history to help make their point. What different points from past history do the following passages make?
   (a) Exod. 13.3–10
   (b) Deut. 26.5–10
   (c) Josh. 24.1–15
   (d) 2 Kings 17.1–18
   (e) Luke 4.21–27
   (f) Acts 7.2–53

DISCUSSION AND APPLICATION

9. What factors help us to decide whether or not to speak out about a particular issue?
10. 'Even if we appear to be completely ineffective, that does not mean that the protest was wrong' (p. 149). How would you reply to a friend who said that there was no point in speaking out unless you had a good chance of being listened to?
11. What examples can you give of local or national leaders paying lip-service to what is right but failing to do anything about it?
12. Imagine you are a leader in your local Church. At a Church meeting one of the members draws the attention of the group to a way in which the Church is disobeying God. The public rebuke is embarrassing; how do you respond?

13. Do those who speak out in your society tend to meet with strong opposition, or are they just quietly ignored? What effect do their protests have? Give examples.
14. Would you rather face strong opposition or be ignored? Give your reasons.

27.1—29.32
Exile and the Prophets

OUTLINE

In these chapters the scene is Jerusalem in the years immediately following the exile of King Jehoiachin. Jeremiah, who remained in Jerusalem, was certain that for many years to come Babylon would continue to dominate the political scene. But many people from Judah, some in exile and others who had remained in the land, disagreed, and hoped for a quick end to the Exile. Once again Jeremiah found himself in a minority and in conflict with other prophets. These three chapters record some of the conflicts. Their common language and style suggest that they form a distinct unit. Although their setting is Jerusalem, they were possibly a collection intended to be sent to exiles in Babylon who were hoping for a quick return to Jerusalem.

27.1–22: This passage announces that Babylon will remain supreme for many years. Verses 1–11 are addressed to various nations bordering on Judah, vv. 12–16 to Zedekiah and vv. 17–22 to officials of the Jerusalem Temple.

28.1–17: The chapter records a conflict between Jeremiah and Hananiah, another prophet, about the length of the Exile. The conflict is accompanied by acts of prophetic symbolism.

29.1–32: Jeremiah sends a message to the exiles in Babylon. In it he declares that those prophets in Babylon who assure them of a speedy return to Jerusalem are false. Verses 1–23 deal generally with the issue; vv. 24–32 are particularly concerned with a prophet called Shemaiah.

INTERPRETATION

RECOGNIZING GOD'S MESSAGE

In 23.9–40 the need for prophets to be sure their message came from God was emphasized. Now a related problem arises; how does the *listener* recognize God's message? The story told in ch. 28 illustrates the difficulty. Jeremiah had been wearing a wooden yoke (see 27.2) as a picture of the way that the people would serve Babylon. Then Hananiah, who also prophesied in Yahweh's name, assured the people that within two years Babylon's dominance would be broken. To drive the point home, he took the wooden yoke from Jeremiah and broke it, a powerful act of prophetic symbolism. The crowd must have been thrilled, and great rejoicing would have followed.

What was Jeremiah to do? In 28.6–9 we see his doubt whether Hananiah was right, but he recognized the possibility that Yahweh had given this message to Hananiah. So for the time being he kept quiet, only breaking his silence later, when told by Yahweh that Hananiah's message was false.

If Jeremiah could not immediately contradict Hananiah, how much less could the average Israelite! The issue of discerning the truth of a prophecy became very important around this time, and is raised both in Jeremiah and in Deuteronomy. How could people decide between two prophets, each speaking in Yahweh's name, whose messages contradicted each other? How did they know if a prophet was truly inspired by Yahweh?

The Old Testament makes some suggestions. Deuteronomy proposes two tests; the prophet's theology (13.1–5), and whether or not the prophecy was fulfilled (18.21f). These hardly go far enough. People could (and did!) argue that Jeremiah was unorthodox (he seemed to many to deny the covenant with David), and that his prophecies were unfulfilled. (From the beginning of his prophecy until Jerusalem actually fell there were forty years: how long should people wait for a prophecy's fulfilment?). Jeremiah suggests that the quality of a person's life *may* be a guide to the prophecy's truth (23.10,14) and that most earlier prophets had proclaimed judgement (28.8f), but these too are generalizations. Nor is sincerity enough, for a prophet could be quite sincere (we have no reason to doubt Hananiah's sincerity) but wrong.

This difficulty springs from the very nature of Old Testament prophecy. A prophecy from God could not be deduced by logic, since it came as something new and startling. While we may think that the people should have recognized that God was speaking to them through Jeremiah, it would not have been so obvious at the time. Similarly, we have no difficulty in agreeing with Paul that a non-Jew who became a Christian need not follow Jewish customs; but in Paul's day the right course of action was not nearly so obvious to most people, and the controversy was fierce. We have the benefit of hindsight.

One conclusion to be drawn is that what God is saying is not always obvious. We may have to struggle to identify it. We would perhaps prefer that this were not so, that the right action was perfectly clear for all to see. But often it is not. God does guide us, but He has also given us freedom to make choices, and He respects that freedom. He desires us to use the freedom to listen carefully and cultivate an openness to His word to us.

This word comes not only through prophets but also through other means – Scripture, people, circumstances, our consciences. Our responsibility is to be open to hear what God may be saying, not to let personal desires blind us to His wishes. Often we shall have to act in faith rather than with cast-iron certainty of God's will, but that is typical of the Christian life. A good general rule is that we continue as we are unless it becomes clear that we should change; Isaiah 30.21 declares that unmistakeable guidance comes when we stray from the right path. This can encourage us: if we really want to do God's will, however uncertain we may be of it, He will make it clear to us.

RELIGION AND POLITICS

During the years after Josiah's death Judah contained parties with varying political attitudes. Some were pro-Babylonian and urged immediate submission. Others were equally strongly urging resistance. Others still tried to sit on the fence, co-operating with Babylon as much as necessary, but no more.

Inevitably Jeremiah became involved. A large part of his message concerned God's activity in history, so he was bound to pronounce on the issues of the day. In many passages he supports submission to Babylon. When Jerusalem continued to resist the Babylonians' siege he even encouraged soldiers to desert; because of this many saw him as a threat to the morale of the troops and a traitor (38.2–4).

In chs 27—29 he takes a pro-Babylonian position, urging the exiles to seek the well-being of their conquerors. At this time such a view would have been politically 'safe', and welcomed by both King Zedekiah and the Babylonians. Jeremiah's opponents were the ones who were running political risks, for the king would be unlikely to welcome the return of his predecessor Jehoiachin (which Hananiah promised), and the Babylonians would have regarded the messages of prophets such as Ahab and Zedekiah (a different man from the king) as revolutionary. But to patriots of Judah, longing for deliverance from Babylon, Jeremiah's position would have made him seem a traitor.

Where did Jeremiah's loyalty really lie? Was it to his own people or to their enemy? Was it to himself? Personal safety and comfort can have a large influence on the policies we choose, and the way the Babylonians treated Jeremiah after they had captured Jerusalem shows they knew that he had encouraged Judah's submission. It was because Jeremiah's loyalty was to God above all else that it was difficult to define his politics. So at one time he could urge that Jerusalem surrender to Babylon and in the next breath declare God's coming judgement on Babylon. His consistency did not lie in following a particular party line in international politics but in trying to proclaim what he found God saying at that time. Only humanly speaking might this seem inconsistent.

The relationship between religious leaders and those in political power is a very fragile one. In many countries the amount of political freedom is very limited, and any criticism of party policies or of the head of state can be presented as subversion. In such situations religious leaders must weigh words carefully. To be entirely supportive of a government and never breathe a word of criticism can compromise the gospel and lose credibility for the Church. To criticize everything means that the force of criticism is blunted. Somewhere there is a middle way, identifying those issues on which it is vital to protest and accepting those where fundamental principles are not at stake. When there is protest there needs also to be a readiness to take the consequences that may result from protest – unpopularity, imprisonment, or death. Archbishop Luwum of Uganda and Archbishop Romero in El Salvador are just two of the many Christians who have faced such consequences in our own times.

It is a difficult path; the leader will never please everyone. Some would argue that the approach of those like Archbishop Desmond Tutu in South Africa has not gone far enough, others that he has been too controversial. Those who are called to lead need the wisdom to discern when to be silent, when and how to speak.

NOTES

27.1: In the beginning of the reign of Zedekiah: Some Hebrew manuscripts read 'Jehoiachin' instead of Zedekiah, and the whole phrase is absent from the Greek. Events in chs 27 and 28 clearly take place about the same time, according to 28.1 the fourth year of Zedekiah. Since he only reigned for ten years it is difficult to describe this as the beginning of his reign. Probably this phrase was originally copied by mistake from 26.1.

27.3: Edom ... Sidon: Why these rulers were present is not known. Disturbances in Babylon around 595–594 BC fostered the belief that

Babylon could be overthrown and in 593–592 BC Judah joined an anti-Babylonian coalition. This gathering might have been preparatory to this coalition. (If v. 1 was retained unchanged they could have been present for Zedekiah's coronation.)

27.6: Nebuchadnezzar: In these three chapters (except at 29.21) this form is used, rather than Nebuchadrezzar as found in the rest of the book. Variant spellings of the names Jeremiah and Zedekiah are also used several times in these chapters.

27.7: His son and grandson: Nebuchadrezzar was succeeded by his son Amel-marduk, but then, possibly after a coup, by his son-in-law Neriglissar.

27.9: Prophets . . . sorcerers: Deuteronomy 18.10f contains a similar list. The various terms are here used not technically but generally of religious officials who claimed to have messages from the gods.

27.10: A lie: The word recurs in vv. 14–16 and 29.9, 21; see note on 7.4.

27.12: Bring your necks under the yoke of the King of Babylon . . . and live: The significance of the yoke as a symbol of submission is at the heart of this chapter; Jer. 21.9 and 38.2 also promise that those who surrender to Babylon will have their lives spared.

27.16–22: The vessels of the LORD's house: 2 Kings 24—25 reports that sacred Temple furnishings were taken to Babylon at the exiles of both Jehoiachin and Zedekiah. The present passage refers to those taken with Jehoiachin, which had obviously been used in the Temple for many years. Possession of such sacred items would establish a claim for the legitimacy of the possessors. In later years this would contribute to the tension between the returned exiles and those who had remained in Judah during the years of Babylonian domination.

27.18: Let them intercede: This verse illustrates the way that a prophet's role was expected to include intercession.

28.1: That same year . . . the fourth year: See note on 27.1.

Hananiah . . . the prophet from Gibeon: The description may suggest that he was officially attached to the Jerusalem Temple. Gibeon (see Map 3, p. 236) was about 10 kms north-west of Jerusalem.

28.3: Bring back: The word here and in v. 4 is again *shub*; see 'Returning to God', p. 33. By making his prophecy so definite, Hananiah is risking a lot; if it does not happen . . .!

28.6: Amen: Jeremiah may be saying that he prays Hananiah is right, or there may be a sarcastic tone in his voice.

28.8–9: The prophets who preceded you and me: Earlier prophets like Ahijah (1 Kings 14—15), Elijah, Micaiah (1 Kings 22), Amos, Isaiah and Micah were well known for their grim outlook, not for cheerful messages.

28.10: Took the yoke-bars ... and broke them: The yoke was a strong object and so the breaking required great physical power; it was thus seen as a sign of great spiritual power.

28.11: Jeremiah ... went his way: Presumably because he had nothing to say at this time.

28.13: Wooden bars ... bars of iron: Wood could be broken, chopped or burned, while iron was almost indestructible. So the rule of Nebuchadrezzar would be irresistible.

28.14: Even the beasts of the field: So great will be Nebuchadrezzar's power (see also 27.6).

28.15–16: Not sent ... will remove you from the face of the earth: The Hebrew contains a play on words which we can illustrate by translating, 'Has not sent you (to say this) but will (now) send you away (to die)'.

28.16: You shall die: Hananiah's harsh fate is pronounced as a covenant curse on a covenant breaker. Note also the curses on Pashhur (20.6), and Shemaiah (29.32).

29.1: The letter: The letter was clearly addressed to all the exiles, but particularly to the leaders of the community. Although it was taken by a member of a government delegation (v. 3), Zedekiah need not have known about it. The exact date is unknown.

29.2: Queen mother ... eunuchs: The queen mother was a person of influence in Judah; see note on 13.18. Eunuchs was a term for officials; unless they were in charge of the royal harem, they were not necessarily castrated.

29.5–7: Build houses and live in them ...: A good example of the very positive attitude Jeremiah could show towards Babylon. We can compare it with his attitude to Jerusalem in 16.2–4.

29.8–9: Do not listen to the dreams: Although we are not told the content of these messages, the context makes it clear that they concerned the speedy end of Babylonian domination.

29.10: Seventy years: See note on 25.12.

29.12: Then: The translation is misleading. The verse is not concerned with a specific time when these things will happen, but is more general.

29.14: Restore your fortunes: This phrase recurs eleven times in the book. See the discussion in the next section, p. 161.

All the places: As at 23.8 it is unclear what places are in mind and whether the whole range of exiles is in view. Most of this verse and all of vv. 16–20 are absent from the Greek.

29.17: Vile figs: See note on 24.2.

29.19: Persistently: See note on 7.13.

29.21–22: Ahab ... Zedekiah: These prophets are otherwise unknown. Such prophecies could well lead to conflict with the Babylonian authorities, and were perhaps the cause of their deaths.

29.24: Nehelam: This could be a place name or a family name.

29.25: Zephaniah: Zephaniah also appears at 21.1; 37.3; 2 Kings 25.18.

29.26: Priest instead of Jehoiada: Zephaniah had presumably succeeded Jehoiada when the latter died or was retired.

29.27: Why have you not rebuked: The Hebrew sees Zephaniah being rebuked for his failure to control Jeremiah; Shemaiah is accusing Jeremiah of playing at being a prophet. The Greek omits 'not', thus criticizing Zephaniah for rebuking Jeremiah.

29.29: Zephaniah the priest read this letter: Probably he intended this as a threat to Jeremiah, though some scholars have seen his action as reflecting support for Jeremiah.

29.32: Talked rebellion: Shemaiah and his family must die for the apostasy. We can compare with Deuteronomy 13, though in the present passage there is no suggestion of the people being charged to carry out the death sentence.

STUDY SUGGESTIONS

REVIEW OF CONTENT

1. Why was it often difficult to tell if a prophecy was genuine? What are the main tests suggested in Jeremiah and Deuteronomy for the genuineness of a prophecy?
2. In what ways may God's word come to us today?
3. Why could patriots of Judah have thought that Jeremiah was a traitor to his country?
4. Why would many people have been delighted when Hananiah broke Jeremiah's wooden yoke?
5. What would the authorities' attitude have been towards prophecies of a speedy return from exile?
6. Why could some people argue that Jeremiah was inconsistent in his politics?

BIBLE STUDY

7. Consider each of the following passages as a guide to the accuracy of a prophecy:
   (a) Deut. 13.1–5   (c) Jer. 23.10,14
   (b) Deut. 18.21f   (d) Jer. 28.8f

How might you try to apply them to the situation posed by ch. 28?

8. By what means did the following people find guidance?
   (a) Moses: Exod. 18.13–24
   (b) David: 2 Sam. 11.1—12.15
   (c) Jesus: Luke 4.1–13
   (d) Cornelius: Acts 10.1–48
   (e) The Church at Antioch: Acts 13.1–3
   (f) Paul: Acts 16.6–15
9. How does Jeremiah's attitude towards the state compare with:
   (a) Jesus's position in Matt. 22.15–22?
   (b) Rom. 13.1–7?
   (c) Revelation's picture of the state as an enemy of God's people?

DISCUSSION AND APPLICATION

10. What methods have been most helpful to you for finding out God's will?
11. Have there been times when you have had to decide between two opposites, each being presented as God's will? If you have, what has helped you to decide?
12. 'I think God should make what He wants more obvious.' How would you comment on that statement?
13. Jeremiah's loyalty was to God rather than to politics. If this principle is applied to our own situations, does it make it impossible for a Christian to be an active member of a political party? Give reasons for your answer.
14. Jeremiah could have been accused of inconsistency in his attitude towards Babylon: are there times when your Church's political attitudes have been faithful to God but have seemed inconsistent to others? Give examples.

30.1—31.40
A Ray of Hope (1)

OUTLINE

The message about Shemaiah at the end of ch. 29 finished by saying that he would have no share in the good that God planned for His people. These good plans are central to chs 30—33. A variety of short oracles and narrative pieces, which probably date from a wide range of time, have been brought together and make a very encouraging section in a book which contains much that makes sad reading. (Although there are short hopeful passages elsewhere in Jeremiah, for example 3.14–18; 12.14–17; 16.14f; 17.24–26; 22.2–4; 23.5–8; 24.4–7; 29.10–14; 42.7–12, they are embedded in material that concentrates on God's judgement.) For this reason these chapters are often known as the 'Book of Consolation'. Most of the material in chs 30—31 is poetry, while chs 32—33 are mainly prose; this makes a convenient division of the material.

30.1–3: A short introduction to the collection which can be regarded as a text for the four chapters.

30.4–17: Judgement is unavoidable, but hope is equally certain to follow. This is the central theme of three short oracles found in vv. 4–9,10f and 12–17.

30.18–22: A poem about the wonder of being the people of God.

30.23–24: A short passage, also found at 23.19f, about the fury of God's judgement.

31.1–20: Three messages of joy: 31.1–6 tells of the future unity of the peoples of Judah and Israel; 31.7–14 celebrates the joy of the restored community; and 31.15–20 proclaims the end of weeping over the Exile.

31.21–22: An exhortation to the people of God to return and experience His salvation.

31.23–25: A short message about Judah's restoration.

31.26: This verse may suggest that part of the prophecy came in the form of a dream, but the meaning is uncertain.

31.27–34: The future will bring the reversal of an old proverb (vv. 27–30) and a new covenant (vv. 31–34).

31.35–37: A poem that links God's sovereignty over the world to the certainty of His remaining faithful to Israel.

31.38–40: A short statement about the way that Zion will be transformed.

INTERPRETATION

THE JOY OF RESTORATION

'I will restore the fortunes' occurs eleven times in Jeremiah, seven of which are in chapters 30—33 where it is an important theme. After the devastation of God's judgement comes delight at His restoration, a restoration as glorious as it is unexpected. The joy of those restored is expressed, especially in 30.18–22 and 31.1–14, with an exuberance that bubbles up and spills over; the greater the sense of forgiveness, the greater the joy (cf. Luke 7.47).

Such a picture of delight in God, reflected in daily life and supremely in worship, is frequent in the Old Testament. With such joy there goes spontaneity; you cannot always organize it in official channels – if you try to, it will burst out in other ways. (One handbook on worship which describes an exchange of the Peace as being 'spontaneous but restrained' makes nonsense of the idea of spontaneity.) Joy can be shown in many different ways, varying with culture and tradition, but it should be there and needs to be expressed.

Christian joy in worship is one of the most attractive features of the Christian faith. However, often we do not see it as we should. Sometimes this is because our worship has become stale, having lost the freshness of our Christian experience so that we go through a routine. Perhaps we see joy most often in the new convert, or in a time of revival, or – especially in recent years – in the enthusiasm and spirit of praise that has been a feature of the charismatic movement. We need to be warmed by such joy, so that our own joy in God and in the wonder of His salvation is rekindled.

At other times we may lack joy in worship because the material we are using in worship, whether set or spontaneous, does not meet the needs of the worshippers or the particular occasion. It is still the custom in many Anglican Churches in different parts of the world to sing hymns which were written and composed in England in the eighteenth and nineteenth centuries. Such tunes may still be suitable in the context in which they arose, but the ways in which present-day Africans or Asians will naturally express joy in worship may be very different from that of the nineteenth-century English. The search for the most natural ways to express Christian praise and joy is one of the most urgent of the moment. Worshippers need to draw on the resources of their own cultures to help the Christian faith take deep root in those cultures, so that it does not seem a foreign religion. Of course, we can learn much from others' expressions of worship; the heritage of faith is deep and rich. But, although others' cultural inheritances can enrich our worship, they must not deny the place of our own culture in our worship.

UNITY THROUGH GRACE

These chapters of Jeremiah have many contrasts with the earlier ones. Instead of judgement there is to be blessing; instead of tears there will be joy; fertility will replace devastation. One of the sharpest contrasts concerns the relationship of Judah and Israel.

Both Judah and Israel looked back to the experience at Mount Sinai in the period of the Exodus with the conviction that that was the time when they had become the people of God, a nation. But, once in the Promised Land, the whole history of the children of Israel reveals tension and disagreement between the two groups. They had different emphases in their understandings of the faith. The northerners were distrustful of the south's desire to rule over them; they suspected that the covenant with David was just a device the south was using to assert its authority. After the death of Solomon the temporary union of north and south which David had negotiated collapsed. For the next two centuries Judah and Israel were separate kingdoms, often in tension with one another. Then, late in the eighth century BC, the northern kingdom was overrun by Assyria, many people were deported, and settlers were moved in.

In these chapters we are told that part of the hope for the future is that Israel as well as Judah will be restored and the two enjoy unity with one another. The changes in the north since Israel's overthrow by Assyria make it hard to know just what kind of restoration was pictured. But the twin ideas of the restoration of the whole land, and of unity among people who had been deeply divided, are among the marks of excitement of these chapters.

We live in a divided world: north and south; rich and poor; educated and illiterate; divisions between countries and within countries; differences in language and culture; the multiplicity of tribes within many African and Asian countries. One of the most powerful witnesses to the gospel is the demonstration of unity among peoples who in human terms are so different, or who have traditional and deep-rooted hostility towards one another. When Christian unity is really demonstrated between denominations which have a history of mutual suspicion and opposition, and between those of widely different ethnic and cultural backgrounds, then the power of the gospel will be clearly displayed. As long as people's first loyalty is to a particular clan or tradition before it is to Christ, the gospel is denied. People said of the first Christians, 'See how they love one another'; this needs to be seen today also. Only in the restoration that Christ brings does it begin to be possible.

One factor vital for world peace—demonstrated here when Nigeria's Military Governor welcomed the UN Secretary General U Thant—is agreement between nations. Sadly, such agreements are often broken, just as Judah broke the old covenant with Yahweh. But Jeremiah hinted that God would one day offer a new covenant; agreement between Christians of different cultures and denominations is one of the most powerful witnesses to this gospel.

THE NEW COVENANT (31.31–34)

The message about the new covenant is one of the Old Testament's great visions for the future. We do not know how the prophet envisaged its fulfilment: whether he thought of the renewal of the covenant already in existence, or of something totally new; or whether he could do no more than say that something wonderful would happen. But even if he was only pointing towards a new direction in which God was going to work, he was undoubtedly doing that. And this was no small step. For centuries the covenant at Sinai had been one of the great landmarks in the history of God's people, even if – as Jeremiah had been forcefully pointing out – Judah had been neglecting it.

But now Jeremiah speaks of something else. He sees that the old covenant of Sinai, as it stands, has a fatal defect; it cannot change human nature and make people follow the Law. But in spite of this there need not be despair, for God will initiate a new plan. By one means or another, God will act to bring hope to a situation that, humanly speaking, offered only despair.

The world situation could often lead us to despair. Some problems seem insoluble, the future outlook bleak. The message of the new covenant came in a similarly hopeless situation. Judah's freedom was over; Jerusalem's destruction was in sight (or may already have occurred); there was nothing to encourage optimism and Jeremiah was no escapist. Nevertheless, in spite of these discouragements, he is presented as having the faith to continue to be open to God, and so able to receive a new word of hope for the future. The placing of 31.35–37 is significant; this vision of the supremacy of God is joined to the failure to give way to despair. It is when *God* is the focus that problems can be seen in their true light; if we concentrate on the problems, they will surely dominate us.

NOTES

30.2: Write in a book: There is no indication exactly what collection of oracles is meant; 25.13 and chapter 36 also refer to books.

30.7: Yet he shall be saved out of it: Possibly this should be understood as a question. In this case, it may originally have expected the answer, 'No, there is no hope'. But now, followed as it is by vv. 8f, a positive answer must be expected.

30.8: I will break the yoke: The yoke is one of several images of bondage and captivity from earlier chapters which are totally reversed in chapters 30—33.

30.9: David their king: See further on 33.14–26, p. 169.

30.10–11: Fear not ... unpunished: These verses recur as 46.27f; they seem to fit better here.

By no means: This brings out the strong emphasis of the Hebrew. The phrase itself does not follow well from what has gone before (the same is also true of 'therefore' in verse 16), though it does lead naturally into the following verses.

30.21: One of themselves ... from their midst: Once more Judah will be independent and self-governing. Some commentators find in the verse a suggestion that kingship and priesthood will be combined in the same person, but this may read too much into the idea of **draw near.**

30.22: My people ... your God: The link between God and His people is very old and very important (see e.g. 7.23; 11.4; 24.7; 31.1; 32.38; Exod. 6.7; Deut. 7.6; 30.6,14; Hos. 2.23; Zech. 13.9).

30.23–24: Behold the storm of the LORD: These verses are also found as 23.19f. There 'the wicked' are the false prophets, while here they are those who oppress God's people. This is a good example of how an oracle may be adapted and re-used.

31.1: All the families of Israel: See note on 2.4.

31.5: Again you shall plant vineyards: The doom of Amos 5.11 is reversed. The allusion to Amos is even closer in Isa. 65.21f.

Shall enjoy the fruit: Most English versions have something like this, though the NEB finds a reference to the worship of Baal.

31.7: The chief of the nations: A term for God's people (cf. Amos 6.1).

31.9: With weeping: Probably these are tears of joy at the return, though there may also be sadness for those lost and the state of Jerusalem.

31.11: Ransomed ... redeemed: To 'ransom' was to make a payment to secure the release of someone or something. Traditionally, the first-born belonged to God and needed to be redeemed by animal sacrifice (see note on 15.21).

31.15: In Ramah ... Rachel is weeping for her children: Rachel, the mother of Joseph and grandmother of Ephraim and Manasseh, died when giving birth to Benjamin. The verse is probably an allusion to the tragedy of her descendants. According to one tradition, 1 Samuel 10.2f, Rachel's tomb was at Zelzah, not far from Ramah which was about 8 kms north of Jerusalem (Map 3, p. 236); another old tradition, Genesis 35.19, puts her tomb at Bethlehem. It has been suggested that before the exiles were taken to Babylon they were first collected in a camp at Ramah.

31.16: Your work: This refers to her work of mourning.

31.18: I have heard Ephraim bemoaning: The Hebrew is emphatic, 'I have surely heard'. In the character of Yahweh lies the hope of restoration; in His power lies its possibility.

31.19: Smote upon the thigh: This was a sign of pain and lament.

31.22: How long ...?: Compare the question in 13.27.

The LORD has created ... a man: The diversity of suggested English translations shows that the meaning of this phrase is uncertain. Perhaps it is just a proverbial saying about something radically new.

31.26: Thereupon I awoke: There is no earlier mention of sleep, and this is probably an editorial insertion. Though it may be intended to imply that part of the prophecy came as a dream, there is no other evidence of this. It seems to be suggesting either how wonderful it is that God will manage to do these things, or how unlikely they appear when the realities of the situation are considered.

31.29: The fathers have eaten sour grapes ... on edge: The same proverb is quoted at Ezekiel 18.1–4,20. In Ezekiel God is protesting about the way in which earlier generations are being blamed for the problems of the present generation; but here it is emphasizing a change of fortunes.

31.32: Though I was their husband: Literally, 'I was *baal*'; *baal* means lord. We should remember the authority of husband over wife in ancient Israel, an authority still found in many traditional societies.

31.34: I will forgive: The Hebrew word used here for 'forgive' is only ever found with God as the subject.

31.39: The measuring line shall go out farther: This description of the city suggests that it has expanded beyond its traditional boundaries.

31.40: Dead bodies and the ashes ... sacred to the LORD: What was defiled now becomes dedicated. The 'ashes' would have been the dumped remains of altar fires, possibly including the remains of human sacrifices (see note on 7.31).

STUDY SUGGESTIONS

REVIEW OF CONTENT

1. What was the cause of the great joy shown in these chapters?
2. If such joy is to be particularly marked in worship, what may be the causes of *lack* of joy in worship?
3. What contrasts do you find between the emphases of these chapters and those in the earlier part of the book?
4. What differences had developed between Israel and Judah?
5. What weakness did Jeremiah find in the old Sinai covenant? What hope did he see in its place?

BIBLE STUDY

6. Look up all the references given in the note on 30.22 to form a picture of the strength of the bond between God and His people.
7. Read Ezek. 37.15–28, and compare it with what the present passage has to say about the reuniting of Judah and Israel.
8. Compare 31.31–34 with Ezek. 36.24–32. What themes do the passages share and what different points do they make?
9. Compare the following covenants:
   (a) The covenant with Abraham: Gen. 15.1–21 and Gen. 17.1–21
   (b) The Sinai covenant: Exod. 19.1—23.18
   (c) The Davidic covenant: 2 Sam. 7 and Ps. 89.1–37
   (d) The new covenant: Jer. 31.31–34

DISCUSSION AND APPLICATION

10. What reasons do you think that Christians have for joy? How does the worship of the Church to which you belong help you to demonstrate true joy? In your experience, why is some Christian worship lacking in joy?
11. What are the major divisions between people in your society? In what ways do the Churches in your country demonstrate the unity that Christ can bring? In what ways do they fail to demonstrate this unity? What can they do about this?
12. What personal experience, if any, do you have of God healing divisions?
13. The new covenant brought hope in a situation where hope seemed inconceivable. Are there situations in your society where hope seems impossible? What relevance has the Christian message for these situations?

32.1—33.26
A Ray of Hope (2)

OUTLINE

The 'Book of Consolation' continues with two further chapters which are mainly in prose. They reinforce and develop points made in the previous two chapters, especially ideas about the future of the Davidic covenant.

32.1–15: A vivid story about Jeremiah's buying of a family field at a time when the dominance of Babylon is about to become complete.

32.16–25: A prayer in which the prophet reflects on God's goodness and the problems that now face the people.

32.26–44: Yahweh replies to Jeremiah's prayer and its questions. The reply falls into three sections: a summary of the reasons for judgement, vv. 26–35; a promise of God's will for good for the future, vv. 36–41; an assertion that Jeremiah was right to buy the field, vv. 42–44.

33.1–13: A further passage declaring that restoration will surely come, and with it forgiveness, worship and fertility.

33.14–26: A series of short passages gives assurance that the covenant with David is not ended by the fall of Jerusalem, but has a certain and exciting future.

INTERPRETATION

FAITH IN THE DARK (32.1–44)

The story of Jeremiah's purchase of the family field is a powerful example of faith that endures in the dark. In Israelite society land was not supposed to pass outside the family or be sold to members of other tribes (cf. 1 Kings 21.3). We are not told why Jeremiah's cousin, Hanamel, wanted to sell the field, only that he asked Jeremiah, as a next of kin, to buy it. In human terms it was a bad investment. Babylon had already overrun the territory of Benjamin, which included Anathoth, and there was no likelihood of its ceasing to be occupied territory in the near future. Jeremiah himself must have been well over fifty years old, as his call to be a prophet had come forty years earlier.

God, however, had told Jeremiah that Hanamel would come. Because of this Jeremiah decided that it would be right to buy the land and he did so, going through normal legal procedures. The purchase is another act of prophetic symbolism, an assurance that restoration will come. But it still lies far ahead; an earthenware vessel will keep the documents for many years. Jeremiah's hope is very different from Hananiah's.

In performing this action Jeremiah must have given the impression of great confidence. But behind the scenes he was in turmoil. The public action done, he pours out his heart in prayer to God, sharing just how he feels. He has done what he thought right, and yet, confronted with the realities of the situation, he wonders whether he is not being stupid. He can look back to the past in which God's goodness and greatness have been displayed to Israel, but now he looks at the present and sees a grim and depressing outlook. So what about the future – can it really make sense to buy the field?

God's answer begins by quoting Jeremiah's own words, (compare vv.17 and 27); 'If you really meant what you said, why are you now doubting?' It then re-states the reasons for judgement, and moves to a fresh assurance of restoration and a new covenant. Finally, Jeremiah is told that he was right to buy the field; both land and people have a future.

This story shows us a familiar tension: on the one hand there is a real faith in God, on the other an uncertainty because of the surrounding problems. For Jeremiah it was a case of hoping in spite of the situation: of 'Lord, I believe; help my unbelief'. Today, as in the past, many are called to this kind of faith. When whole generations grow up knowing only famine conditions, or civil war and violence, it is not easy to face the future positively. And yet, faith is not stifled in such situations. A Ugandan pastor was talking about his experiences. For more than fifteen years the country had known violence and war, inflation was crippling and stability still seemed far away. Within the past three years his family had lost everything they possessed, their home had been destroyed and for part of that time they had been refugees in another part of the country. But, 'God is good', he was saying; and the look on his face showed that he meant it.

We are often much less positive than that. We too easily identify with Jeremiah's hesitation and leave out his faith. We need not be ashamed of our fears and uncertainties when faced with the harsh realities that sometimes confront us. But we can also draw help from Jeremiah's prayer; it faces the present but does so while trying to reflect on God's great acts in the past and on His nature and character. It is honest and genuine, and God's response is not harsh but understanding. He is the one who holds the future. In the words of a hymn:

> I do not know what lies ahead,
> The way I cannot see;
> Yet one stands near to be my guide,
> He'll show the way to me.

A FUTURE FOR DAVID (33.14–26)

We have seen Jeremiah very critical about Judah's trust in God's promise to David, and the people's blind assumption that God's care for them would be automatic. He had also declared that no future king would come from Jehoiachin's family (22.30). From such passages it appears that he believed that the Davidic covenant was finished and had no future.

But, just as we find talk of a new covenant to supersede the old covenant of Sinai, we learn here of a future for the covenant with David. Only rarely in Jeremiah is David spoken of positively, but these few passages (23.5f – virtually identical with 33.14–16 – and 30.8f, together with the whole of 33.14–26) cannot be ignored. All these passages are very general; they do not specify how or when there will be a Davidic king, but they declare boldly that there will be. As with the message of the new covenant, we can imagine the speaker pointing beyond what he could clearly see or imagine. He was dealing with a paradox; the common understanding of the Davidic covenant was ended, but not the covenant itself.

All human understanding is provisional. What may seem a contradiction to us is not necessarily so. This is not to claim that black is white, that words mean nothing; but it is to say that, in relation to God, man's understanding is necessarily limited. Whatever the origin of the various statements in Jeremiah, the editors were prepared to put side by side what seemed paradoxical. They must have done so because they believed that each side of the paradox contained something important that should be preserved.

With the fall of Jerusalem in 587 BC the line of Davidic kings reigning in Jerusalem came to an end. Many people felt that the Davidic covenant had ended or been proved false. But others could not reconcile that conclusion with their conviction of God's faithfulness. They wrestled with the issue and came to a new appreciation of the covenant, one which had been true all along but which only appeared now. The old understanding of the covenant with David had become an idol, and only when it was shattered could the deeper truth be discovered.

This is often the case. The crucifixion seemed to the disciples to mark the end of their hopes; in fact it became the very centre. Before his conversion Paul was sure that the Jews were the true focus of God's plan; his understanding of that plan was turned upside down. Our vision of God's purposes can collapse in ruins, but out of those ruins we can find a truer vision emerging. 'Our' idea of God, 'our' theology can all too easily become an idol. Only when it is shattered can we perceive the living God more clearly.

NOTES

32.1: The tenth year of Zedekiah: This would be 588—587 BC.
32.2: Shut up in the court of the guard: Chapter 38 records Jeremiah's being placed in the court of the guard so this incident must

have occurred after that time; 37.21 suggests that it was a sort of house arrest, whereby Jeremiah could receive visitors, but not move out of the building or area.

32.3–5: Why do you prophesy . . .: Zedekiah complains because he does not like what Jeremiah says about him. Micaiah (1 Kings 22.1–28) and John the Baptist (Mark 6.17f) faced opposition for similar reasons.

32.9: Seventeen shekels: A shekel was 11.5 gms.

32.11: Sealed deed of purchase: In such a transaction two copies were made, a sealed one for permanent record and an open one for consultation; if forgery was suspected the sealed one would be opened.

32.12: The Jews: Although used earlier, this term for God's people became widespread after the Exile.

Baruch: Baruch acts as Jeremiah's scribe in the story in ch. 36; he also appears in ch. 45.

32.14: Earthenware vessel: At this time the standard method of preserving documents was to put them in a pottery jar and seal the lid onto the jar with pitch. This protected the documents from decay.

32.18: Showest steadfast love . . . does requite the guilt: Compare this with the thought of Exodus 34.6f.

32.23: They did not obey thy voice or walk in thy law: This general accusation reflects editorial language. See 7.1–15 and 11.1–17 for expansion of these ideas.

32.29: On whose roofs incense has been offered to Baal: See note on 19.13.

32.30: Work of their hands: This could refer specifically to idols, as it does at 1.16, or more generally to their behaviour.

32.33: Turned to me their back . . . persistently: See note on 2.27 for the first phrase, and that on 7.13 for the second.

32.38: They shall be my people, and I will be their God: The same thought occurs at 30.22.

32.40: I will make with them . . . not turn from me: This verse is equivalent to the promise of the new covenant in 31.31–34.

32.44: In the land of Benjamin . . . cities of the Negeb: See the note on 17.26 and see also 33.13. Although the Book of Consolation as a whole includes both Israel and Judah, in this verse only the territory of Judah is included in the restoration. This passage was probably originally placed in another context but has now been re-used here.

Restore the fortunes: See 'The Joy of Restoration', p. 161.

33.3: Call to me and I will answer: God invites His people to ask Him to show them something of the good plans that He has for their future. These plans are beyond their dreams.

33.9: This city ... a name of joy: What happens to Jerusalem will reveal God to the world. The thought of Ezekiel 36.22–38 is related; God will restore His people for the sake of His Name.

33.11: Voice of mirth: The gloom of 7.34; 16.9 and 25.10 is reversed.

Give thanks ... for ever: This may be a quote from a Psalm; cf. Pss 106.1; 107.1; 118.1; 136.1.

33.13: Pass under the hands of the one who counts them: This was the shepherd's normal way of counting the flock to make sure that all were safely in for the night.

33.14–16: Behold ... The LORD is our righteousness: See note on 23.5f, for these verses are identical. This is one of the ideas that were developed to contribute to the understanding of the Messiah.

The name: In these verses this refers to Jerusalem (and Judah?); this is different from 23.6, where it is the name of the ruler that God will send.

33.18: The Levitical priests: God's covenant with the tribe of Levi is referred to in Numbers 25.12f; Nehemiah 13.29 and Malachi 2.4–9. In Zechariah there are suggestions that the Davidic and Levitical covenants will be fulfilled in the same person (Zech. 6.11–13). Here, in vv. 17 and 18, two different persons are distinguished.

Burnt offerings: These were particularly linked with dedication and were the most frequent sacrifice during the latter part of the monarchy.

33.19–26: The word of the LORD ... mercy upon them: These verses are parallel to the guarantee of 31.35–37. In both passages the established order of the universe guarantees that God will keep His promises. In ch.31 it is applied to the continuity of the people of God, here to the continuity of the institutions of kingship and priesthood.

33.21: David my servant: The same phrase comes at v.26. Note the earlier references to 'Nebuchadrezzar my servant' at 25.9 and 27.6.

STUDY SUGGESTIONS

REVIEW OF CONTENT

1. What message did Jeremiah symbolize by his buying of his cousin's field?
2. What tensions does this passage show to have existed within Jeremiah?
3. Why did most people think that the fall of Jerusalem would mean that the Davidic covenant was ended?
4. How did the fall of Jerusalem, together with a conviction of God's faithfulness, lead to a fresh understanding of the Davidic covenant?

BIBLE STUDY

5. Compare the inner tension which this passage shows to have existed within Jeremiah with the faith of:
    (a) Abraham: Gen.15.1–6
    (b) Elijah: 1 Kings 19.1–10
    (c) Job: Job 19
    (d) The writers of Psalms 13, 73 and 74
6. 'Only when it was shattered could the deeper truth be discovered' (p. 170). What ideas, totally new to most people, did the following passages bring?
    (a) Isa.52.13—53.12
    (b) Amos 5.18–24
    (c) Luke 10.25–37
    (d) Acts 10.1—11.17

DISCUSSION AND APPLICATION

7. How far did Jeremiah's prophecy of a new covenant depend upon his earlier prophecies concerning the destruction of Jerusalem?
8. Should we be surprised if we find tensions between our outward profession of faith and inward questions? If we have inward questions should we always voice them? Give reasons.
9. In what ways is our understanding of the gospel provisional? How much confidence can we have in our understanding of the Christian message?
10. How might we try to help people who say that their faith is shattered because God had not helped them as He had promised?
11. Do you think that an honest faith is bound to have struggles with doubt, or is it natural for some people to find that they are untroubled by problems that worry others? Give your reasons.
12. What experience do you have, if any, of situations which seemed to shatter your faith, but then rebuild it in a new way?
13. Have you been encouraged by others whose faith has shone brightly although they were in great difficulty? Give examples.

34.1—36.32
Lost Opportunities

OUTLINE

These three chapters tell of Judah's rejection of the final opportunities to turn and escape God's judgement. We find sharp contrasts between the actual behaviour of Judah (as represented by its leaders) and the ideal behaviour required. Once again, the arrangement of the material is theological and not chronological.

34.1–7: A message for Zedekiah promises him personal safety in spite of the coming destruction of Jerusalem.

34.8–22: A report tells of leaders in Jerusalem making a covenant to free their slaves, but then breaking the covenant. Jeremiah declares God's judgement for this.

35.1–19: The Rechabites, a 'sect' within Judaism, are praised for their faithfulness to their founder's teaching: their behaviour is a rebuke to the faithlessness of the people of Judah.

36.1–32: This chapter tells the story of a scroll containing Jeremiah's messages. Verses 1–7 describe its writing, vv. 8–19 its public reading by Baruch, and vv. 20–26 King Jehoiakim's destruction of it. Lastly, vv. 27–32 concern a new scroll that Jeremiah produces.

INTERPRETATION

FAITHLESSNESS AND FAITHFULNESS (34.8—35.19)

Chapter 34 is set in the Babylonian siege of Jerusalem. The city's defenders were becoming desperate. Finally, seeing no human hope, they decided that they would try to please God by releasing all the Jews who were slaves in Jerusalem, in the hope that He would spare the city. The phrase used is '*proclaimed liberty*' a technical term used elsewhere in the Old Testament, and linked with the Jubilee Year which occurred every fifty years (cf. Lev. 25.10,39–46 and Ezek. 46.17). All the leaders agreed on this, and a decree was published at a solemn ceremony held in the Temple. However, it seems that very shortly afterwards the Babylonians heard news of Pharaoh's army advancing from Egypt (37.5), and temporarily withdrew from Jerusalem in order to deal with this threat. No sooner had they withdrawn than the Jerusalem rulers reversed the decree about freeing the slaves, thereby breaking their solemn promise.

The account of the Rechabites in ch. 35 stands in total contrast, and was probably placed in its present position for that reason. The Rechabites originated in the northern kingdom of Israel in the time of Jehu. Their founder, Jonadab, appears in 2 Kings 10.15–27 (where he is called Jehonadab), though there is no information about the group's beginnings. Like the Hutterites (an Anabaptist group founded during the Reformation) and some of the African Independent Churches of today, they had a distinctive way of life. For the Rechabites this meant refusing to live in houses (remaining in tents instead), to grow crops or to drink wine. Because of the pressures of the Babylonian invasion they now had to move, like refugees, into Jerusalem. Jeremiah summons a group of their representatives to a meeting in a room in the Temple and there invites them to drink wine. On the basis of their founder's instructions over 200 hundred years earlier they refuse.

Jeremiah proceeds to draw a contrast between the faithfulness of these people to their founder's instructions (he does not comment on whether or not he approves of those instructions), and the faithlessness of Judah and Jerusalem to Yahweh. The contrast is within ch. 35, but it becomes even stronger when the previous chapter is linked with it. The emphasis on faithfulness is one close to the heart of Jeremiah, as it was to his predecessor Hosea. It is another aspect of his attack on the breaking of the Sinai covenant. The Rechabites were faithful to a merely human tradition, the people of Jerusalem broke the commands of God. The faithfulness of the one was a public rebuke to the other.

Although the Rechabites belonged to the children of Israel, most Israelites probably regarded them as strange and extremist. Yet they had a lesson to teach the rest. It was a lesson not in extremism but in commitment. They were sure that what they believed was important and were determined to hold to it. In doing so they exposed how weak was the faith of many others, a faith based on political convenience, crying out to God in difficulties but ignoring Him the rest of the time. If we really believe the Christian faith we should hold fast to it, and not let other pressures divert us from it. The conviction and commitment of some of the 'minority' and 'fringe' groups can rebuke us. We may not want to follow all their beliefs or practices, but we should imitate their commitment; if we fail in this we are open to the criticism of the Laodicean Church made in Revelation 3.14–22.

A FAITH OPEN TO CORRECTION?

A theme that emerges from chs. 26—36 is the rejection of opportunities for turning back to God. The story of ch. 36 is one more example of a lost opportunity. In the fourth year of Jehoiakim's reign Jeremiah had prepared a scroll which contained a number of his early prophecies. During the following year, on the occasion of a great fast when there would have been a very large congregation, Baruch read the scroll publicly in the Temple. Probably he spoke out of a window, addressing the crowd assembled in the courtyard below. (It was at about this time that the Babylonians overthrew Ashkelon in the plain of Philistia, and this warning of the growing power of Babylon might have been the reason for the fast.)

One of Baruch's hearers was Gemariah's son, Micaiah. His grandfather was the court secretary (an important member of the cabinet), and Micaiah immediately told some of the government leaders what had happened. They summoned Baruch so that he could report in person. When they heard the scroll's contents they realized that the king would be very angry; so they urged Baruch (and through him Jeremiah) to stay hidden, and went to report to the king. The king's response was as they had expected. As each piece of the scroll was read, the king cut off the piece and threw it into the fire that was keeping him warm. If this was not just an act of contempt it may have been a kind of prophetic symbolism, the burning of the scroll representing the cancelling of its contents.

The description of Jehoiakim's response should be compared with that of Josiah when the 'Book of the Law' was found during Temple-clearing operations (2 Kings 22.8–20). In both cases a scroll is read to senior government officials who report the matter to the king. The king has the scroll brought and read to him. Josiah tears his clothes in repentance, but Jehoiakim is unmoved and has the scroll torn (the same Hebrew word) and burnt. Then follows a prophetic oracle: a good future is decreed for Josiah, but a bad one for Jehoiakim. Josiah was open to correction, but Jehoiakim was not.

A wise leader considers the advice of others. The greater a leader's power, the more important it is to be open to correction. Some leaders are authoritarian, and see any questioning of their policy as rebellion or treachery. Early last century the Duke of Wellington, who had been a very successful British general, became Prime Minister. He recorded his own account of his first day in office. 'I met my cabinet for the first time this morning and gave them my instructions. The most extraordinary thing happened: they started discussing them!'

Such authoritarianism is common in Church circles, as it is in politics. Bishops or pastors who insist on their own ideas and make decisions without reference to others may temporarily exert their authority, but in the long run they will greatly weaken their effectiveness. A Church leader who thinks and behaves as though there is nothing to learn from others about Christian truth will cause parish and ministry to suffer. An openness to new ideas and to correction is invaluable.

JERUSALEM'S FATE IS SEALED

In Special Note B, p. 21, we indicated that the central theme of chs 26—36 is God's offer of forgiveness if the people repent. We have seen, for example in the Temple sermon (7.1–15 and 26.1–24), how forgiveness is promised if the people turn back to God. Even at the start of ch. 36 repentance is a possibility. But by the end of the chapter the last chance has been thrown away. Jehoiakim may think that he is putting an end to Jeremiah's message, but in fact he is putting an end to Jerusalem and his own family. The progress to judgement is now inevitable. There are no more suggestions that it may be avoided. Jehoiakim has gone too far.

The invitation of the Christian message is an invitation to forgiveness and fellowship with God. It is for all people, and God would like all to accept it. But there is a cutting edge to the Christian message, for God respects the freedom that He has given us. If we will not have God then finally He will not have us. If we persist in rejecting God's invitation the time will come when He confirms that decision. We may rightly turn away from some of the ideas of, for instance, hell-fire, and their presentation by our Christian ancestors. But the whole of Scripture, Old and New Testaments, suggests the possibility that people may fail to receive what God would love to give them. If this happens it is not God's fault, but theirs. We are not judges; that role belongs to God: but our ministry is carried out against such a possibility – the Gospel *does* matter.

NOTES

34.1: All the kingdoms ... peoples: This includes the soldiers from nations conquered by Babylon.

34.3: Eye to eye ... face to face: The picture is not of friendship but of confrontation. Zedekiah will be summoned before an angry conqueror and pay dearly for his rebellion.

34.4–5: You shall not die by the sword. You shall die in peace: It is difficult to relate this to Zedekiah's subsequent experience; he sees his sons killed, he is blinded and then dies a prisoner in a foreign country (52.10f; 2 Kings 25.7). It has been suggested that this is a promise conditional on earlier submission, e.g. 38.17, but that is not stated in the present text.

Spices were burned: Incense was burned ceremonially at a funeral. The dead Zedekiah will be remembered far more positively than the dead Jehoiakim (22.18).

34.7: Lachish . . . Azekah: Two towns to the south-west of Jerusalem in the foothills of the Shephelah (see Map 3, p. 236). They were among the last towns in that area to surrender to Babylon. We have some letters from Lachish which date from this period.

34.11: Afterward: That is, when the Babylonian army moved away from Jerusalem to counter the Egyptian threat.

34.17: I proclaim to you liberty: There is irony here. Jerusalem had denied freedom to the slaves, and will now lose all freedom except to be devastated by others.

35.4: Keeper of the threshold: A title given to three important Temple officials, 2 Kings 25.18. Possibly, each was responsible for one of the three principal Temple entrances.

35.5: Pitchers: Large containers for pouring wine; many English versions translate as 'bowls'.

35.13: Will you not . . .?: An emphatic 'No!' is the expected answer. A stubborn and deliberate refusal to listen to God is part of Jeremiah's picture of Judah; cf. 5.3; 6.8–10; 32.33.

35.14: Persistently: Also in v. 15; see note on 7.13.

35.15: Turn . . . you shall dwell: There is another play on words here; in Hebrew the two words sound similar.

35.19: Jonadab the son of Rechab: The Rechabites are not mentioned elsewhere, so we do not know their subsequent history.

36.1: Fourth year: This was 605 BC, the year of the Battle of Carchemish which firmly established Babylon's dominance.

Scroll . . . all the words: The scroll was probably made of papyrus. We do not know the extent of the document (though it could be read three times in one day) but can be confident that it consisted entirely of poetic oracles. Many, if not all, of them are probably found within the present book of Jeremiah, either as poetic oracles or edited in the form of prose sermons.

36.2: Israel: Some English versions follow the Greek and read 'Jerusalem'.

36.4: Baruch: See note on 32.12.

36.5: I am debarred: Unless there was some ritual reason, Jeremiah had probably been banned from the Temple area as a trouble-maker (cf. 20.1–6; 26.7–16). He cannot yet have been locked up or he would not have been able to hide (36.19, 26).

36.9: Fifth year . . . ninth month: There was thus an interval of perhaps a year between the making of the scroll and its public reading.

36.10: Secretary: The secretary was a leading government official.

New Gate: See note on 26.10.

36.16: In fear: Obviously the officials expect the king to be very hostile to the scroll. Their fear may have been out of concern for the safety of Baruch and Jeremiah, or because they themselves were genuinely alarmed by the scroll's content.

36.22: The winter house: Judah's climate meant that the rich preferred different living conditions in winter and summer. The building in question probably had two storeys, the ground floor being used in winter (the Hebrew is literally 'autumn' or 'harvest' house) with the better ventilated upper floor being used in the warmer summer months.

36.26: The king's son: This could refer to a member of the royal household who need not be a direct descendant of the king.

The LORD hid them: The Greek, less colourfully, reads, 'They had hidden themselves'.

36.30: He shall have none to sit upon the throne of David: In fact his son Jehoiachin did reign, though only for three months. Compare 22.18f and the note on it for a similar statement about Jehoiakim's burial.

Cast out: The Hebrew word is the same as that used in v. 23 for Jehoiakim's throwing the scroll into the fire. What he did to the scroll will be done to him.

36.32: And many similar words: A further example of irony. Not only did Jehoiakim fail to obliterate the prophecies of judgement; his action led to even greater denunciation. He was indeed playing with fire!

STUDY SUGGESTIONS

REVIEW OF CONTENT

1. What led the people of Jerusalem to change their minds about freeing their slaves? Why did Jeremiah regard this behaviour as unacceptable?
2. What lesson did Jeremiah draw from the behaviour of the Rechabites?
3. What was King Jehoiakim's attitude to the scroll containing oracles of Jeremiah?
4. Why, once the events of ch. 36 had taken place, was there no suggestion that Jerusalem might be spared?

BIBLE STUDY

5. Make a full comparison of Jer. 36.1–32 and 2 Kings 22.8–20, noting all the points of similarity in the way that the stories are

presented and the contrast between the characters of the two kings.

6. What do the following passages have to teach about faithfulness and consistency? 1 Kings 22.1–28; Ps. 15.4; Dan. 6.1–13; 2 Cor. 1.17–20

7. According to the following passages, which of the people described was open to correction?
   (a) Cain: Gen. 4.1–16
   (b) Balaam: Num. 22.1—24.25
   (c) David: 2 Sam. 11.1—12.25
   (d) Jehoiakim: Jer. 36.1–32
   (e) Nebuchadrezzar: Dan. 4.1–37
   (f) Jonah: Jonah 1.1—3.5
   (g) The rich young ruler: Mark 10.17–22
   (h) Simon Peter: John 13.1–11

DISCUSSION AND APPLICATION

8. When Christians are under pressure, what helps them to be true to their faith, and continue to trust in God?

9. 'The conviction and commitment of some of the "minority" and "fringe" groups can rebuke us' (p. 175). What lessons can your Church learn from such groups? How is it possible to believe passionately in a balanced expression of the gospel?

10. How would you advise Church leaders who want to remain open to fresh insights in their faith?

11. Sometimes people feel threatened when criticized. Is it possible in your Church for such criticisms to be made without the leaders feeling personally threatened? In what ways can we help our leaders to receive criticism and learn from it?

12. How would you comment on a statement that the love of Jesus shows that He accepts all and will never finally reject anyone, whatever their attitude to Him?

37.1—39.18
The Last Days of Zedekiah

OUTLINE

The narratives in chs 37—44 cover the time from the final period of Zedekiah's reign, through the fall of Jerusalem and the assassination of Gedaliah, to the Exile of a group of Jews to Egypt. The chief theme is the way that the inevitable destruction of Jerusalem works out, and how, even after it, those who survive in Judah remain stubbornly opposed to God. The first three of these chapters deal with the end of Zedekiah's reign.

37.1–10: This passage re-emphasizes that Jerusalem's destruction is inevitable; nothing at all can now prevent it.

37.11–21: A story telling of Jeremiah's arrest because of the suspicion that he was intending to desert to the Babylonians. He appeals to the king and the conditions of his detention are improved.

38.1–28: Another story (probably an alternative account of 37.11–21) of Jeremiah's arrest, rescue from death and subsequent house arrest.

39.1–10: A report of the fall of Jerusalem and the fate of Zedekiah.

39.11–14: A short footnote giving Nebuchadrezzar's instructions for the treatment of Jeremiah.

39.15–18: A further footnote, dating from an earlier period, in which Jeremiah gives a word of reassurance to a man who had rescued him from probable death.

INTERPRETATION

One common way for preachers to use the Old Testament is as a source of moral illustrations. We can find in it many examples which show what we consider good or bad behaviour. It would be very easy to do that with these chapters about Zedekiah. But should we? For our account of the message of the Old Testament should be directly related to our understanding of the intended message of the writer. Otherwise we can fall into the trap of using the Old Testament (or, for that matter, the New Testament) to say what we want to say, even though the intended message may be quite different.

We can use Jer. 38.24–28 to illustrate this. In these verses we find Zedekiah instructing Jeremiah what to say when government officials ask him about his conversation with the king. He is to give a deliberately misleading report. We could apply this passage in various ways. We could say that here Jeremiah compromises himself, and that under no circumstances should he have agreed to do this. Or we could use it as an example of telling a 'white' lie: although it is a lie, in these circumstances it protects the king and so is a good thing to do. Or again, we could see it as an example of obeying the head of state, respecting those in authority. Whichever application we chose we would in fact be arguing, on the basis of a belief reached *on other grounds*, that this passage supported our belief. In actual fact, as presented here it supports none of them; it is an incident mentioned without any comment, favourable or unfavourable.

Before we attempt to apply a passage to our own situation we need to identify its original meaning and purpose. So what is the chief concern of these three chapters? Clearly an important part is to report the coming of the promised destruction of Jerusalem. The final warning had been rejected (ch. 36) and now the judgement must be effected. And so, under Zedekiah's weak leadership we see the catastrophe approach and arrive. The certainty that God will fulfill what He has promised is a constantly recurring theme in the whole book, and we shall not consider it further at this point.

Of course it is not always easy to draw the line between an illustration or incident that reinforces the main theme and a sub-theme which, while being of secondary importance, is also present. But in the present chapters two sub-themes may be suggested as having been in the mind of the editors; to these we now turn.

LIKE MASTER, LIKE SERVANT

A substantial part of the book of Jeremiah is stories about the prophet. We cannot use it to compile his life history, for the biographical material is selected and edited to make particular points. But the sheer quantity of such material suggests that the writers were interested in Jeremiah's own experience. This is especially so with the present chapters.

Jeremiah has been presented as faithfully proclaiming that Babylon will destroy Jerusalem. As we saw in ch. 36, that message has been finally and fatefully rejected. Now that Jeremiah's message is to be proved true, and Jerusalem's doom is at hand, what will be the fate of the messenger? The answer given is that prophet and message received similar treatment. The brutalities of his treatment were similar to the horrors of the final days of the siege of the city. While a few listened and showed concern for Jeremiah, many were indifferent or hostile and some worked for his death.

This latter group's attack on Jeremiah is presented in two different accounts in chs 37—38. Although the details vary, the basic pattern of each passage is the same. Jeremiah was accused of activities hostile to the state, arrested, and dealt with summarily without any proper trial. He was imprisoned in a cistern where he would have died but for his rescue by Ebed-melech. Subsequently he managed to have a meeting with King Zedekiah, after which he remained under arrest but experienced greatly improved conditions.

The writers affirm two points. On the one hand, those who follow the Lord faithfully can expect harsh treatment from His opponents. On the other hand, and this is applied also to Ebed-melech (39.15–18), and Baruch (45.1–5), God can be trusted to protect His servants. There is a tension here: as it had been earlier (26.1–19), Jeremiah's life was spared; but Uriah had been killed (26.20–23). The present passage affirms both God's protective care for His servants and the hostility they will face, without concluding how the relationship between these principles will be worked out.

When we also take into account the New Testament we can see the balance between these two principles from a fresh perspective, that of belief in a life beyond this one. But within this life they still remain in tension. There is real opposition to Christianity. Sometimes it occurs in States that are openly opposed to Christianity; but just as often it may be elsewhere, in a State that is, in theory, sympathetic to Christians but which wishes to silence a protest at injustice or a campaign for freedom of speech. Hostility to Christians is known the world over. But so also is Christian testimony to God's protection. Sometimes it may be a miraculous deliverance; Peter's rescue in Acts 12 is one of many such deliverances. But more often it may come through the help of friends, as it did for Jeremiah. And, more importantly, Christians who have been through great hardship and even torture will often bear witness that their awareness of God's love and care was greater in their difficulties than they had ever known it before. In the middle of opposition the protection of God is clearly experienced.

FAITH WITHOUT CONVICTION

Although it is tempting to view the story of Zedekiah as a source of moral teaching, this is not the main concern of the editors. They are in fact more sympathetic to Zedekiah than to his brother Jehoiakim, and are much more concerned to expose the folly of a particular approach to faith.

Zedekiah's faith is one that hopes for the best but refuses to face reality. He asks for Jeremiah's prayers but refuses to listen to what Jeremiah actually says. He tries to please everyone and ends by pleasing no-one. He fears the members of his government more than the message of Jeremiah, and allows them to dictate what happens. He surrenders his responsibility to others, being himself too frightened to lead.

Zedekiah's problem was lack of conviction. When Indonesia became independent in 1965 all citizens were required to subscribe to one or other of four 'recognized' religions. As a result, the four approved faiths all recorded a marked growth in followers. For most of the new followers this was just a matter of convenience and had no conviction. Such faith is superficial; it has no real effect on character or behaviour nor, in the case of leaders, on policies. People with such faith look for a pleasant life, trying to keep on the right side of others and avoiding hard decisions of principle. When trouble comes they call for help, but in a helpless fashion, without real hope and without the will to change anything radically. They look for easy ways out, often hoping that they will have to make no decision at all. Such faith leads to a denial of responsibility, and those led – in Church or nation – can find themselves shipwrecked.

NOTES

37.2: People of the land: This may be a general term for the population, but it sometimes seems to refer to a group of important landowners in Judah and may have that meaning here.

37.3: Pray for us: A further example of the way that a prophet was expected to be an intercessor; see note on 7.16.

37.5: They withdrew from Jerusalem: See the discussion of ch. 34, p. 174.

37.10: Only wounded men: The Hebrew means those who are desperately wounded and out of the fight. Even a few such people would be enough to destroy Jerusalem.

37.12: Jeremiah set out ... to receive his portion: This cannot refer to the land that Jeremiah bought from Hanamel, since in ch. 32 Jeremiah was already under arrest. 'Portion' is an uncertain translation, but there is general agreement that it refers to some kind of property.

37.13: You are deserting: Since Jeremiah had been encouraging people to desert to Babylon (21.8–10; 38.2,19) Irijah's accusation was reasonable. In the Greek the account of Jeremiah's arrest is quite different; it is ascribed to the influence of a man who lodged with Jeremiah.

37.15: The princes were enraged ... beat him ... imprisoned him: The attitude of these government officials was quite different from that of the officials described in ch. 26. The earlier officials would have

'Zedekiah's faith is one that hopes for the best, but refuses to face reality.' The sick people queueing at a mobile clinic in India have faith that doctors and nurses will heal them. But only those who accept the treatment and medicine given are likely to be made well. Those who refuse because they fear it will be painful may continue to suffer.

been deported ten years earlier with Jehoiachin, and there is no reason to assume that their successors should have had the same attitude towards Jeremiah. Moreover, in ch. 26 the charge was basically of apostasy, whereas here it was of treason; we would expect political leaders to see the two charges differently.

37.16: Dungeon cells: It is literally 'to the house of the pit and to the cells'. For this 'pit' see note on 38.6.

37.17: Is there any word ...? ... There is: Zedekiah's initial reaction was probably one of delight, to be shattered by the message that followed.

37.19: Where are your prophets: Jeremiah, imprisoned for making a true prophecy, asked ironically what punishment had been given to the false prophets!

37.21: Until all the bread of the city was gone: 52.6f reports that the ending of the bread supply coincided with the breaching of the city wall.

38.1: Jucal ... Pashhur: Jucal is the Jehucal of 37.3; Pashhur was a member of the earlier delegation from Zedekiah reported at 21.1.

38.4: He is weakening the hands of the soldiers: One of the letters from Lachish (see note on 34.6) also criticizes defeatist elements among Jerusalem officials.

38.5: The king can do nothing against you: This was probably not just flattery. Since Zedekiah was only reigning by Nebuchadrezzar's permission, any complaint about him by a government official might lead to his deposition.

38.6: The cistern: This may have been some kind of solitary confinement or punishment cell, or even a pit latrine. Although there was no water in it, the muddy slime at the bottom would have been extremely insanitary, leading to quick death.

Malchiah, the king's son: The Greek omits these words. For 'king's son' see note on 36.26.

38.7: Ebed-melech, the Ethiopian, a eunuch: His name meant the king's servant, and he came from the region of Ethiopia or Sudan. For 'eunuch' see note on 29.2.

38.11: A wardrobe of the storehouse: This involves a slight emendation of the Hebrew. Different English translations make different suggestions.

38.14: Third entrance: The location of this is unknown. It was perhaps one of the three main entrances to the Temple (cf. the three keepers of the threshold); alternatively, it may refer to the king's private entrance to the Temple.

38.16: Swore secretly: Although the conversation was in view of others (vv. 25–27), it was not overheard. Zedekiah's fear of the princes is again stressed.

38.17: If you will surrender ... your life shall be spared: Zedekiah is offered only one hope of survival: surrender; prosperity is beyond the bounds of possibility. The following verse spells out the consequence of rejecting this advice.

38.19: I am afraid of the Jews who have deserted to the Chaldeans: Again Zedekiah is presented as afraid of others. He would have opposed these Jews' policies, so they might well be ill-disposed towards him.

38.22: Your trusted friends ... turn away from you: There is irony in this verse. It had been Jeremiah who was stuck in the mud; now it will be the king.

38.26: House of Jonathan: This is the first mention of Jonathan in this chapter (cf. 37.15). The context clearly assumes this house to be identical with the cistern of Malchiah in v.6.

39.1: Ninth year ... tenth month: This would be January – February 588 BC. For accounts parallel to this chapter see 2 Kings 25.1–12; Jer. 52 and Ezek. 24.1–2.

39.3: All the princes: Comparison of the English translations shows that the names and titles of these officials are not entirely clear.

39.4: They fled: Having resisted Babylon for so long, to stay would be to invite quick death; to flee was the only hope.

The Arabah: Here this refers to the Jordan valley; elsewhere the term can also refer to the continuation of the Rift Valley south of the Dead Sea.

39.5: Riblah: This was an ancient Syrian town, south of Kadesh, on the river Orontes (see Map 1, p. 234). It was a strategic base where the military highways for Egypt and Mesopotamia met. Nebuchadrezzar directed his campaign from here.

39.8: The house of the people: In the light of the parallel account in 52.13 the NEB reads 'the house of the LORD and the houses of the people'.

39.9: Nebuzaradan: The guard in question was probably the imperial bodyguard.

Carried into exile ... those who had deserted ... who remained: In 21.8f and 38.2 we find that Jeremiah promises life to the deserters and death to the others. Now it appears that both deserters and those left alive in the city were deported.

39.14: Gedaliah: Gedaliah was the son of Ahikam, one of Jeremiah's earlier benefactors (cf. 26.24).

Home: This was probably the official residence that he occupied by virtue of his status as governor.

39.16: Ebed-melech the Ethiopian: See note on 38.7.

39.18: Life as a prize of war: The same phrase occurs at 21.9; 38.2; 45.5.

STUDY SUGGESTIONS

REVIEW OF CONTENT

1. Why would it be wrong to use these chapters merely to comment on Zedekiah's moral behaviour?
2. What steps must we take before we can apply a passage like this one to our own situation?
3. How can we try to relate God's promise to care for His children with the suffering that some have to endure?
4. What reassurance would Ebed-melech find in Jeremiah's message to him?
5. What was the weakness of Zedekiah's faith?

BIBLE STUDY

6. Consider Jeremiah 26.20–23; in the light of the present passage what if anything, could you say to Uriah's relatives about God's care for His servants? Do Mark 10.28–30 and Hebrews 11 add anything further?
7. In what ways is the behaviour of Felix (Acts 24.1–27) and Herod (Matt.14.1–12) similar to that of Zechariah?

DISCUSSION AND APPLICATION

8. What sort of suffering or injustice concerns the members of your Church most? Do they see God as genuinely concerned about it? What things can they do to help those experiencing it?
9. Many things in the world speak of heartache. How do we try to reassure those who have experienced tragedy (whether through persecution or through some other sort of suffering) of God's love?
10. What are the main reasons for weak or 'nominal' faith in your society? How does the Church try to show people that such faith is only nominal, and lead them on to a real faith?
11. In what ways have you felt the temptation to follow Christ on the surface but not from the heart? What has helped your commitment grow deeper?
12. Why, in your opinion, do we sometimes value other people's opinions of us more highly than God's opinion?
13. Why do you think God allowed Jeremiah to be thrown into the cistern, and to suffer because of the prophecy he had been given?

40.1—43.7
From Gedaliah to Egypt

OUTLINE

This section traces the course of events after the fall of Jerusalem. Gedaliah is appointed governor of Judah by Nebuchadrezzar but is then murdered; one influential group then decides to escape to Egypt. Jeremiah is present at the start, going to join Gedaliah at Mizpah, but is not mentioned again until he is asked for advice by those intent on going to Egypt.

40.1–6: Jeremiah, in captivity with those awaiting exile to Babylon, is released and given the freedom to decide his own future.

40.7–12: Gedaliah proclaims an amnesty for those who have been resisting Babylon and for some who have returned from exile in neighbouring countries.

40.13–18: Gedaliah is warned that a former guerilla leader called Ishmael plans to kill him, but disbelieves the warning.

41.1–3: Ishmael and his supporters murder Gedaliah.

41.4–10: After committing more murders, Ishmael takes hostages and flees east.

41.11–18: Johanan leads a rescue operation which frees the hostages, though Ishmael escapes. Johanan and those with him decide to go to Egypt.

42.1–6: Johanan and his associates seek Jeremiah's advice about going to Egypt.

42.7–22: Jeremiah replies that God's will is for the people to stay in Judah, and warns of severe consequences if they go to Egypt.

43.1–7: Jeremiah's advice is rejected and the group goes to Egypt, taking Jeremiah with them.

INTERPRETATION

THE TRAGEDY OF REJECTED ADVICE

'If only I had known', people sometimes say, 'I would never have made that decision.' Failure in communication causes many problems. People forget to deliver messages or decide that they are not urgent. The postal service is not able to deliver a letter in time. The telephone is not working. Advice is not received. Problems follow.

But problems also have another cause. Advice is received but not heeded. Smokers are warned that they are more liable to get lung cancer, but they continue to smoke. Alcoholics are warned that they can die from liver failure, but they continue to drink. A political leader is advised that his policy will lead the country into a disastrous war, but he goes ahead and the country suffers.

In these chapters we find two different examples of ignored advice. First come Johanan's words to Gedaliah, 40.13–16. Both Ishmael, who came from the royal family (41.1) and Johanan were among the leaders of some small resistance groups which had made as their bases cities that the Babylonian army had earlier devastated. Babylon knew well how difficult it was to deal with small guerilla groups, and wanted to find a compromise solution that would satisfy the guerillas and at the same time release Babylonian troops for service in other parts of the empire. So Gedaliah, the governor that Nebuchadrezzar had appointed, proclaimed a general amnesty and these guerilla leaders came to him to discuss the proposals.

The peace talks were successful. However, a little later, Johanan warned Gedaliah that Ishmael was planning to assassinate him. We do not know what evidence he had. Whatever it was, it did not convince Gedaliah, who probably just thought that it was a case of rivalry between the two men. He continued to treat Ishmael as a trusted friend and paid for it with his life.

We can sympathize with Gedaliah's difficulties in trying to discover where the truth lay. Politics is a tricky business, full of jugglings and uncertainties. Today's friend may be tomorrow's enemy. Two thousand years ago the Roman leader Julius Caesar found that his friend Brutus was among his assassins. In recent years President Thomas Sankara of Burkina Faso was overthrown by political colleagues led by the man who had been his closest ally. A president is unhappy about a vice-president or general and removes him from office. His move may be successful, but the person newly appointed may prove to be an even bigger threat; alternatively, the one ousted and now disaffected may lead a rebellion. Gedaliah's murder was just one more example in the ongoing history of political misjudgements.

The second example, which we find in 42.1–43.7, is quite different. After they had freed the hostages that Ishmael had taken, Johanan and his colleagues decided that Babylon might well take reprisals, and that they would be likely to suffer. So they made plans to go to Egypt, which was then the only neighbouring country not under Babylonian control. But first they asked Jeremiah to tell them God's wishes, promising that they would follow them. When the advice came it was the opposite of what they had hoped and expected; it did not fit with their wishes. Jeremiah reminded them that they had sworn to do God's will, and warned them of disastrous consequences if they went to Egypt. But they declared that he was a liar who had not understood God's message. Then they set off for Egypt, taking Jeremiah with them.

Not to know the will of God is one thing, but it is quite another to spurn it deliberately. What Johanan and his colleagues really wanted was God's approval for the plans on which they had already decided; they were not interested in finding and following God's plans. Because of this, they lost any remaining chance of a prosperous future. The story makes quite clear why there could be no hope that any 'remnant' would come from those who were left in Judah and now planned to go to Egypt. Even after Jerusalem's destruction they remained totally indifferent to God's will. So the hope for the future would lie with those in Exile in Babylon.

When we have a strong desire for something we may try to convince ourselves that it is God's will. We try to select passages of Scripture that will fit our wishes, rather than allowing Scripture to guide us. We may appeal to our personal feelings: 'The Lord has told me', said an unqualified person to a famous preacher, 'that I'm to preach from your pulpit next Sunday'; 'Excellent, my brother', replied the preacher, 'When He tells me as well, then you can!'

This reminds us once again that we need to cultivate an openness to what God may have to say to us, and then to follow it. We do well to remember that we should not normally come to major decisions on our own without first seeking the advice of others we respect. The Spirit of guidance, the Holy Spirit, comes to us not on a purely individual basis but within the family of the Church. If all the family members advise us against something it will be very rare that we should disregard them. We need to listen to others and not prejudge the issues.

NOTES

40.1: The word that came to Jeremiah: This verse makes a heading to what follows. In view of 39.12 it is surprising to find Jeremiah in chains at Ramah. Some scholars have suggested that, after his release in Jerusalem, a unit of the Babylonian army picked him up, ignoring his protests; the discipline of conquering troops frequently breaks down. Alternatively, this story and that in 39.14 may be two versions of a single tradition: in both accounts Jeremiah is released by Babylon, stays in Judah, and is associated with Gedaliah.

40.2: The LORD your God pronounced this evil: Similar ideas are expressed at 22.8f. Is Nebuzaradan here sincere or mocking?

40.4: Come with me to Babylon: The invitation to go to Babylon must have had many attractions for Jeremiah. He would have found a well-appointed city with a comfort lacking in the ruined territory of Judah. Also, it could be argued, since God's future for Judah lay with Jehoiachin's fellow-exiles, that he could influence these exiles for good. But it seemed right to him to remain in Judah and so he declined the offer.

40.5: If you remain: This follows the Syriac; the Hebrew is unclear. **Gedaliah ... appointed governor:** This is the first mention of Gedaliah being governor. His family had been sympathetic to Jeremiah (see 26.24 and 36.10–12, 25).

Allowance of food: This would have been for Jeremiah's journey to Mizpah.

40.6: Mizpah: The new administrative capital lay 13 kms north of Jerusalem (Map 3, p. 236). Not only was the old capital in total ruins; it would have been Babylon's deliberate policy to shun it.

40.7: Captains ... their men: This describes various small guerilla groups that had continued to resist Babylon.

40.8: Johanan the son of Kareah: The RSV follows the Greek; some English versions follow the Hebrew, which reads, 'Johanan and Jonathan the sons of Kareah'.

40.10: Gather wine and summer fruits and oil: Although this implies that the harvest could be enjoyed, no doubt some of it would go as tribute to Babylon! **Taken:** This is literally 'seized', or 'captured'. We should think of these units reoccupying some of the cities destroyed and abandoned by the Babylonian army; this is much more probable than imagining that the guerillas had defeated the Babylonians in a full-scale battle.

40.12: Then all the Jews returned: Those returning from voluntary exile in neighbouring countries may have been Babylonian sympathizers or political refugees from the days of Jehoiakim or Zedekiah. Alternatively, they may have been Jews who, in order to avoid being exiled to Babylon, fled abroad as Judah and Jerusalem fell.

40.14: Baalis: Perhaps Baalis was still partly resisting Babylon and did not want a Babylonian sympathizer as governor in Judah.

41.1–2: As they ate bread: To eat bread was a sign of fellowship; to kill in such a context was a total betrayal of traditional hospitality. Ishmael's motives are not known; it would hardly have been realistic for him to have expected that he himself could have become governor. No year is stated and the initial assumption would be that these events closely followed those of the previous chapters, so that it was still very soon after the actual fall of Jerusalem. However, since there was obviously time for refugees to return and gather harvest it is much more likely that there was an interval of perhaps a couple of years. In this case, the third Exile reported at 52.30 may have been a reprisal for Gedaliah's murder.

41.5: Eighty men arrived: This delegation from the north was going to the ruins of the Jerusalem temple, mourning its fate. The seventh month (41.1) was the time of the great autumn festival and of the Day of Atonement, and this may have been the occasion of the pilgrimage.

41.6–7: Ishmael ... slew them: The Greek states that it was the pilgrims who were weeping. Why Ishmael should have wished to kill these men is unclear.

41.8: We have stores: Which fields were they referring to? Since they came from the north they could hardly have had these stores with them.

41.9: Which King Asa had made: 1 Kings 15.22 records the building of Mizpah by Asa; this took place late in the tenth century or early in the ninth century BC.

41.10: King's daughters: A general term for any of the women connected with the royal family. Ishmael obviously hoped to use these hostages to ensure his safe escape to the east; he succeeded.

41.17: Geruth Chimham: Chimham was a son of the Barzillai who assisted David (2 Sam. 19.31–40). The precise site is unknown.

42.2: Pray to the LORD your God: Once again the prophet is seen as an intercessor. 'Your' is singular, and so refers to Jeremiah's God who may not necessarily be theirs. Jeremiah's immediate reply, v. 4, makes it clear that the LORD is also their God (or should be!).

42.7: At the end of ten days: As at 28.11f, Jeremiah has to wait for God's answer.

42.10: I repent of the evil: Usually we use 'repent' to mean that we change our mind and regret our past behaviour, but it would be misleading to understand it in exactly that way here. The NEB's 'I grieve for' carries the right idea. God's activity towards the people has now reached a new stage. God's 'repentance' comes because there is a changed situation which means that His policy can now also change (cf. 18.7f).

42.12: Let you remain: This requires a slight change of the Hebrew; those versions which retain the Hebrew unchanged read 'let you return'. The general point is that these people are in God's hands and not just in Nebuchadrezzar's.

42.14: Shall not ... hear the sound of the trumpet: See note on 4.5; they hope to be free from battle.

42.18: Execration: An 'execration' was a fierce curse, often accompanied by a ritual action which was believed to set the curse into operation.

43.2: The insolent men ... telling a lie: 'Insolent' refers to godless, rebellious men. Earlier (see p. 49) we saw that Jeremiah accused the people of Jerusalem of being false; now the charge is thrown back at him.

43.3: Baruch: See further on ch. 45, p. 202.

43.7: Tahpanhes: See note on 2.16. There Tahpanhes was an enemy, taking advantage of Judah; now it is regarded as a refuge. But in fact it will give no security, for its days are numbered like the days of those who seek refuge there (cf. Ezek. 30.18).

STUDY SUGGESTIONS

REVIEW OF CONTENT

1. What are the likely reasons for Gedaliah's ignoring the warning about Ishmael?
2. (a) Why did Johanan and his associates wish to go to Egypt?
   (b) What reasons did they give for ignoring Jeremiah's advice? What do you think were their real reasons for ignoring it?
3. What reasons does this chapter give for God's continued rejection of those who remained in Judah after the fall of Jerusalem?

BIBLE STUDY

4. Note the following examples of advice given, the reasons for it, whether or not it was taken, and the final outcome:
   (a) Gen. 41.1–57
   (b) Exod. 18.13–27
   (c) 1 Kings 12.1–20
   (d) Acts 5.33–40
   (e) Acts 23.12–35

DISCUSSION AND APPLICATION

5. How do we try to assess the advice that other people give us? What tests do we apply?
6. Describe any occasions when you have asked others for advice but have in fact already made up your mind?
7. How can we avoid the temptation to try and twist the Bible to say what we want it to?
8. Imagine that your Church leader is convinced that the Church should follow a particular plan, but no-one in the congregation agrees. What would happen?

43.8—44.30
Jeremiah in Egypt

OUTLINE

These verses are our only record of Jeremiah's activity in Egypt. Like the previous chapters they stress the stubbornness and apostasy of the Jews who have come to Egypt. They also re-emphasize that Yahweh's sovereignty extends to Egypt.

43.8–13: A short account of an act of prophetic symbolism which Jeremiah performed soon after the exiles arrived in Tahpanhes. It declares that one day Nebuchadrezzar will control this region.

44.1–14: A sermon declaring God's total judgement on the Jews in Egypt because of their apostasy.

44.15–19: The exiles respond that it was when they had worshipped other gods in addition to Yahweh that things had gone well for them.

44.20–30: Jeremiah replies, confirming God's judgement.

INTERPRETATION

INTERPRETING HISTORY

Both Jeremiah and the Jewish exiles knew the recent history of Judah. Not many would have been old enough to remember the reign of Manasseh, but they would all have known about it. However, the ways in which they understood the past eighty years were quite different.

Jeremiah saw the destruction of Jerusalem by Babylon as the consequence of God's judgement on the sin of Judah. Throughout the long reign of Manasseh the worship of many other gods and goddesses was practised as well as that of Yahweh. Josiah attempted a reform, but after his death the reform lapsed, and once again many different gods were worshipped. Jeremiah believed that Jerusalem lay in ruins because Yahweh had not been faithfully followed.

The exiles in Pathros saw things very differently. They looked back to the time of Manasseh as a time of peace and stability, and believed that this had been so because the people had been worshipping not only Yahweh but also these other gods. They claimed that it was only when King Josiah prevented people from worshipping other gods that the problems began. Since that time Josiah had been

killed in battle, and Judah had been continuously under the domination of foreigners, first Egypt and then Babylon. The key to
restoration, they argued, was a return to the worship of many gods.

The two groups came to different conclusions although they
started with the same evidence. Although we might argue that the
exiles' theory ignored the fact that for the past twenty years many
gods *had* been worshipped in Jerusalem, the main reason for the
different conclusions lay elsewhere. They started with different
assumptions.

Jeremiah began with the conviction that Yahweh was the true
God, the God of Israel, and that the people of Judah should worship
only Him; failure to do this would lead to problems. By contrast, the
exiles believed that there was no harm in worshipping a variety of
gods; indeed there was safety in numbers! They believed that the
failure to acknowledge all these deities had caused the present
problems. Both sides could look at history and find evidence to
support their beliefs; we could compare this with the way that the
understanding of Jeremiah's willingness to conceal the content of his
conversation with Zedekiah could depend on the starting point of
the interpreter, see p. 182.

As in the case of the contradictory prophecies in chs 27—29, it
would not be easy for hearers to decide who was right. Evidence can
be used selectively, to confirm our natural instincts or what we
would like to believe. This is perhaps particularly so in the sphere of
religious faith, where we are not dealing with something that can be
either established or disproved by evidence of a 'scientific' kind.
There may be very good reasons for faith, but reasons and proof are
distinct. One Christian leader used to say that when he prayed he
found 'coincidences' happening, and when he stopped praying they
ceased to happen; in matters of faith we are seldom dealing with
conclusive 'proof'.

This whole issue is a useful reminder that our starting point
influences our conclusions; we can often find evidence supporting
the conclusions that we wish to reach. For instance, if we consider
the variety of theological attitudes to Jesus over the past 150 years
they often tell us more about the attitudes and values of the various
theologians than about Jesus Himself. One of the positive insights
that has emerged in recent years is the recognition of the close link
between gospel and culture, and the corresponding need to try and
distinguish the two. The way the gospel is appropriately applied in
one culture may be very different from the best way to apply it in
another. To be able to apply the gospel rightly we need a right
starting point for our understanding of God. This was where
Jeremiah and the exiles disagreed.

OUR IDEAS OF GOD

The real difference between Jeremiah and the exiles lay in their concepts of God. The exiles saw no reason why, if there were many gods, they should not worship them all (or at least many of them). Each god, they thought, might be responsible for particular geographical areas or different aspects of life, and one who was neglected and offended might cause the people to suffer. So the safest path lay in trying to keep all the gods happy.

Jeremiah believed this was utter folly. He saw Yahweh as not only their God but *the* God. Other gods were not even to be considered. Yahweh was far, far greater than these exiles realized. They had in fact made a god in their own image, one who was limited and whom people could choose to worship as they wished. Jeremiah could not accept this, for he had grasped something of the fact that God is king over every part of the universe and every aspect of life. Such a God, he insisted, required total commitment.

The need for total commitment to God is one that constantly recurs. We can see this in the Western world in situations where Christianity has become part of the established routine of life. Once it takes on this role, some people will wish to try and 'tame' it, so that it is kept in its proper 'place'. According to such a viewpoint, Christianity should be controlled and not controller, since it is considered to be a personal matter which should not 'interfere' in politics or public affairs. But, in reality, if God is truly the Lord of all He cannot be omitted from certain parts of it. Commitment to Him requires a faith that affects every part of life.

Another way that faith in God requires total commitment is in the search for religious truth. Some believe that all religions lead to God and that people should therefore be left to follow their particular faith, whether it be a major world religion or a more local traditional one. It is possible to be unduly negative about other religions, and we should welcome the insights that we may receive through members of other faiths. It is simply not true that there are no valuable insights about the nature of God in, for example, Islam, or Hinduism or traditional religions.

However, just as Jeremiah asserted that Yahweh was the one, true God, the Christian faith acknowledges Christ as the way, the truth and the life. If we accept that, we are surely foolish or inconsistent to divide our loyalties between Christ and some other revelation: the Christian faith calls for nothing less than a total commitment.

'Jeremiah believed that Yahweh was the true God.' The people exiled in Egypt saw no harm in worshipping many different gods.' Some people today believe all religions lead to God; others believe there is no God at all. And some, like those Jeremiah condemned, believe that true worship can be combined with calling upon spirits, for example through the practice of Obeah or Voodoo, as in Haiti.

NOTES

43.9: Pharaoh's palace: 'Government building', as in the GNB, gives the right idea. The Pharaoh did not live in Tahpanhes, but would have stayed in this building when he visited the town.

43.10: Nebuchadrezzar ... my servant: See note on 25.9.

He will set: Here, and at v. 12 ('he shall kindle'), the Hebrew reads 'I'. These things result directly from God's activity.

Royal canopy: This was a sign of Nebuchadrezzar's presence, much as today a flag may indicate the presence of a head of state or diplomatic representative. It probably refers to a pavilion or tent, though a special carpet has also been suggested.

43.11: Giving to the pestilence ... sword: Cf. 15.2.

43.12: Temples of the gods: These were supposed to be the centres of power for Egyptian religion; they will be shown to be powerless.

He shall clean ... as a shepherd cleans: The image is that of a shepherd carefully checking his clothes to rid them of lice. An alternative translation pictures the shepherd wrapping his garment round him to keep warm at night; similarly, Egypt will be so completely under the power of Babylon that it will be wrapped round Nebuchadrezzar at his will.

43.13: Obelisks of Heliopolis: Obelisks were sacred stone pillars, not unlike the *masseboth*, the pillars which Jeremiah condemned in Judah. Heliopolis (Map 1, p. 234), 8 kms north-east of Cairo, was the site of a great temple dedicated to the Sun. In 568–567 BC, while Amasis was Pharaoh, Nebuchadrezzar conducted a campaign into part of western Egypt; it was a raid rather than a total subjugation of the country.

44.1: Migdol ... Tahpanhes ... Memphis ... Pathros: Whereas 43.8–13 concerned only the group of exiles under Johanan's leadership, this chapter is addressed to all Jewish exiles in Egypt; there were obviously several such communities. Those who make the response in vv. 15–19, and to whom Jeremiah further speaks in vv. 20–30, are representatives from Pathros. Migdol and Tahpanhes were near the mouth of the Nile; Memphis was the chief city of Lower (northern) Egypt, and Pathros a general term for Upper Egypt, the southern part of the country (see Map 1, p. 234).

44.3: Burn incense: Here and later in this chapter a better translation is probably 'sacrifice' (see note on 1.16).

44.4: Persistently: See note on 7.13.

44.8: Works of your hands: The context suggests that this means idolatry; the phrase can also refer more generally to behaviour.

44.11: I will set my face: Compare also 'Those who have set their faces' in v. 12. See note on 21.10.

44.12: Execration: See note on 42.18.

44.17: We will do: The Hebrew is emphatic, 'We will certainly do . . .'

Queen of heaven: See the discussion of 7.18, p. 52. There the **libations** were offered to other gods, here they are offered specifically to Astarte. Chapter 7 focused on the fact of family worship, here attention is directed towards the women's role in it.

44.19: Was it without our husbands' approval: This is perhaps a further allusion to the husband's authority in Jewish society. According to Numbers 30.6–8, a husband could cancel his wife's vow.

Cakes for her bearing her image: See the discussion of 7.18, p. 52, and also Amos 5.26.

44.21: People of the land: Here, the term is best seen as a general one for the whole population, not just a particular group within it (cf. the note on 37.2).

44.23: His law . . . statutes . . . testimonies: These terms are used here (as they often are in Deuteronomy) in a general sense. Strictly, 'statutes' were written laws which had become part of the official behaviour required, while 'testimonies' were conditions attached to the covenant, and were particularly solemn since there was stress on their divine origin.

44.25–26: Perform your vows: We could paraphrase the thought here as God saying, 'By all means keep your vows, but you had better note Mine..!'

I have sworn by my great name: For the significance of such an oath, see note on 22.5.

44.27: I am watching over: See 1.12 and the note on it.

44.28: Shall know whose word will stand, mine or theirs: As in ch. 28, the passage of time will eventually show who is right.

44.30: Hophra: Hophra became Pharaoh after Neco and ruled from 598–570 BC. It was he who had promised to help Zedekiah in 588 BC and was the cause of Nebuchadrezzar's temporary withdrawal from Jerusalem. From 570 BC he was joint ruler with Amasis, who deposed him and had him executed in 567 BC.

STUDY SUGGESTIONS

REVIEW OF CONTENT

1. (a) What different conclusions did Jeremiah and the exiles in Egypt reach about the reasons for the fall of Jerusalem?

   (b) Why do you think they came to these different conclusions?

2. Why does our starting point often influence our conclusions?

3. How would you compare the different views of God held by Jeremiah and the exiles? Make a list of the similarities and the differences that you think would stand out.
4. What kind of commitment does the Christian faith call for in the search for religious truth?

BIBLE STUDY

5. What different views of God are suggested by each of the following passages?
   (a) 1 Kings 18.20–29
   (b) 1 Kings 20.23
   (c) Ps. 32
   (d) Isa. 40.12–31
   (e) Acts 17.22–31
   (f) Phil. 2.5–11
6. How determined do you think the following were to seek out and follow the truth?
   (a) Ahab and Jehoshaphat: 1 Kings 22.1–28
   (b) Josiah: 2 Kings 22.1—23.25
   (c) The Jewish leaders: Matt. 22.15–22
   (d) Niocodemus: John 3.1–15
   (e) The Ethiopian: Acts 8.26–40

DISCUSSION AND APPLICATION

7. How would you try to decide between two groups, both linked with the Church and yet giving you contradictory advice?
8. How closely do you think the Christian gospel is linked with your own culture? Is it possible to distinguish the two?
9. What kinds of things do you think that Christians can learn from other faiths? If you can, give examples of what you have learned from another faith?
10. What effect does John 14.6 have on your attitude to other faiths?

45.1–5
A Message for Baruch

OUTLINE

Chronologically, this short chapter stands quite separate from what has gone before. It relates to the time of ch. 36, the production of the scroll read to Jehoiakim. The verses warn Baruch that, in view of the collapse of the world around him, he should not hold great personal ambitions. But together with this warning comes an assurance that his own life would be spared.

Although it does not follow directly from ch. 44, in two ways this chapter rounds off chs 37—45. Firstly, it provides a link back to ch. 36, where Jerusalem's fate was sealed; since then we have seen that fate enacted. (We should note that Baruch is also prominent in ch. 36.) Secondly, like 39.15–18, which is also out of chronological sequence, it follows a story of great devastation. In ch. 39, in spite of the approaching destruction of Jerusalem, Ebed-melech is promised his personal safety. Now, in ch. 45, although it has been declared that God's judgement will fall on those who go to Egypt, Baruch is exempted from that threat. He too, in a world that is collapsing, has a future.

INTERPRETATION

REALISTIC PRIORITIES

Although later Jewish tradition developed many stories about Baruch and his relationship to Jeremiah, within the book of Jeremiah we learn little about Baruch. He appears in just four passages: 32.12–15 and 36.4–32, where he seems to be some sort of assistant to Jeremiah; 43.2–6, where, having opposed those with Johanan who want to go into Exile in Egypt, he is accused of having falsely influenced Jeremiah; and the present passage.

Traditionally, in the light of ch. 36, Baruch has often been described as Jeremiah's secretary. Some scholars have developed this idea and imagined him as the one responsible for the biographical material and the editing of a large part of our book of Jeremiah. This suggestion has certain attractions and cannot be ruled out; however, it remains a suggestion that we have no way of confirming.

A brother of Baruch called Seraiah appears at 51.59. Both brothers were used as Jeremiah's messengers. Baruch conveyed the written word of doom to the people of Judah and to Jehoiakim in particular; Seraiah conveyed the written word of doom to Babylon (and so implicitly a message of deliverance for Judah). Since Seraiah was accompanying Zedekiah he is likely to have been a person of some importance; this and 43.2–6 suggest that Baruch too could have been an influential person.

All of us have ambitions. We need to be sure they are appropriate. Sometimes we fail to recognize that when circumstances change our ambitions may also need to change. We make the mistake of keeping the same goals even though they are no longer suitable. There are times when to be content with mere survival is close to being heretical; there are other times when just to survive is a great triumph. In prison in Hitler's Germany in the 1940s, Dietrich Bonhoeffer recognized that the country and its society were bound to experience great destruction. This would have to take place before there could be any thought of building for the future. And so he wrote, 'It will be the task of our generation, not to "seek great things", but to save and preserve our souls out of the chaos, and to realize that it is the only thing we can carry as a "prize" from the burning building.'

In our own situations we need to recognize the time, and shape our goals accordingly. This is true for both individuals and the Church as a whole, locally and nationally. In no situation, least of all when there is great social upheaval, should personal ambition dominate our attitudes. Over the past fifty years some countries have faced a whole series of upheavals. Tragically, in such situations public figures have sometimes made personal profit at the country's expense. Public service should be service, not exploitation. When it is, God does remember the individual for good.

This is the core of the message for Baruch. In more settled times he could have expected to rise to an important post within the administration of Judah. As it is, he is destined to go to Egypt as an exile in very depressing circumstances. He might have felt his life was wasted and hardly worth living. The message for him makes two points. On the one hand, when all is crumbling round him traditional priorities must be radically altered; how wrong he would be to set his heart on human triumph and importance. But on the other hand, even in the middle of so much death and destruction God will continue to care for him, and his life will be preserved.

NOTES

45.1: These words in a book: Since the content of chs 37—44 comes from a time much later than that of Jehoiakim, **these words** cannot refer to the preceding chapters. Since the date in 45.1 is the same as that of 36.1 we may be intended to recognize a reference to the scroll of ch. 36. If this is correct, the message was probably originally an encouragement to Baruch, who at that time was risking a successful career by being linked with Jeremiah against King Jehoiakim.

45.3: Woe is me: Jeremiah frequently expressed such an attitude; here it is found in one of his associates.

45.4: What I have built ... whole land: The language can be compared with 1.10. Baruch is not alone in his grief for there is at least a hint of divine agony here. By implication, God is asking, 'Do you imagine that it is easy for Me to treat My creation in this way?'. Baruch may feel that he is suffering agony, but God's sorrow should put Baruch's feelings into perspective.

45.5: Do you seek great things for yourself: The GNB translates, 'Are you looking for special treatment for yourself?' Since Jerusalem is collapsing, why should Baruch expect to be better off than others? Some English versions see it as a statement rather than a question, but the point is unchanged.

A prize of war: See note on 21.9.

STUDY SUGGESTIONS

REVIEW OF CONTENT

1. What do we know about Baruch? Why have some people suggested that he was Jeremiah's secretary?
2. Why are personal ambitions sometimes inappropriate?
3. What other sorrow is mentioned in the chapter, other than Baruch's?

BIBLE STUDY

4. In what ways do you note God's concern in the following passages? Exod. 3.7–10; Jonah 3.3—4.11, Luke 1.68–79; 2 Pet. 3.9.
5. What do you think were the basic ambitions of the following people and where did their ambitions lead?
   (a) Abimelech: Judges 9.1–57
   (b) Rehoboam: 1 Kings 12.1–24
   (c) Haman: Esther 3.1—7.10
   (d) Daniel: Dan. 6.1–24
   (e) James and John: Mark 10.35–44
   (f) Simon Magus: Acts 8.9–24

6. Compare what, in the light of this passage, you understand to have been Baruch's attitude with Paul's approach in Phil. 3.4–14.

DISCUSSION AND APPLICATION

7. Sometimes, because we think of God as omnipotent, we do not think of His having emotions: how important is it for people to realize that God feels real sorrow? What difference does it make to realize this?
8. Is it good to have high ambitions? How would you advise someone of ability who had high ambitions?

Special Note G
Oracles Against the Nations

The story of Balaam in Numbers 22—24 illustrates one widespread feature of life in Ancient South-western Asia, the denouncing by a religious leader of various nations. Jeremiah 28.8 regards such oracles as a recognized feature of Israelite prophecy and within the prophetic books are several collections of such messages: e.g. Isaiah 13—23, Ezekiel 25—32, Amos 1—2, Zephaniah 2—3. The whole of Obadiah and Nahum are given over to the denunciation of foreign nations.

Like prophetic symbolism, such oracles were believed to be highly effective. Sometimes they were delivered as part of a political conflict (e.g. Num. 22.4), while at others they may have been used to claim the power of one religion over another. Within ancient Israel their use may have originated in the political sphere or the cultic (religious) one: because of the people's understanding of life as a unity these two could not, in fact, be completely distinguished. By the time of Jeremiah we are dealing with a kind of literature that has become traditional. Both language and imagery are often conventional, and we find that very similar ideas recur in different oracles. Some passages used elsewhere in Jeremiah are re-used in chs 46—51, and some closely related material is found in other Old Testament books. This demonstrates well the fact that often a common stock of material is being used; we should therefore interpret it in general terms and not be too concerned with all the details.

As well as being stylized, such oracles often include references to various places in the countries concerned. We cannot always identify these places and shall not spend time discussing their location. Our focus will be the basic point of the verse or passage.

STUDY SUGGESTIONS

1. Why do you think that in ancient Israel it was difficult to distinguish between the political and the religious spheres of life? Would it be equally difficult to distinguish between them in your country today? Give your reasons.
2. Why should we concern ourselves chiefly with understanding the oracles against the nations in general terms, and not try to give accurate interpretations of all the details they contain?

46.1—49.39
Judgement on the Nations (1)

OUTLINE

The last major section of the book of Jeremiah, chs 46—51, illustrates Jeremiah's role as a 'prophet to the nations' (1.5,10). It contains oracles of judgement on various nations, most of them near neighbours which had caused Judah problems at different times in the past.

Because so much of it is general in nature we cannot tell just when the material in these chapters was produced. Some may have taken its earliest form before Jeremiah, and further material may have been added after Jeremiah's own activity. We need have no doubt that Jeremiah himself did deliver oracles against various nations.

The order in which the nations are addressed is quite similar to that in 25.19–26, though not all the nations mentioned in ch. 25 are found here and ch. 25 does not include Damascus. There may be some kind of geographical arrangement with a gradual move from the nations in the west to those in the east. There is clearly a climax with Babylon. As mentioned in Special Note F, p. 145, the Greek version places these oracles in a different order and much earlier in the book, after 25.13a and before 25.15–38. The location of the countries concerned is shown on Map 1, p. 234.

46.1: A heading for chs 46—51.

46.2–28: The focus of this chapter is Egypt. Verses 2–12 describe the total defeat of its army and vv. 13–24 the ruin of the land. Two footnotes follow, the first (vv. 25f) concerned with Egypt's judgement, the second (vv. 27f) an assurance of a future for Israel.

47.1–7: A message of judgement for the Philistines.

48.1–47: This long chapter contains a series of oracles against Moab and its people. Moab was a very rocky area with fortresses in the mountains. Its main wealth lay in sheepbreeding.

49.1–6: An oracle against Ammon. Its king, Baalis, was apparently involved in the plot to assassinate Gedaliah (40.13f), and it was to Ammon that Ishmael, the plot's leader, made his escape.

49.7–22: The subject of this section is Edom, whose people, according to tradition, were descended from Jacob's brother Esau.

49.23–27: An oracle against Syria.

49.28–32: These five verses concern Kedar and Hazor, two groups of nomadic people.

49.33–39: The final oracle in the chapter is addressed to Elam.

INTERPRETATION

PRIDE COMES BEFORE A FALL

When we looked at ch. 25, p. 136, we saw that God was regarded as the judge of all the earth. This belief lies behind the chapters we are now studying. That God has the right to act as judge is not discussed; it is merely assumed. We are not always told why these nations are judged; for instance, no reason is stated for the judgement of Philistia. But in several cases the nation concerned is charged with pride or some other kind of human confidence. Thus, one way to read these chapters is as an extended commentary on these nations in the light of Jeremiah 9.23f.

So, for instance, 46.7f refers to Egypt's pride and political ambition to assert authority over other nations and peoples. Edom's pride is reported at 49.16, and the same charge is made against Moab, who in self-confidence despises Yahweh as one who does not need to be considered (48.29f,42). 49.4 is difficult to translate but clearly relates to some sort of confidence on the part of Ammon. Damascus appears to be relying on its past reputation (49.16), while Kedar and Hazor are 'at ease', i.e. confident (49.31). Finally, Elam boasts of its archers' skill (49.35).

No doubt the reason why these nations were singled out for attack is that they had been opponents of the people of Israel and Judah. But this is not the reason given for the coming judgement of God; the reasons given relate to the nations' confidence in someone or something other than God. People are for ever given to self-assertion, taking to themselves the rights of God: such behaviour is as old as the story of Adam and Eve. That they ought to know better is declared by both Old and New Testaments. Even without any special revelation such as Israel received, these nations should have known better. There was enough evidence around them to make it clear to them that they ought to depend on a divine power and not on their own skill or effort.

There is a story told of a woman in Asia who found none of the religions around her satisfying. When Christians came to the area she heard for the first time the Christian message. 'I always knew there ought to be a God like that', was her response. Saint Augustine put the same thought in a different way, 'Our hearts are restless until they find their rest in God'. We are created to depend on our creator; unless we do so we shall fail to find true fulfilment, for we cannot rebel against our creator and remain unhurt. Whatever our human goals may be, they will pass away just as these nations are destined to do.

CAN THERE STILL BE HOPE?

Four of the oracles finish with a short word of promise: 46.26b; 48.47; 49.6; 49.39. Because these words about restoration make a total contrast with the surrounding material some scholars think that at least some of them may have been added to the text later. Whether or not they are right, since the passages occur in the final text we need to ask how we should understand them.

We are not given an explanation. There is no clear evidence that the promises all come from a time when the nation concerned had shown signs of revival. We may have to leave it a mystery. But a different possibility may be suggested by the book of Amos. These chapters and Amos both assert the sovereignty of Yahweh as the lord of life and destruction. Although the chief concern of Amos's message was God's judgement on Israel, just because Yahweh *was* sovereign the possibility that hope might follow judgement could not be ruled out – and so we have the 'It may be' of Amos 5.15. Similarly here, since God is supreme it is possible for Him to have a future for these nations beyond their destruction. With God the future remains open. Just as a hope that seems impossible for Judah may emerge, so hope may emerge outside Judah also. Beyond this we cannot go.

NOTES

46.2: Carchemish: The battle of Carchemish in 605 BC was one of the decisive battles of the ancient world. Egypt's defeat by Babylon decided Babylon's supremacy in world affairs.

'The swift cannot . . . escape . . . prepare yourselves baggage for exile' (Jer. 46.6,19). We are not always told why these nations are judged, just as we find it difficult to understand why so many people should be driven from their homes as refugees simply because of the pride and political ambitions of national leaders.

46.3–4: Prepare ... harness ... put on ... mail: We are shown an army parading in its splendour, ready for a great victory. But when the battle comes, instead of triumph there is a total rout, vv. 5f.

46.5: Terror on every side: See note on 6.25.

46.6: The swift cannot ... escape: The 'swift' are the very people whose speed should enable them to escape; the warrior is the one expected to be able to fight his way out of trouble. Defeat is total.

46.7–8: Rising like the Nile: Egypt's prosperity lay in the annual flooding of the River Nile; without it crops were poor. The image is of the power of Egypt rising like the Nile in flood. When it comes, nothing can resist that flood.

46.9: Put ... Lud: Both places provided mercenaries for the Egyptian army. Their precise location is debated, but both were in northeast Africa; Put was probably either Somalia or Libya.

46.11: Gilead ... balm: See note on 8.22.

Virgin daughter: The same idea recurs in v. 24, and it is used of Israel at 14.17; 18.13; 31.4,21.

46.14: Migdol ... Memphis ... Tahpanhes: See note on 44.1.

46.15: Apis: Apis was a bull sacred to the Egyptian god Ptah, the guardian of the city of Memphis.

46.17: Noisy one who lets the hour go by: The Pharaoh is full of talk, but his actions do not match his boasts.

46.18: Tabor ... Carmel: Mount Tabor in Galilee and Mount Carmel in north-west Israel both stand out conspicuously from the surrounding countryside. The one who comes (vv. 2, 26 imply that Nebuchadrezzar is meant) will be similarly dominant over Egypt.

46.20: Gadfly: An insect that gives a sharp nip or sting.

46.21: Fatted calves: Calves that were specially fattened to provide the best veal for feasts. The mercenaries prove to be like them, without any muscle.

46.22: A sound like a serpent gliding away: The snake was an important symbol of deity in Egypt. For 'gliding away' the Greek has 'hissing' which some English versions follow.

46.25: Amon: Amon was the god of the important Egyptian city of Thebes.

46.26: Afterward ... LORD: The first of four places in these chapters where hope is expressed (see Interpretation, p. 208).

46.27–28: But fear not ... unpunished: These verses occur earlier as 30.10f.

47.2: Out of the north: Coming after 47.1 (and note also 46.8) the enemy is most naturally understood to refer to Egypt; in this case the phrase should be taken as a general term for a frightening enemy (unless it is understood to mean the Egyptians as they retreat from their defeat at Carchemish). If 'the north' is meant literally, the reference must be to a coming devastation by Babylon, and the editorial introduction of v. 1 is misleading.

47.4: Every helper: It seems that there was some kind of treaty between the Philistines and the people of Tyre and Sidon. English versions differ as to whether the help is going to Philistia or coming from it.

Caphtor: The Philistines had originally migrated from Caphtor, which is to be identified with Crete and possibly more widely with the area of the Aegean Sea.

47.5: Baldness ... gash yourselves: Both these customs were signs of mourning. Gaza and Ashkelon (see Map 2, p. 235) were two of the leading towns of the Philistines (Joshua 13.3). The **Anakim**, which follows the Greek and makes a slight change to the Hebrew, were giants who had traditionally lived in that area (Joshua 11.22).

48.5: At the ascent ... destruction: This verse is also found at Isaiah 15.5.

48.6: Wild ass: This follows the Greek: others find the name of a bush or a place-name, Aroer, here. Whichever we choose, the general picture is of a struggle to exist in the wilderness.

48.7: Chemosh: The name of the chief god of Moab; he was unable to save his people.

48.9: Give wings ... no inhabitant: A picture of devastation. The variety of English translations for the first part of the verse shows that the meaning of the Hebrew is unclear.

48.10: Cursed is he: This verse, which may be an editorial note, urges those appointed to bring the judgement to do their work thoroughly.

48.11–12: On his lees ... tilters: Wine is allowed to settle and then men carefully tilt it and decant it, leaving the sediment behind. Moab has been lying undisturbed; now men will come and attend to her, but instead of treating her gently they will be like people hurling the wine about, breaking all the jars and spilling their contents.

48.13: Shall be ashamed: Moab's trust in Chemosh will be exposed as worthless, just as Israel's trust in the gods they worshipped at Bethel was shown to be empty. Bethel (Map 2, p. 235) was an important sanctuary in Israel. It may also have been a god's name, but more probably the point being made here is that worship of Yahweh at Bethel had been strongly corrupted both by King Jeroboam I (see 1 Kings 12.23–33) and by Canaanite beliefs.

48.17: Sceptre ... staff: The 'sceptre' was the staff a king used as a sign of his royal office. The 'staff', here parallel to sceptre, was used by a shepherd; for the king being pictured as a shepherd, see note on 3.15.

48.28: Be like the dove ... gorge: A picture of a very insecure existence; to find any safety is extremely difficult.

48.29–30: We have heard ... false: Parts of these verses are also found at Isaiah 16.6–10. Isaiah 15—16 is also about Moab.

48.43–44: Terror, pit and snare: These three words sound very similar in Hebrew. These verses are almost identical to Isaiah 24.17f.

48.45–46: In the shadow ...: The Greek omits these verses. They are similar to Numbers 21.28f; 24.17.

48.47: I will restore the fortunes: This is the second of the promises for the future in these chapters. For the phrase, see note on 29.14 and the discussion on chs 30—31, p. 161.

49.2: Rabbah: Rabbah was the capital of Ammon.

Dispossess ... dispossessed: All the English versions bring out the wordplay of the Hebrew.

49.3: Hedges: These hedges would be the fences of the sheepfolds. Many English versions slightly emend the Hebrew to read 'in mourning' or 'with gashes' (a sign of mourning).

49.6: Restore the fortunes: See note on 48.47.

49.7–22: Concerning Edom: Several parts of this attack on Edom are very similar to parts of Obadiah.

49.7: Wisdom ... counsel: Obviously Edom was famous for its wisdom.

49.11: I will keep them ... trust in me: The positive nature of this verse seems out of harmony with the surrounding material.

49.12: Drink the cup: For the cup of Yahweh's wrath, see notes on 13.13f and 25.15.

49.13: I have sworn by myself: See note on 22.5.

49.16: Clefts of the rock: 'The rock' might be translated 'Sela', a place in Edom, but the general meaning is not affected. The defenders of Edom are proud that their position is impregnable.

49.17: Edom ... disasters: This verse also occurs at 19.8.

49.18: Sodom and Gomorrah and their neighbour cities: These cities were proverbial for the way in which they were destroyed; see note on 20.16. The 'neighbour cities' were probably Admah and Zeboiim (Deut. 29.23).

49.19–21: Like a lion ... Red Sea: As a lion comes from the lush area around the River Jordan (see note on 12.5) and the shepherds are powerless to protect their sheep, so Yahweh's attack on Edom will be irresistible.

Red Sea: This is better translated as 'Reed Sea'. It refers to an area of papyrus marsh near the Mediterranean coast of eastern Egypt. These verses recur at 50.44–46.

49.22: The heart of the warriors of Edom: This is almost identical to 48.40f, but with the substitution of Edom for Moab.

49.23: Damascus ... Hamath ... Arpad: The capital cities of three Syrian states. The Hebrew of the second half of the verse is difficult, but apparently means that the people's anxiety at the news of approaching trouble prevents them from sleeping.

49.27: Ben-hadad: This was the name of several Syrian kings, and was also used as a general term for Syria (Amos 1.4). Hadad was the Aramaean storm god, the equivalent of the Canaanite Baal.

49.29: Terror on every side: See note on 6.25.

49.31: No gates or bars: Since they were nomadic peoples there were no permanent settlements or defences.

49.32: Cut the corners of their hair: See note on 9.26.

49.39: I will restore the fortunes: The final declaration of hope; see note on 48.47.

STUDY SUGGESTIONS

REVIEW OF CONTENT

1. What examples of pride do you find in these chapters?
2. How might Jeremiah 9.23f help us to understand the purpose of these chapters?
3. What vital attitude does human pride prevent?
4. What idea can lie behind the glimmer of hope found in Jer. 46.26b; 48.47; 49.6 and 49.39?

BIBLE STUDY

5. Many of the nations condemned showed pride in their achievements. How would you describe the attitudes towards God shown in the following passages?
   (a) Exod. 8.8–14
   (b) Jer. 2.34f
   (c) Luke 18.9–14
   (d) Acts 5.1–11
6. What do the following passages have to say about the relationship between the future and God's sovereignty?
   (a) Exod. 3.1–12
   (b) Isa. 41.11–20
   (c) Jer. 32.26–28
   (d) Acts 17.22–31
   (e) Rev. 1.4–18

DISCUSSION AND APPLICATION

7. Do you think that delight in personal skills and achievements automatically decreases our trust in God? Describe any times when your own successes have led you away from dependence on God.

8. What achievements does your nation take pride in? Do you think that this pride makes it difficult for your national leaders to trust in God or not? Give examples.
9. What hope or encouragement can we offer, if any, to people whose nations have been utterly ruined by war or some other disaster?

50.1—51.64
Judgement on the Nations (2)

OUTLINE

The remaining part of the oracles against the nations is directed to Babylon, then the greatest world power. Babylon has been deliberately placed last so that the message of its downfall comes as the climax of the whole section. Within these two chapters are brought together a large number of short oracles with two alternating themes. The dominant one is the approaching judgement of Babylon; interspersed with this are a number of short passages about the restoration of Israel.

50.1–3: After an introductory verse, a short oracle serves as a text for the material that follows: 'The Fall of Babylon'.

50.4–5: A short passage declares the return of Israel's exiles when Babylon falls. Babylon's end thus marks a new start for God's people.

50.6–7: A further reminder that the Exile was a consequence of the sin of Israel.

50.8–10: The advance of the enemy towards Babylon is announced.

50.11–16: A poem about Babylon's disgrace; vv. 11–13 are directed to Babylon itself and vv. 14–16 to the attackers.

50.17–20: A prose declaration that the downfall of Babylon will be accompanied by the restoration of Israel.

50.21–30: A further poem about Babylon's destruction.

50.31–32: A short poem about the humbling of Babylon, the proud one.

50.33–34: Another short piece about Israel's restoration.

50.35–40: A picture of Babylon as a scene of sword and slaughter.

50.41–46: Despair will grip Babylon so that it becomes paralysed and powerless.

51.1–14: A poem asserting that Babylon's downfall is the Lord's judgement.

51.15–19: This poem, which interrupts the attack on Babylon, emphasizes Yahweh's sovereignty.

51.20–26: Babylon, who has been the great destroyer, is now to be destroyed.

51.27–58: A final collection of short oracles which pronounce the completeness and permanence of Babylon's fall.

51.59–64: A report of a final act of prophetic symbolism which Jeremiah arranged to be performed.

INTERPRETATION

THE END OF THE TYRANT

In the years before Jerusalem was overthrown, the power of Babylon had steadily increased. Its influence grew wider and wider until it seemed as though it would dominate the world for ever. By the time Jerusalem fell, Babylon's power seemed irresistible; it was almost impossible to imagine that it could be successfully overthrown.

Confronted with such a powerful military presence it was natural to feel overwhelmed and crushed by it; resistance seemed futile. That is equally true today. When a nation's border is occupied by a powerful invading force, opposition may seem to be the road to disaster. Yet these chapters take a wider perspective. The days of Babylon are numbered; its defeat is sure to come, and with the downfall of Babylon will come a revival for the people of God. Babylon's pride and hostility towards God's people will bring it to judgement. Babylon took the credit for its own power; this defiance of the creator will bring its own reward.

As the greatest power of the day, Babylon stands here (and elsewhere in the Old Testament, e.g. Isa. 13—14) for the human assertion of power. And the final experience of Babylon – defeat – will be the final experience of all human power. No human tyranny will last; it is doomed to fall. The experience of history supports such a verdict. Past centuries are littered with the rise and fall of great and small empires. Though for a time they may appear to carry all before them, their time will come. People whose nation lies in the shadow of another can take heart from this, whatever the nature of their oppressor. So too can those who find themselves under an oppressive or brutal regime, for the principle applies within countries as well as between them.

The map of history is constantly changing. Dictatorships and democracies continually develop in new directions. At the present time there is ferment in parts of Eastern Europe, South-western Asia is in a state of flux, the barriers of apartheid are crumbling. A list of heads of state drawn up now will soon be out of date. To realize this is to see with a truer perspective. When a new tyranny arises it is not the end of the world, for the days of that tyranny are already numbered. God's perspective is wider than ours.

THE END OF EVIL

To write in this way may be true from the point of view of history, but it hardly comforts people suffering oppression now. To know that one day, perhaps in twenty years, perhaps in two hundred, our oppressors will no longer be able to oppress is not of much help to us in the present. However, these chapters permit a further assertion. For Babylon is becoming more than just an example of human tyranny. It is starting to become the personification of evil, the symbol of opposition to Yahweh. (This idea is developed much more fully in the New Testament book of Revelation; there the power opposing God is Rome, but Rome is given the name 'Babylon'.) And so Babylon is not merely proud, it is totally opposed to God and His people. It is evil.

Such evil is real. It is brutal. But it will finally be overthrown. The Christian hope for the future is only developed in the New Testament; for much of the Old Testament period the hope of God's people was far more this-worldly. But in passages like these chapters we are moving towards a declaration of the final and total overthrow of all evil. Part of the basis for this is found in the way that the Old Testament as a whole, and Jeremiah in particular, clearly assert the absolute sovereignty of God over the world that He has created and continues to sustain.

Sometimes, when we look at the world around us and see the extent of human greed and crime, we can be tempted to despair of the future. This is nothing new; those who remained faithful in Israel must have felt the same, confronted as they were with the tyranny exerted by the powers of the day. To them, and so to us also, comes a message of encouragement: 'Thus shall Babylon sink, to rise no more'. More than a century earlier Isaiah had put it more generally, 'The Lord of hosts has a day against all that is proud and lofty' (Isaiah 2.12). The struggle with evil will not last for ever; the day will come when accounts will be settled and all wrong put right. Only God knows how and when this will happen, but He declares that it *will* happen. If we protest that we cannot imagine such an end to evil, we have to remember that no more could the Israelites among the ruins of Jerusalem imagine a hope for the future. We are dealing, not with what human effort may be able to attain, but with the activity of the living God. Such was Jeremiah's basis.

'No human tyranny will last ... God's perspective is wider than ours'—though this
hardly comforts the people who suffer death and destruction in war, or face execution
on the order of ruthless dictators, as this man did under Idi Amin in Uganda.

A conviction like this has a profound effect on a Christian understanding and approach to life. Christians should indeed be firmly committed to work for a fairer and juster society in this world, trying to improve the lot of its citizens. They should resist evil in its many shapes and forms. This world matters. But Christians also have another perspective, for they look towards a future in which God will make all things new; that newness requires the final and total overthrow of all that is evil. The coming of this remains a mystery, hidden in the purposes of God; but without it our theology remains incomplete. 'If in this life only we have hoped in Christ, we are of all men most to be pitied', concluded Saint Paul (1 Cor. 15.19). Such an understanding takes us beyond Jeremiah, but part of its foundation lies in his assertion of the overthrow of evil. Jeremiah would have rejoiced in the fuller vision that we now have.

NOTES

50.2: Bel ... Merodach: 'Bel' and 'Merodach' (or Marduk) were two names for the same god, the chief Babylonian god in the time of Nebuchadrezzar.
Her idols: The Hebrew is insulting, 'pellets of dung'.
50.3: Out of the north: The same thought recurs at 50.9,41; 51.48. Here it is clearly a general term for an enemy's approach; see note on 1.14.
50.4: Note that **Judah** *and* **Israel** will together share in restoration.
50.6: Their shepherds: As at 23.1f, kings are probably meant.
50.13–14: The wrath of the LORD: The cause of Yahweh's wrath has not yet been stated. (The Greek omits the last phrase of v. 14.)
50.16: Every one shall turn to his own people ... own land: This probably refers to mercenaries and others who have grown rich through Babylon but now escape in desperation; Isaiah 13.14b is identical.
50.17: The king of Assyria devoured him: This most naturally refers to the destruction of the northern kingdom in 722–721 BC. That it should refer to Sennacherib's attack on Jerusalem in the reign of Hezekiah is much less likely.
50.19: Carmel ... Bashan ... hills of Ephraim ... Gilead: All these areas were well-known for good pasture.
50.21: Merathaim ... Pekod: Merathaim, to the south of Babylon, and Pekod, to the east, were both part of Babylon's territory. They are singled out because of plays on words, Merathaim meaning 'Rebel of rebels' and Pekod 'Punishment'.
50.23: Hammer of the whole earth: See note on 23.29.

50.27: Slay all her bulls: Bulls were killed at a time of sacrifice. Some English versions translate as 'warriors'; her finest men are to be sacrificed in battle.

Time of their punishment: See note on 6.15. This phrase or the related 'year of punishment' occurs nine times in Jeremiah.

50.29: She has proudly defied the LORD: Pride is again the focus of condemnation.

The Holy One of Israel: This title, common in Isaiah 40—55, is found in Jeremiah only here and at 51.5.

50.30: Her young men . . .: This verse is also found at 49.26.

50.32: The proud one shall stumble . . .: This verse is close to 21.14.

50.34: Redeemer: The noun occurs only here in Jeremiah; the verb is found at 15.21 and 31.11.

50.36: Diviners: This is literally 'boasters'. The Hebrew word is very similar to the name of the Babylonian baru-priests who practised hepatoscopy, divination by the examination of animals' livers. In Isaiah 44.25 liars and diviners are equivalent.

50.38: A drought upon her waters: If the great rivers, the Tigris and Euphrates, are dried up it is indeed a drought! Some make a slight change in the Hebrew which emends 'drought' to 'sword'; if we follow this, war has caused the irrigation system to fall into disrepair.

A land of images . . . mad over idols: A wide variety of translations has been proposed for this half of the verse.

50.39–40: Wild beasts shall dwell . . .: Isaiah 13.19–22 is closely similar. The creatures mentioned are variously translated; v. 40 is also found at Jeremiah 49.18.

50.41–43: A people comes . . .: These verses are also found at 6.22–24.

50.44–46: Like a lion . . .: These verses are very close to 49.19–21.

51.1: Chaldea: This follows the Greek. The Hebrew is Leb-Kamai which is probably a code for Babylon; it means 'heart of those who rise up against me'.

51.5: The land of the Chaldeans: The Hebrew reads 'their land' and could equally refer to the land of Israel.

Holy One of Israel: See note on 50.29.

51.7: Golden cup: For the Lord's cup of wrath, see notes on 13.13f and 25.15.

51.11: The kings of the Medes: This is a prose insertion and may be editorial. It is the first time the Medes are mentioned by name. The mother of Cyrus, the Persian emperor who eventually overthrew Babylon, was a Mede. It is also possible that Babylon expected a Median invasion around 561 BC.

51.14: Sworn by himself: See note on 22.5.

51.15–19: It is he ... name: These verses are identical to 10.12–16, where they fit more naturally.

51.20–23: You: The GNB translates as 'Babylon' and is probably right: this is the role that Babylon has exercised for Yahweh in the past. Alternative suggestions are that 'you' is the destroyer of Babylon, or else Israel – the nations are judged on the basis of how they treat the people of God.

51.25: A burnt mountain: Babylon is like a spent volcano; she has exploded and can do no more.

51.27: Prepare ... Ararat, Minni, and Ashkenaz: 'Prepare' is literally 'sanctify'; the nations were called to a special task, a holy one. Those named were in Armenia.

51.30: Her bars are broken: These are the bars of the city gates; the defences are wide open to the enemy.

51.31: Runner ... messenger: Babylon was famous for her courier system.

51.32: Bulwarks: Most English versions translate as some sort of fortifications here; a few read 'marshes', seeing these as part of the city defences or as being burnt to prevent people from hiding in them.

51.41: Babylon: The Hebrew is *Sheshak*; see note on 25.26.

The praise of the whole earth: Because of its power, Babylon is the centre of attention; the nations offer praise because they are forced to!

51.42: The sea has come up on Babylon: This verse may be intended as a reverse of the Babylonian myth according to which Marduk, Babylon's god, defeated the waters of chaos.

51.49: For the slain of Israel: A specific reason is now given for Yahweh's judgement. Babylon will be receiving the treatment it inflicted on others.

51.51: We are put to shame: This reflection by the exiles could show despair or repentance.

51.58: Broad wall ... levelled to the ground: Under Nebuchadrezzar Babylon had a double wall of defensive fortifications; the historian Herodotus claimed that it enclosed 200 square miles! The Hebrew emphasizes how total is the ruin; not one stone will be left standing on another. Verse 58b is the same as Habakkuk 2.13b.

51.59: With Zedekiah: The Greek reads 'from Zedekiah'. The dating given for this incident is the same as that for chs 27—28: there, Jeremiah could have been accused of being pro-Babylonian; here, he could not. See the interpretation of chs 27—29 (p. 154) for the relationship between these attitudes.

Seraiah was the quartermaster: The job of Seraiah, Baruch's brother (see ch. 45, p. 202), was literally 'ruler of the grain offering'. He would have been responsible for the catering and the overnight stops on the way to Babylon.

51.60: A book: Presumably it contained part of chs 50—51 or equivalent material.

51.61: See that you read all these words: The reading was of great importance; without it, the significance of the act would be lost.

51.63–64: When you finish reading this book: After the reading comes a final act of prophetic symbolism. Just as in ch. 19, once the flask was broken, nothing could prevent Jerusalem's destruction, there is now nothing that can prevent Babylon's overthrow.

Upon her: By mistake, 'and they shall weary themselves' has been copied in the Hebrew from the end of v. 58.

Thus far are the words of Jeremiah: A formal conclusion to the content of Jeremiah's preaching. The following chapter is an epilogue quite independent of the prophet.

STUDY SUGGESTIONS

REVIEW OF CONTENT

1. What encouragement is there in these chapters for those being oppressed by a greater power?
2. Why can we be tempted to despair of hope for the world?
3. What added element of hope comes clearly into view in the New Testament?

BIBLE STUDY

4. What expectations for the future does each of the following passages show?
   (a) Deut. 28.1–14
   (b) Job 7.7–10
   (c) Job 19.23–27
   (d) Pss 6; 37; 73
   (e) Eccles. 3.19–21
   (f) Dan. 12.1–3
   (Note that in some cases the translation is uncertain because the meaning is not clear.) Compare these attitudes with those shown in the present passage.
5. Study 1 Cor. 15. According to this passage what are the distinct elements of hope for the future?
6. What does Rev. 20.1—22.5 have to say about the final overthrow of evil?

DISCUSSION AND APPLICATION

7. How would you answer the charge that encouraging people with
   a hope for the future is just an attempt to distract them from the
   difficulties of the present?
8. 'This world matters' (p. 218). In what ways does your Church
   demonstrate this?
9. How can we keep the right sort of balance between encouraging
   action to change the world in the present, and giving assurance
   about God's total victory in the future?
10. What effect does a firm conviction of the final overthrow of evil
    have on our lives today?
11. Why do you think that Paul said, 'If for this life only we have
    hoped in Christ, we are of all men most to be pitied' (1 Cor.
    15.19)?

52.1–34
A Historical Appendix

OUTLINE

The material in this final chapter is very closely parallel to the
account of the fall of Jerusalem given in 2 Kings 24.18—25.30; it
also has a close link with that given in Jeremiah 39. Within the
chapter there is no mention of Jeremiah. The recounting of the
historical facts serves as an epilogue to what has gone before, and as
a vindication of the prophet. The fall of Jerusalem, predicted by
Jeremiah for so long, has finally taken place.

52.1–11: An account of Zedekiah's rebellion, the siege of Jerusalem
and Zedekiah's subsequent fate.

52.12–27: A report of the destruction of the Temple and city of
Jerusalem, and also of the fate of various citizens and Temple
artefacts.

52.28–30: A statement about the numbers of people Nebuchadrezzar
had taken to Exile in Babylon.

52.31–34: A final footnote about Jehoiachin's release from prison in
Babylon.

INTERPRETATION

THE VINDICATION OF JEREMIAH

The picture of Jeremiah given by the book bearing his name is of a prophet who faced great opposition and found himself perpetually in a minority. Help given him by certain sympathizers in high places enabled him to survive, but his experience was one of continuous struggle. Although the book's editors clearly believed that Jeremiah was a prophet sent by God, they were equally clear that his view (and theirs) was a minority one. The majority either refused to accept that Jeremiah was a true prophet or they found his message too uncomfortable.

Although this final chapter makes no mention of Jeremiah, it serves to vindicate him. The long-promised destruction of Jerusalem was finally a fact. It happened, not partially, but totally. God *had* sent him. There was no need for Jeremiah to appear and say, 'I told you so'; history had shown he was correct.

There is a further point to make. For Jeremiah had talked not only of Jerusalem's destruction but also of the hope that lay beyond it, which would arise from among those who had gone as exiles with Jehoiachin. Placed where it is, the appendix not only asserts that Jeremiah's message about the city's destruction had been proved true; it also declares the rest of his message to be true. Yahweh was Lord of heaven and earth, of nature and history, of past and future; Babylon's dominance was only by the permission of Yahweh and for a limited time.

Because of this there was a future hope for Judah, and for Israel too; in the future God would establish a new covenant. The bearers of this hope were in Babylon. The final verses of this chapter, with their report of Jehoiachin's release from prison, do not demand an optimism about the future – indeed, they inform us that Jehoiachin had died – but they do indicate that the future was not closed. With God the future remains open. So the appendix not only testifies that one part of Jeremiah's message has been proved accurate; it also endorses the whole of it as having God's authority. It does not invite us to select what we believe we can without doubt attribute to Jeremiah and leave out the rest (in any case, scholars' conclusions on this would never agree!). It takes the complete book, both material coming directly from Jeremiah and that which we owe to later editors.

In taking the book as a whole we must try to avoid two opposing dangers. One is to magnify the tensions within the material so that we produce a mass of contradictions. The perspectives and emphases will depend, in part, on where the writer stands; that alone can account for much variety in outlook. The other danger is to blend the differing insights together so completely that they no longer speak with their distinctive voices. We need to take it as a whole on its own terms, not filtered and tamed by our predetermined views.

To accept the epilogue's endorsement of the whole of the book of Jeremiah is not to insist that the prophecies need be fulfilled as Jeremiah or his editors expected. Clearly Jeremiah was deeply disturbed by the way that some of his prophecies did not seem to be fulfilled! When he began his ministry he obviously had no idea that forty years would pass before his message about Jerusalem's destruction would be proved true! Time after time Old Testament prophecies are 'fulfilled' in a most unexpected way. The New Testament declares that Christ is the fulfilment of Old Testament prophecy, and the Christian Church agrees. But the nature of Christ's ministry could never have been deduced merely from the relevant Old Testament passages, for Christ far transcended bare words and expectations.

Jeremiah could have learnt from the way Jerusalem's judgement finally came that prophecy and expectation are two separate things. He doubtless had no idea how some of the things to which he pointed would be fulfilled. But he declared that they *would* come. God had declared judgement on Jerusalem; that judgement had come. God had declared His good purpose for the future; He would bring that about also. For the future belongs to God.

NOTES

52.1: Hamutal: Zedekiah's mother was also the mother of Jehoahaz (2 Kings 23.31).

52.4–6: In the ninth year ... fourth month: The siege began in January 588 BC and ended in July 587 BC.

52.7–11: Then a breach ...: See 39.4–7.

52.11: Till the day of his death: This phrase is not found in 2 Kings 25.7, nor in the account given in Jeremiah 39, so it is likely to be later than these passages; the same is true at 52.34.

52.12: On the tenth day of the month: 2 Kings 25.8 reads 'seventh day'.

52.13: He burned the house of the LORD: Just as the entry into the city recorded in the previous verse was ceremonial, the destruction may also have been ceremonial. Certainly it was brutal. For Judah's reaction to the Temple's destruction, see Pss 74.1–11; 79.1; Isa. 64.10f; Lam. 2.7.

52.17–23: And they took away the pots: see also 27.19–22 for reference to the Temple vessels being taken to Babylon. 1 Kings 7.13–50 contains details of the furnishing of the Temple.

52.20: The two pillars: These would be Jachin and Boaz, the two pillars that stood by the temple entrance.

52.22: Pomegranates: These were commonly carved as decorations in Ancient South-western Asia.

52.24: Seraiah ... Zephaniah ... keepers of the threshold: These were the leading priests. Seraiah was the grandson of Hilkiah, the chief priest at the time of Josiah's reform (see 2 Kings 22.8 and 1 Chron. 6.13–15). Zephaniah may be the priest mentioned at 29.24–32; 37.3.

52.25: Seven men: 2 Kings 25.19 reads 'five men'.

52.27: Put them to death: The punishment was exemplary, and intended as a deterrent to others who might consider opposing the system.

52.28–30: In the seventh year, three thousand and twenty three: According to 2 Kings 24.14,16 the number deported with Jehoiachin was far larger. To avoid this difficulty, the NEB emends 'seventh' to 'seventeenth' and understands the figure to refer to exiles taken from the general territory of Judah as it came under Babylonian control; those exiles in the following year are understood to have come from Jerusalem after it finally fell. John Bright has made the alternative suggestion that the figures in Jeremiah are those of adult males, while 2 Kings gives the total number of people deported. Both suggestions are speculative attempts to solve a problem. We may note that the later account in 2 Chronicles 36 implies that all the inhabitants of Jerusalem who were not killed during the siege of the city were taken into Exile in Babylon.

52.31: Thirty-seventh year: This would be 561 BC.

Twenty-fifth day: The Greek reads 'twenty-fourth', while 2 Kings 25.27 has 'twenty-seventh'.

Evil-merodach: The real name of this son of Nebuchadrezzar, who reigned only briefly, from 561–560 BC, was Awel-marduk, meaning 'Man of Marduk'. This has been deliberately corrupted to Ewil-marduk, meaning 'Stupid of Marduk'.

52.32: The kings who were with him: This is most naturally understood to refer to other kings who had been exiled to Babylon.

52.34: Until the day of his death: See note on 52.11.

STUDY SUGGESTIONS

REVIEW OF CONTENT

1. What is the purpose of the final chapter of the book of Jeremiah?

2. How does this final chapter vindicate Jeremiah?
3. By the time the book was completed Jerusalem had been destroyed. What parts of Jeremiah's message remained to be demonstrated?
4. There are tensions within the material of the book of Jeremiah. How should we understand the relationship between the various elements?

BIBLE STUDY

5. Make a close comparison of this passage with 2 Kings 25 and Jeremiah 39. What differences do you find? Which, if any, of them are significant?
6. In the following New Testament passages the authors explain how Old Testament prophecies have been fulfilled in Christ:
   (a) Matt. 1.23, cf. Isa. 7.14
   (b) Matt. 13.34f, cf. Ps. 78.2
   (c) Matt. 27.3–10, cf. Jer. 32.6–15
   (d) John 19.24, cf. Ps. 22.18
   (e) Acts 2.14–21, cf. Joel 2.28–32
   (f) Acts 8.32f, cf. Isa. 53.7f
   (g) Acts 13.35, cf. Ps. 16.10
   (h) Heb. 2.5–9, cf. Ps. 8.4–6
   How many of these Old Testament passages would you have expected to have been explained in the way described? Does this matter?

DISCUSSION AND APPLICATION

7. Jeremiah was disturbed because God did not act in the way he expected. How confident can we be of how God will act? If we cannot have any confidence about details, what kind of assurance *do* Christians have?
8. If there are tensions between the different elements within the book of Jeremiah, there are even greater tensions between different elements of the Old Testament as a whole. How do we try to hold together different insights within our own understanding?
9. Does your Church take a very rigid approach or does it allow a variety of understanding in some areas of Christian doctrine? When there is such a variety of understanding, what helps us to retain a genuine unity and fellowship?

Special Note H
The Understanding of God of the
Book of Jeremiah

Because the Book of Jeremiah is large it may be helpful to try and summarize its chief themes. Some of these re-echo constantly through the book, others – such as the new covenant – occur much less frequently, but are nevertheless of great importance in any outline of Jeremiah's theology. We shall briefly consider five themes, each having an important place in the book's overall understanding of God. More detailed consideration of these themes will be found in discussion of the passages where they are most prominent; the passages to which reference is made below are merely examples of passages illustrating the theme in question.

A GOD WHO IS SOVEREIGN

One of the first impressions gained from the poetic material in the book concerns the sovereignty of the God whom Jeremiah represents. This can be seen in various ways.

He is sovereign over *creation* (5.20–24; 10.12f; 14.1–9). Yahweh, declares Jeremiah, is none other than the creator of the universe, responsible both for its origin and for the ongoing cycle of nature. He is responsible for sending or withholding rain and harvest, for enabling creatures to reproduce.

He is also sovereign over all *nations* and so of all *history* (10.1–16; 18.1–10; 25.15–38; discussion of 43.8—44.30). Jeremiah's God is not local and limited, His power and control exceed all human imagination. Past, present and future belong to Yahweh; so does the experience not only of Judah and Israel, His specially chosen people, but of all other nations.

Finally, as part of His sovereignty, He remains *inscrutable* to men and women (15.15–21; 20.7–10; 24.1–10). This is no easy doctrine for Jeremiah; he does not gladly take refuge in it, but is forced into it by his own experiences. For often he cannot understand what God is doing; His promises appear misleading, His servants face great difficulties. He is a God who remains mysterious even when he reveals His plans and will. This is part of His sovereignty.

A GOD WHO JUDGES JUSTLY

Within the Book of Jeremiah the sovereignty of God is closely linked with the fact that He is the judge of all peoples, a just judge. The

'One of the first impressions gained from the Book of Jeremiah concerns the sovereignty of God ... who is creator of the whole universe.' His power and control exceed all human understanding, whether relating to the smallest everyday actions and experiences of His people, or to the unimaginably vast distances of space and time we are only just beginning to explore.

grounds on which He judges His own people are clearly laid down, and concern their allegiance to Him (7.1—8.3 and many other passages). This allegiance is reflected, not by the outward show of a sacrifice, but by the consistency of their religious worship and the quality of their moral behaviour. Their worship is judged according to whether it is pure or contaminated by practices from other religions. The acceptability of their moral behaviour depends on its fitting with the pattern that God had given His people through Moses.

When it comes to the judgement of other nations, no clear basis is given, other than the peoples' contempt for God Himself or their disregard of His people. But there is no suggestion that He is capricious. On the contrary, it is assumed that the peoples should know better, and the dominant impression given is that the chief focus of God's displeasure is the pride of the nations (46.1—51.64). This pride is basically self-satisfaction; people make the mistake of seeing themselves as self-sufficient, without need of any God. If they only thought, believes Jeremiah, they would know that this is dreadful arrogance. They must face the consequences of this attitude.

A GOD WHO SPEAKS AND ACTS

If God is to judge His people justly, they need to understand what He requires of them; He has to communicate with them. Jeremiah indicates two main ways in which this happens. The first is the Law, handed down and developed over the years and now all linked with the figure of Moses. For Jeremiah the Law is bound up with the promises of God; if the Law is neglected the people can no longer rely on God's promises, for these are conditional upon observance of the Law (7.1–15). This does not mean that there is a strict legalism, for again and again forgiveness and a fresh start are offered if the people will repent and return. But the Law is of permanent significance: the importance of the new covenant (31.31–34) is that it will make it possible for the Law to be truly followed, from the heart rather than merely outwardly.

Together with the law, and developing from it, come the prophets (see discussion of 13.1–11; 23.9–40). Today we may see the prophets as bringing fresh revelation, but in their own day, while they were recognized as having new messages from God, these new messages were seen to be in harmony with the Law already given and not in opposition to it. The prophets talk of what the people have done (or not done), what they should do (or not do) and what are the consequences of these actions (which may sometimes be avoided by a change of behaviour); they relate both past history and the future to the people's allegiance to Yahweh. The prophets assume the Law to be the foundation, and Jeremiah is no exception to this.

The revealing of God's wishes and plans through the Law and the prophets is followed up by His activity in the world of nature and history. This links back to the teaching of His sovereignty. But without the interpretation of the prophets, and (to a lesser extent) of the Law, there would be no clear understanding or interpretation of what was happening in the realm of history.

A GOD OF HOPE

Despite the sombre tone of much of the book the element of hope must not be discounted. It occupies a significant position in the final shape of the book, holding an importance greater than the proportion of the book that it occupies. The book as a whole is not just an indictment of the past evil of Judah (and to a smaller extent Israel) and an explanation of the fall of Jerusalem, though that is an important part of the total message. The finished book declares God's good plans for the future of His people, and His will to bring these plans to effect.

Thus the hope of the new covenant outlined in ch. 31 and that of the restoration of Judah and Jerusalem, together with the reuniting of Judah and Israel, form a distinct core of encouragement and hope for the future (3.12–18; 30.1—31.40; 33.14–26). Even for the nations of the world there are elements of hope (46.26b; 48.47; 49.6,39), for the sovereignty and goodness of God make it possible that hope may be more widespread than for the people of God alone.

A GOD WHO CALLS TO FAITH

A final element in the book's understanding of God is that God calls to faith. This faith is practical, not theoretical; if it is real it must issue in repentance and obedience, and the results of such obedience can be seen in daily life (3.12–23 and discussion; 7.1–15; 17.5–8; 34.8—35.19). We may illustrate this faith with reference to three areas of life.

1. The relationship between the faith of which Jeremiah speaks and *politics* is varied. At some times it may call for decisions that are in harmony with practical politics, at others it may recommend a course that is political suicide. The determining factor is not the policy in question, but what is in harmony with the God in whom faith is placed (26.1—29.32; 43.8—44.30). Allegiance to Him must come before all questions of political expediency or desirability.

Inevitably this leads to tensions between people with faith and the policies of the government of the day.

2. Yahweh must also come first (and exclusively so) in the realm of *religion* (7.16—8.3; 10.1–16). The common practice in the ancient world of acknowledging a number of deities is unacceptable to the God of Jeremiah. This too can obviously lead to tensions and opposition; it caused Jeremiah himself no small difficulty, provoking antagonism from many of those who took part in other religious practices in addition to the worship of Yahweh.

3. A third important element of faith emerging from Jeremiah is that it must often hold on *in the dark* (20.14–18; discussion of 32.1–44). It can be hard to continue believing when things seem to be going wrong, but true faith will hold on through great difficulties to the end. Its path never becomes easy, but can be a call to believe in spite of what is happening. The nature of true faith is such that it will not permit the believer to give up – even if torn in two by inward tensions.

STUDY SUGGESTIONS

1. What five themes are suggested as central to Jeremiah's understanding of God?
2. What do you understand by the sovereignty of God? In what ways does the book of Jeremiah show a belief in the sovereignty of God?
3. On what basis does Jeremiah believe that God judges:
   (a) His own people?
   (b) Other nations?
4. How do you think that Jeremiah would have said that God spoke? Do you think that God speaks in the same ways today? If not, how do you think that He does speak?
5. If you were summarizing the message of Jeremiah would you include anything hopeful? Give your reasons.
6. How would you explain what you understand by faith? Do you think that Jeremiah would mean the same thing by faith? In what ways, if any, can Jeremiah's understanding of faith help your own?

Special Note I
Jeremiah and the Book of Lamentations

The Greek version of the Old Testament Book of Lamentations begins by stating that the book was composed by Jeremiah after the fall of Jerusalem. Because of this the book has sometimes been called the Lamentations of Jeremiah. The statement in the Greek version is not found in the older Hebrew version, and was probably based on a misunderstanding of 2 Chronicles 35.25, believing the 'Laments' to be our Book of Lamentations.

The Book of Lamentations was written shortly after the fall of Jerusalem. It comes from those people who were not exiled to Babylon but remained in Judah, and it contains a number of poems reflecting on the situation. In various ways its emphases match themes found in the Book of Jeremiah; four examples will be given. First, Lamentations declares that Jerusalem's judgement was deserved and came from Yahweh (e.g. 1.8; 2.1–8); second, the poems show a heart bleeding as it reflects on the city's shattered ruins (1.16; 3.48–51); third, because of God's mercy and concern there can be hope for the future in spite of the devastation (3.22–33; 4.22); fourth, there is evidence of a struggle for faith when so much seems to be going wrong (5.19–22).

The fact that Lamentations and Jeremiah share these common themes does not prove that there is any direct link between the two books. Although the mood of Jeremiah's 'Confessions' (see Special Note E, p. 107) shows some similarities to that of Lamentations, the most we could argue is that it was the faith and experience of people such as Jeremiah that formed a vital part of the theology expressed in Lamentations.

We just do not know who wrote Lamentations: it may have been one person or more. What we do know is that the poems express vividly the anguish and hopes of those caught up in shattering events. Because of this the book became regularly used by the Jewish people on the ninth day of the month of *Ab* (about mid-July), as part of a festival commemorating the destruction of Jerusalem by Babylon (and subsequently also its later destruction by the Romans in AD 70).

STUDY SUGGESTIONS

1. Why is it sometimes suggested that Jeremiah was the author of the Book of Lamentations?

2. What similarities are there in the themes of the Books of Jeremiah and Lamentations?
3. When was the Book of Lamentations written?
4. How was the Book of Lamentations later used by the Jewish people?

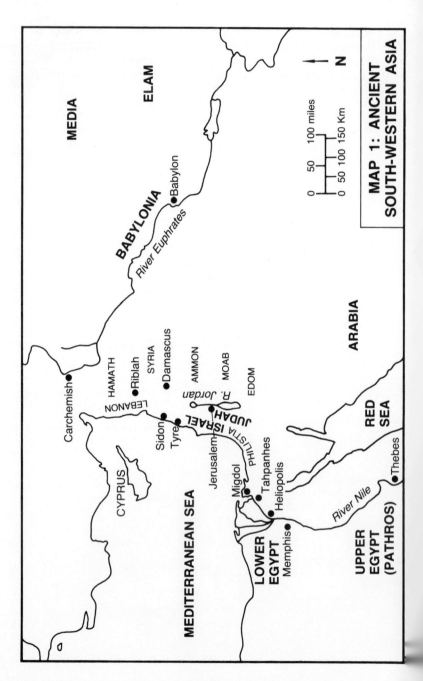

MAP 1: ANCIENT
SOUTH-WESTERN ASIA

N

0   50   100 miles
0 50 100 150 Km

MEDIA

ELAM

BABYLONIA

Babylon

River Euphrates

Carchemish

HAMATH

Riblah

SYRIA

Damascus

AMMON

MOAB

EDOM

LEBANON

R. Jordan

JUDAH

ISRAEL

PHILISTIA

Jerusalem

Sidon

Tyre

CYPRUS

MEDITERRANEAN SEA

Migdol

Tahpanhes

Heliopolis

LOWER
EGYPT

Memphis

ARABIA

RED
SEA

Thebes

River Nile

UPPER
EGYPT
(PATHROS)

234

MAP 2:
JUDAH
AND
ISRAEL

•Dan

•Hazor

SEA OF
GALILEE

Mt Carmel

Mt Tabor▲

•Megiddo
Mt Gilboa

MEDITERRANEAN SEA

River Jordan

GILEAD

•Samaria
Mt Ephraim
•Shechem

ISRAEL

AMMON

•Shiloh

•Bethel
BENJAMIN

ARABAH

•Ekron
Ashdod•
Ashkelon•

•Jerusalem

PHILISTIA

•Gath

SHEPHELAH

•Lachish

DEAD SEA

•Gaza

JUDAH

MOAB

NEGEB

ARABAH

0   5   10 miles

0   5   10 15 Km   N

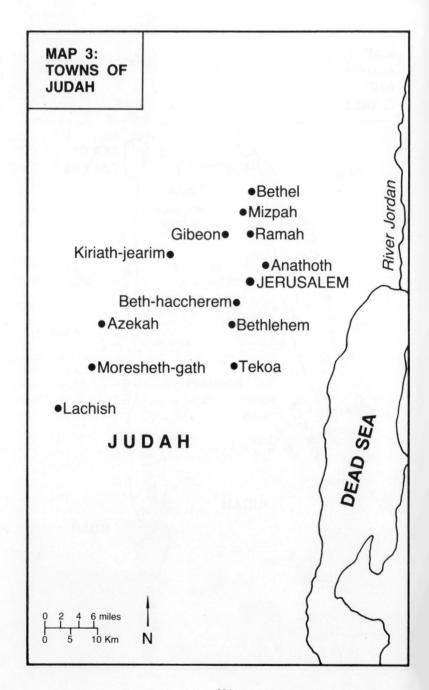

MAP 3:
TOWNS OF
JUDAH

●Bethel
●Mizpah
Gibeon● ●Ramah
Kiriath-jearim●
●Anathoth
●JERUSALEM
Beth-haccherem●
●Azekah ●Bethlehem
●Moresheth-gath ●Tekoa
●Lachish

JUDAH

River Jordan

DEAD SEA

0 2 4 6 miles
0   5   10 Km

N

Further Reading

The following books may be helpful in different ways for those who wish to explore the book and message of Jeremiah further.

BOOKS ON JEREMIAH

Bright, John, *Jeremiah* (Anchor Bible Commentary). Doubleday, New York 1965.

Brueggemann, Walter, *To Pluck up, To Tear Down; Jeremiah 1—25* (International Theological Commentary). Eerdmans, Grand Rapids, and The Handsel Press, Edinburgh 1988.

Carroll, Robert P., *Jeremiah* (Old Testament Library). SCM Press, London 1986.

Davidson, Robert, *Jeremiah 1—25* and *Jeremiah 26—52 & Lamentations* (Daily Study Bible). St Andrew's Press, Edinburgh 1983 and 1985.

Harrison, R.K., *Jeremiah & Lamentations* (Tyndale Old Testament Commentary). Inter-Varsity Press, Leicester 1973.

Jones, Douglas Rawlinson, *Jeremiah* (New Century Bible Commentary). Eerdmans, Grand Rapids, and Marshall Pickering, London 1992.

Kidner, Derek, *The Message of Jeremiah*. Inter-Varsity Press, Leicester 1987.

Nicholson, E.W., *Jeremiah 1—25* and *Jeremiah 26—52* (Cambridge Bible Commentary on the NEB). Cambridge University Press, Cambridge 1973 and 1975.

Skinner, John, *Prophecy and Religion*. Cambridge University Press, Cambridge 1926.

Thompson, J.A., *The Book of Jeremiah* (New International Commentary on the Old Testament). Eerdmans, Grand Rapids 1980.

MORE GENERAL BOOKS

Ackroyd, P.R., *Israel under Babylon and Persia* (New Clarendon Bible). Oxford University Press, Oxford 1970.

Bright, John, *A History of Israel*. SCM Press, London 1981.

Bright, John, *Covenant and Promise*. SCM Press, London 1977.

Herrmann, Siegfried, *A History of Israel in Old Testament Times*. SCM Press, London 1973.

Hinson, David F., *History of Israel* (TEF Study Guide 7). SPCK, London 1973, revised 1991.

Southwell, Peter, *Prophecy*. Basil Blackwell, Oxford 1982.

Key to Study Suggestions

Introduction

1. See p. 1, the first line of each of the 4 numbered paras.
2. See p. 2, paras 2 and 3.
3. See p. 2, para. 2, last 6 lines.
5. See p. 2, last 3 paras and p. 3.

1.1–3

1. See p. 6, note on 1.1.
2. See p. 5, para. 3, lines 2–5, and para. 5, lines 2–5.
3. See p. 5, paras 3–5, and p. 6, para. 3.
4. See p. 5, para. 5, lines 3–4.
5. See p. 6, note on 1.3, lines 2–7.

Special Note A

1. See p. 8, para. 4, line 2; p. 10, para. 2, line 4; p. 10, paras 4–6. See also Time Chart on p. 11.
3. See p. 7, last line and p. 8, lines 1–2.
4. See p. 8, para. 3.
5. See p. 10, para. 2.
6. See p. 10, para. 4, lines 5–6; para. 5, lines 4–6 and para. 6, lines 1–4.
7. See p. 10, para. 3, line 5, and para. 4, lines 9–10.

1.4–19

1. See p. 13, para. 5, line 1; p. 14, para. 1, line 2; para. 2, line 1; para. 3, line 2 and para. 5, line 2.
2. See p. 15, last para.
3. See p. 16, 'The message of the prophet'.
4. (a) See p. 16, note on 1.12.
   (b) See p. 18, note on 1.15.
   (c) See p. 18, note on 1.17.

Special Note B

1. See p. 20, para. 1, lines 6–8, and para. 2.
2. See Section Headings.
3. See p. 20, para. 2, lines 5–12.
4. See p. 22, last para.

2.1—3.5

1. See p. 24, para. 5; p. 25, para. 4.
2. See p. 26, paras 3 and 4.
3. (a) See p. 25, para. 4.
   (b) See p. 24, para. 5, lines 1–2; p. 25, para. 1, lines 4–11.
   (c) See p. 27, lines 1–3.
   (d) See p. 26, last para., lines 7–8.

3.6—4.4

1. See p. 31, paras 2 and 3.
2. See p. 31, last para. and p. 32, first para.
3. See p. 33, last para. and p. 34, first para.

4. See p. 32, paras 3–5 and p. 33, lines 1–15.

4.5—6.30

1. See p. 38, para. 2, lines 1–2; para. 3, line 1: also p. 38, para. 2, lines 5–13 and para. 3, lines 3–7.
2. See p. 38, last 3 lines and p. 39, lines 1–4.
3. See p. 37, last 2 lines; p. 38, lines 1–2 and last 7 lines; p. 39, lines 1–4 and para. 3.

Special Note C

1. See p. 44, paras 1, 2 and para. 3, lines 1–2.
2. See p. 44, last 3 lines and p. 45, lines 1–6.
3. See p. 45, lines 1–4.

7.1–15

1. See p. 46, paras 2 and 4, especially last 3 lines; and see p. 46 last 2 lines; p. 47, paras 1 and 4; p. 48, para. 3.
3. See p. 47, lines 4–7 and lines 7–11.
4. See p. 48, para. 2, lines 1–12 and p. 50, note on 7.12.

7.16—8.3

1. See p. 52, paras 2–3 and para. 4, lines 4–6; p. 53, lines 1–9.
2. See p. 53, last 2 paras and p. 55, first para.
3. See p. 56, note on 7.31.
4. See p. 53, paras 3 and 4.

8.4—9.26

1. See p. 59, para. 3, lines 1–5 and p. 60, lines 3–6.
2. See p. 60, lines 6–9.
3. See p. 60, last para. and p. 61, first para.
4. See p. 59, para. 3, lines 3–5.

10.1–16

1. See p. 66, para. 3.
2. See p. 66, para. 4, lines 5–12.
3. See p. 67, para. 4, lines 3–8.
4. See p. 65, para. 1, lines 4–9 and p. 69, note on 'Lord of Hosts'.

10.17—11.17

1. See p. 71, para. 2, lines 1–7 and lines 8–12.
2. See p. 72, last para. and p. 73, paras 1 and 2.
3. See p. 73, para. 4.

12.7—13.27

1. See p. 77, paras 2–3.
2. See p. 77, last para. and p. 78, lines 1–7.
3. See p. 78, para. 3; p. 78, para. 4 and p. 80, para. 1.
4. See p. 80, para. 2, lines 2–4 and para. 3, lines 2–6.

14.1—15.9

1. See p. 84, para. 2, lines 8–10 and para. 3.
2. See p. 84, paras 4 and 5.
3. See p. 85, para. 3, lines 4–11.
4. See p. 85, para. 4, and p. 86, lines 1–4.

Special Note D

1. See p. 90, paras 2 and 3.
2. See p. 90, para. 2, lines 6–10.
3. See p. 91, section headings; p. 90, last para., lines 1–3; p. 91, and p. 92, first para.
4. See p. 92, para. 2, lines 1–4 and para. 3, lines 1–4.
5. See p. 92, para. 3, lines 4–11 and para. 4.

16.1—17.27

1. See p. 93, summary of 16. 1–13, and p. 94, paras 1 and 2.
2. See p. 94, para. 2, lines 4–7; para. 3, lines 1–7; and p. 95, para. 2, last 6 lines.
3. See p. 95, last para, lines 3–7.
4. See p. 98, note on 17.19–27.
5. See p. 96, last para. and p. 97, paras 1 and 2.

18.1–17; 19.1—20.6

1. See p. 101, para. 2, last 2 lines.
2. See p. 102, para. 3, lines 10–13.
3. See p. 102, last para. and p. 104, first para.
4. See p. 104, para. 2, lines 5–12 and para. 3, lines 1–4.

Special Note E

1. See p. 107, para. 1.
2. See p. 107, last para. and p. 108, paras 1 and 2.
4. See p. 108, last para.

11.18—12.6; 15.10–21

1. See p. 110, lines 1–4.
2. See p. 110, para. 2.
3. See p. 113, note on 12.5.
4. See p. 111, para. 2, lines 1–5 and para. 4, lines 1–4; p. 112, paras 1 and 2.
5. See p. 111, para. 3 and last para.; p. 112, first para.

17.14–18; 18.18–23; 20.7–18

1. See p. 115, last 2 paras, and p. 116, first para.
2. See p. 116, para. 2, lines 4–7.
3. See p. 116, para. 3, lines 3–5 and 11–13.
4. See p. 116, last 3 lines and p. 118, lines 1–3.
5. See p. 118, para. 2, and para. 3, lines 1–4.

21.2—23.8

1. See p. 122, para. 2, lines 1–3 and para. 3, last 2 lines.
2. See p. 122, para. 3, lines 4–7.
3. See p. 123, para. 2.
4. See p. 126, note on 23.5–6.
5. See p. 123, para. 3, lines 1–4 and 6–7.

23.9–40

1. See p. 129, para. 3, lines 1–5.
2. See p. 130, para. 2, lines 1–5.
3. See p. 131, para. 2, lines 1–3.
4. See p. 130, para. 2, lines 8–11, and para. 3, lines 8–13.

24.1—25.38
1. See p. 135, para. 3.
2. See p. 135, para. 4, lines 7–14.
3. See p. 138, lines 1–3.

Special Note F
1. See p. 142, para. 1, lines 6–8.
2. See p. 142, para. 2.
3. See p. 142, last para. lines 1–2.
4. See p. 142, para. 3.
5. Compare your suggestions with p. 144, paras 2 and 3.
6. See p. 145, para. 1, lines 1–11.
7. See p. 145, para. 1, lines 7–13 and para. 2, lines 5–7.

26.1–24
1. See p. 146, last 3 lines; p. 147, para. 1 and para. 2, lines 2–8.
2. See p. 147, para. 3, lines 1–5.
3. See p. 149, paras 1 and 2.
4. See p. 146, para. 3, and p. 150, note on 26.19.

27.1—29.32
1. See p. 153, last para. lines 1–3: p. 153, para. 4.
2. See p. 154, para. 2, lines 1–2.
3. See p. 154, paras 4 and 5.
4. See p. 153, para. 1, lines 3–8 and p. 157, note on 28.10.
5. See p. 154, para. 5, lines 2–9 and p. 158, note on 29.21–22.
6. See p. 155, para. 1, lines 3–10.

30.1—31.40
1. See p. 161, para. 1, lines 2–7.
2. See p. 161, para. 3, lines 3–5 and para. 4, lines 1–3.
3. See p. 162, para. 2, lines 1–3.
4. See p. 162, para. 3, lines 3–12.
5. See p. 164, para. 2.

32.1—33.26.
1. See p. 168, para. 2, lines 1–2 and para. 3 lines 3–6.
2. See p. 168, last para; p. 169, para. 1 and para. 3, lines 1–4.
3. See p. 169, last para and p. 170, para. 3, lines 1–3.
4. See p. 170, para 3.

34.1—36.32
1. See p. 174, last 6 lines: p. 175, para. 2, lines 1–6.
2. See p. 175, para. 2, last 4 lines and para. 3, lines 1–8.
3. See p. 176, para. 2, lines 6–12.
4. See p. 177, para. 2.

37.1—39.18
1. See p. 181, para. 2, especially lines 5–7.
2. See p. 182, para. 2, lines 1–2.
3. See p. 183, para. 2 and para. 3, lines 1–4.
4. See p. 183, para. 2, lines 3–5.
5. See p. 183, last para. and p. 184, lines 1–4.

40.1—43.7
1. See p. 190, para. 3.

2. (a) See p. 190, last para., lines 2–6.
 (b) See p. 191, lines 2–3, and para. 2, lines 2–5.
3. See p. 191, para. 2, lines 6–10.

43.8—44.30

1. (a) See p. 195, para. 3, lines 1–2 and 6–7; p. 195, para. 4, and p. 196, lines 1–3
 (b) See p. 196, para. 2, lines 5–6.
2. See p. 196, para. 3, lines 7–11 and para. 4, lines 1–8.
3. See p. 197, paras 1 and 2.
4. See p. 197, last 2 paras.

45.1–5

1. See p. 202, paras 3 and 4.
2. See p. 203, para. 2, lines 1–4 and para. 3, lines 1–5.
3. See p. 204, note on 45.4.

Special Note G

1. See p. 205, para. 2, lines 6–7.
2. See p. 205, para. 2, lines 7–15, last para. and p. 206, lines 1–2.

46.1—49.39

1. See p. 207, para. 3.
2. See p. 207, para. 2, lines 6–9.
3. See p. 207, last 2 lines and p. 208, para. 2, lines 6–10.
4. See p. 208, para. 4, lines 10–13.

50.1—51.64

1. See p. 215, para. 4, lines 4–12 and p. 216, last para., lines 9–16.
2. See p. 216, para. 4, lines 1–3.
3. See p. 218, lines 5–12.

52.1–34

1. See p. 222, para. 1, lines 4–7 and p. 223, paras 2 and 3.
2. See p. 222, para. 1, lines 6–7.
3. See p. 223, para. 3 and para. 4, lines 1–3.
4. See p. 223, last para. and p. 224, first para.

Special Note H

1. See Section Headings.
2. See p. 227, para. 3, line 1, para.4, line 1 and para. 5, line 1.
3. (a) See p. 229, para. 1, lines 3–9
 (b) See p. 229, para. 2, lines 1–8.
4. See p. 229, para. 3, lines 3–8; para. 4, lines 1–2, and p. 230, para 2.
5. See p. 230, paras 3 and 4.
6. See p. 230, paras 5 and 6, and p. 231.

Special Note I

1. See p. 232, para. 1.
2. See p. 232, para. 2, lines 6–12.
3. See p. 232, para. 2, lines 1–2.
4. See p. 232, para. 4, lines 4–8.

Index

This index has two main aims. Firstly, it shows where discussion of particular topics or words can be found: bold-type references indicate the pages where a theme or subject is studied in detail. Secondly, it shows where proper names (e.g. those of people or places) are encountered and explained. For proper names and themes which constantly recur throughout the book (e.g. Jeremiah, Judah, Exile, Judgement), only a few of the most important references are given.